POSTSCRIPT
LANGUAGE

REFERENCE MANUAL

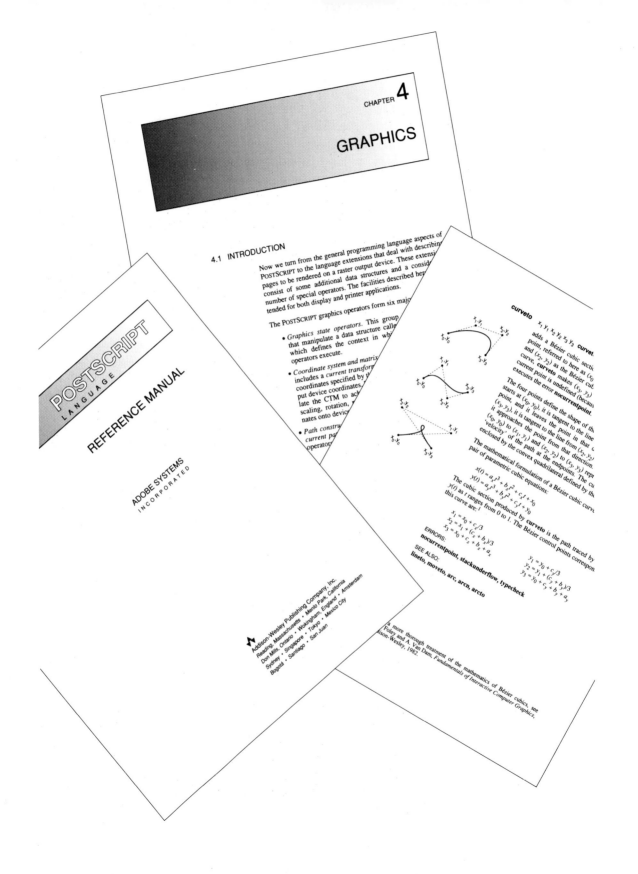

REFERENCE MANUAL

ADOBE SYSTEMS
INCORPORATED

Addison-Wesley Publishing Company, Inc.

Reading, Massachusetts • Menlo Park, California
Don Mills, Ontario • Wokingham, England • Amsterdam
Sydney • Singapore • Tokyo • Madrid
Bogotá • Santiago • San Juan

Library of Congress Cataloging in Publication Data

Main entry under title:

Postscript language reference manual.

Includes index.
1. PostScript (Computer program language)
I. Adobe Systems.
QA76.73.P67P67 1985   005.13′3   85-15693
ISBN 0-201-10174-2

POSTSCRIPT is a trademark of Adobe Systems Incorporated.

TRANSCRIPT is a trademark of Adobe Systems Incorporated.
Times is a trademark and Helvetica is a registered trademark of
    Allied Corporation.
Linotronic 300 is a trademark of Allied Corporation.
Scribe and UNILOGIC are registered trademarks of UNILOGIC, Ltd.
Apple, the Apple logo, and AppleTalk are trademarks of
    Apple Computer, Inc.
Macintosh is a trademark licensed to Apple Computer, Inc.
Diablo, Interpress, and XEROX® are trademarks of Xerox Corporation.
IBM is a registered trademark of International Business Machines Corporation.
UNIX is a trademark of AT&T Bell Laboratories.
ImagiTex is a trademark of ImagiTex Incorporated.

The information in this book is furnished for informational use only, is
subject to change without notice, and should not be construed as a
commitment by Adobe Systems Incorporated. Adobe Systems
Incorporated assumes no responsibility or liability for any errors or
inaccuracies that may appear in this book. The software described in
this book is furnished under license and may only be used or copied in
accordance with the terms of such license.

EFGHIJ-HA-89876
5th Printing, October 1986

Contents

Preface

The POSTSCRIPT language is designed to be a modern standard for electronic printing. This design has benefitted from nearly a decade's experience with several predecessor languages. I would like to present a brief historical background as a preface to the language specification contained in this manual.

The language had its beginnings in 1976 at the Evans & Sutherland Computer Corporation, where it was known as the 'Design System'. It was the outcome of a research project that explored the use of an interpretive language to build complex three-dimensional graphics data bases. The project was successful and the language was used in computer aided design applications.

The major ideas behind the original language are due to John Gaffney, who worked for me at the time. Although the Design System language and its successors bear a superficial resemblance to the FORTH programming language, their conception and development were entirely independent of FORTH.

In 1978, I joined the Xerox Palo Alto Research Center. Martin Newell and I reimplemented the language and called it 'JaM' (for 'John and Martin'). Again the language was used in experimental applications: Martin used it for VLSI design, while I used it for exploring the world of printing and graphic arts. One outcome of the work at PARC was the development of Interpress, the Xerox printing protocol. Many of the ideas found in both Interpress and POSTSCRIPT originated in the Design System and JaM languages.

When Chuck Geschke and I formed Adobe Systems Incorporated in 1982, we undertook a third design and implementation of the language, to which Doug Brotz, Bill Paxton, and Ed Taft made major contributions. This third incarnation, called 'POSTSCRIPT', is again used as an interpretive graphics description language. But this time the language describes two-dimensional printed pages, and the interpreter for the language resides in controllers for raster printers.

I can say without hesitation that the quality of the language, both in its design and in its implementation, has improved and matured greatly during the several stages of its evolution.

John Warnock
June 1985

Production note

Production of this book was an excellent demonstration of the POSTSCRIPT language's capabilities, particularly its device independence and its total integration of text and graphics. The entire production process took place at Adobe Systems, culminating in delivery of camera-ready copy to Addison-Wesley.

A considerable amount of material for this book was derived from three predecessor documents: the *POSTSCRIPT Language Manual*, the *Adobe Font Manual*, and the *Apple LaserWriter Advanced User's Supplement*. The Adobe staff members principally responsible for this material were John Warnock, Doug Brotz, Andy Shore, Linda Gass, and Ed Taft. The original material was reorganized, rewritten, and considerably expanded by Ed Taft. The resulting draft was reviewed and proofread by Doug Brotz and Glenn Reid.

The text for the manual was prepared and edited in the form of an on-line manuscript for the Scribe Document Production System (a product of UNILOGIC, Ltd.) The book design was specified by Robert Ishi and was implemented by Andy Shore (with help from Brian Reid) as a Scribe document definition. This manuscript consisted of commands and text for consumption by Scribe, interspersed with references to POSTSCRIPT programs for describing illustrations and other graphic material. Among the illustrations are two photographs, which were converted to digital form using an ImagiTex scanner and incorporated as POSTSCRIPT sampled images.

Successive drafts of the manuscript were processed by Scribe, each time generating a single POSTSCRIPT page description file for the entire book. This file included all the text and all the illustrations except the frontispiece (opposite the title page). The frontispiece was produced by extracting three pages from the Scribe-generated POSTSCRIPT file, combining them into a single page description, and applying POSTSCRIPT graphics operators to place them in the desired position, size, and orientation.

Proof copy was produced when needed by sending the POSTSCRIPT page description file to an Apple LaserWriter printer. After editing was completed, camera-ready copy was printed from the same file on a Linotype Linotronic 300 typesetter. This final copy was used directly by Addison-Wesley to make plates for publishing the book; no further cutting or paste-up of any kind was required.

REFERENCE MANUAL

CHAPTER 1

INTRODUCTION

1.1 ABOUT THE POSTSCRIPT LANGUAGE

The POSTSCRIPT language is a simple interpretive programming language with powerful graphics capabilities. Its primary application is to describe the appearance of text, graphical shapes, and sampled images on printed pages. A program in this language may be used to communicate a description of a printable document from a composition system to a printing system. The description is high-level and device-independent.

The POSTSCRIPT language's page description capabilities include the following features, which may be used in any combination:

- Arbitrary shapes constructed from straight lines, arcs, and cubic curves; such shapes may self-intersect and contain disconnected sections and holes.

- Painting primitives that permit a shape to be outlined with lines of any thickness, filled with any color, or used as a clipping path to crop any other graphics.

- Text fully integrated with graphics. In the POSTSCRIPT graphics model, text characters (in both standard and user-defined fonts) are treated as graphical shapes that may be operated on by any of the POSTSCRIPT graphics operators.

- Sampled images derived from natural sources (e.g., photographs) or generated synthetically. The POSTSCRIPT graphics model allows sampled images at any resolution and with a variety of dynamic ranges, and it provides a number of facilities to control the rendering of images on an output device.

- A general coordinate system facility that supports all combinations of linear transformations including translation, scaling, rotation, reflection, and skewing. These transformations apply uniformly to all elements of a page description, including text, graphical shapes, and sampled images.

A POSTSCRIPT page description may be rendered on a particular raster printer (or other output device) by presenting it to a POSTSCRIPT interpreter controlling that printer. As the interpreter executes commands to paint characters, graphical shapes, and sampled images, it converts from the high-level POSTSCRIPT description to the low-level raster data format for the specific output device.

Normally, POSTSCRIPT page descriptions are generated automatically by composition programs such as word processors, illustrators, computer aided design systems, and others. Programmers generally write POSTSCRIPT programs only when creating new applications. However, in special situations a programmer may write POSTSCRIPT programs to take advantage of POSTSCRIPT capabilities that are not accessible through a particular application program.

POSTSCRIPT's extensive page description capabilities are embedded in a general-purpose programming language framework. The language includes a conventional set of data types such as numbers, arrays, and strings; control primitives such as conditionals, loops, and procedures; and some unusual features such as dictionaries (associative tables). This enables application programmers to define higher-level operations that are closely matched to the needs of the application and then to generate page descriptions that invoke those higher-level operations. Such a page description is more compact and easier to generate than one written entirely in terms of a fixed set of basic operations.

POSTSCRIPT programs are created, transmitted, and interpreted in the form of source text as defined in this manual; there is no 'compiled' or 'encoded' form of the language. The entire language is defined in terms of printable characters (plus space and newline). This representation is convenient for programmers to create, manipulate, and understand. The limited character set facilitates storage and transmission of POSTSCRIPT files among diverse computers and operating systems; this enhances machine independence.

In this unconventional use of a programming language, POSTSCRIPT defines a standard, extensible, flexible print file format that is the interface between document composition applications and raster printing devices.

1.2 ABOUT THIS MANUAL

This is the programmer's reference manual for the POSTSCRIPT language. It is the definitive documentation for the syntax and semantics of the standard POSTSCRIPT language, the imaging model, and the effects of the graphical operators.

What this manual doesn't provide are guidelines on how to use POSTSCRIPT effectively. As with any programming language, certain techniques yield the best solution to particular programming problems, and there are issues of style that influence the quality and consistency of the results. These matters are the main topic of a companion book, the *POSTSCRIPT Language Tutorial and Cookbook*.

This *POSTSCRIPT Language Reference Manual* begins (chapter 2) with an informal presentation of some basic ideas that underlie the more formal descriptions and definitions comprising the remainder of the manual. We first discuss the properties and capabilities of raster output devices. This leads to a set of requirements for a page description language designed to make effective use of those capabilities. We briefly present the abstract POSTSCRIPT graphical model and describe how that model is realized on a raster output device. The chapter concludes with some pragmatic information about the environments in which POSTSCRIPT interpreters operate and about the sorts of POSTSCRIPT programs that are typically executed.

In chapter 3 we introduce the fundamentals of the POSTSCRIPT language: its syntax, semantics, data types, execution model, and so forth. This chapter concentrates on its conventional programming language aspects, entirely ignoring its graphical capabilities and its use as a page description language.

Chapter 4 introduces the POSTSCRIPT graphical model and describes how, using POSTSCRIPT operators, one may define and manipulate graphical entities such as lines, curves, filled areas, and sampled images. One may then transform these entities into different coordinate systems and render them on a raster output device.

In chapter 5 we describe how the POSTSCRIPT language deals with text. In POSTSCRIPT, text characters are defined simply as graphical shapes, and their behavior is in full accordance with the graphical model presented in the previous chapter. However, due to the importance of text in most printed documents, POSTSCRIPT provides specialized capabilities for organizing sets of characters as fonts and for selecting characters to be printed by means of an efficient encoding.

All of the POSTSCRIPT built-in operators and procedures are fully described in chapter 6. The chapter begins with a categorization of operators into functional groups. Following that, the operators appear in alphabetical order, with complete descriptions of their operands, results, side-effects, and possible errors.

The manual concludes with several appendices containing useful information that is not a formal part of the POSTSCRIPT language standard. Appendix A describes the standard fonts that are generally available in POSTSCRIPT printers. Appendix B specifies certain limits imposed by current implementations of the POSTSCRIPT interpreter (e.g., maximum array length, maximum stack depth, etc.) Appendix C describes a convention for structuring POSTSCRIPT page descriptions to facilitate their handling and processing by other programs.

Appendix D contains detailed information about the Apple LaserWriter, which is the POSTSCRIPT printer most widely available at the time of this writing. This appendix describes how the LaserWriter operates and communicates, and it documents the POSTSCRIPT language extensions that deal with system configuration and special capabilities of the LaserWriter. This information is not part of the POSTSCRIPT language standard and does not necessarily apply to other POSTSCRIPT printers.

If you intend to write applications that generate POSTSCRIPT page descriptions (or to program in POSTSCRIPT directly), it is essential that you have a copy of the *POSTSCRIPT Language Tutorial and Cookbook* in addition to this reference manual. The *Tutorial and Cookbook* is an introduction to effective use of POSTSCRIPT both as a programming language and as a means of achieving high-quality printed output. It includes a large number of techniques and recipes for obtaining results both mundane and exotic.

CHAPTER 2

BASIC IDEAS

2.1 INTRODUCTION

In this chapter we present some basic ideas that are essential to understanding the problems that the POSTSCRIPT language is designed to solve and the environments in which it is intended to operate. We also establish some terminology that will be used throughout the remainder of the manual.

There are two complementary approaches toward describing the POSTSCRIPT language. On one hand, it is a general purpose programming language with powerful built-in graphics primitives. On the other, it is a page description language that includes programming language features. Either of these views could serve as a basis for describing the language, but either one taken alone does not tell the entire story. Both views are equally valid and they interact to provide a complete model for understanding POSTSCRIPT.

2.2 RASTER OUTPUT DEVICES

The need for a page description language of POSTSCRIPT's capabilities is motivated by the properties of the output devices that the language must support. The POSTSCRIPT language is designed to deal with the general class of *raster output devices*.

This class encompasses such technologies as laser, dot-matrix, and ink-jet printers, as well as raster-scan displays.

The essential property of a raster output device is that a printed or displayed image consists of a rectangular array of individually-addressable dots or *pixels* (picture elements). On a typical black-and-white output device, each pixel can be made either black or white; on certain devices, each pixel can be set to an intermediate shade of gray or to some color. By setting large groups of pixels to appropriate colors in appropriate combinations, one can produce an image that includes text, arbitrary graphical shapes, and reproductions of natural or synthetically-generated sampled images.

The *resolution* of a raster output device is a measure of the number of pixels per unit of distance along the two linear dimensions. Resolution is typically but not necessarily the same in the horizontal and vertical directions.

Devices are classified according to their resolutions. Displays in computer terminals have relatively low resolution, typically 50 to 100 pixels per inch. Dot-matrix printers generally range from 100 to 200 pixels per inch. Laser scanning coupled with xerographic printing technology is capable of medium resolution output at 300 to 600 pixels per inch. Photographic technology permits high resolutions of 1000 pixels per inch or more. Higher resolution yields better quality and fidelity of the resulting image but is achieved at greater cost.

2.3 SCAN CONVERSION

An abstract graphical entity (e.g., a line, a circle, a text character, or a sampled image) is rendered on a raster output device by a process known as *scan conversion*. From a mathematical description of the graphical entity, this process determines which pixels to adjust and what values to set them to in order to achieve the most faithful rendition possible at the device resolution.

The pixels of the page to be printed or displayed are represented as a two-dimensional array of pixel values in computer memory. For an output device in which each pixel is either black or white (the most common situation), each pixel is represented by a single bit in memory. In this case, scan conversion consists of laying down a pattern of ones and zeroes in memory. This process is applied in turn to each graphical entity that is to appear on the page. The pixel values are then all read out in row or column order, and by some sort of scanning process an image corresponding to this data is produced on the output device.

Scan converting a graphical shape such as a rectangle or a circle involves determining which device pixels lie 'inside' the shape and setting their values appropriately (e.g., to black). Since in general the edges of a shape do not fall precisely on the boundaries between pixels, some policy is required for deciding which pixels along the edges are considered to be 'inside'. Scan converting a text character is conceptually no different from scan converting an arbitrary graphical shape; however, characters are additionally required to be legible and to meet certain other objective and subjective measures of quality.

Rendering gray-scale images on a device whose pixels can be only black or white is accomplished by a technique known as *halftoning*. The array of pixels is divided into small clusters according to some pattern (called the *halftone screen*). Within each cluster, some pixels are set to black and some to white in proportion to the level of gray desired at that point in the image. When viewed from a sufficient distance, the individual dots become unnoticeable and the resulting illusion is of a shade of gray. Natural images such as photographs and synthetic images such as gray-filled regions may thus be approximated on a black-and-white raster output device. (The chapter headings in this manual illustrate synthetic gray-scale images produced by halftoning.)

2.4 PAGE DESCRIPTION LANGUAGES

Levels of description

In principle, a page to be printed on a raster output device can be described simply as an array of pixel values. An application program can describe the desired output as a full-page pixel array and transmit it to the printer. Pages containing arbitrary combinations of text, graphics, and sampled images can be described in this way.

Such an arrangement is unsatisfactory for many reasons. Chief among them are:

- The description is bulky and is expensive to transmit and to store.

- The pixel array is device-dependent: it is valid for output devices of only one particular resolution and one choice of possible data values per pixel.

- Scan conversion is a difficult and time-consuming process. Requiring an application program to perform scan conversion is not only burdensome but is a serious violation of modularity principles. Furthermore, the processor or memory requirements for performing scan conversion may be beyond the means of many small machines such as personal computers.

In today's computer printing industry, raster output devices with different properties are proliferating, as are applications that need to generate output for those devices. Meanwhile, aspirations are also rising. Typewriter emulation (text-only output in a single typeface) is no longer adequate. Users desire to create and print documents that combine sophisticated typography with arbitrary graphics.

With low-level raster descriptions inadequate to satisfy these aspirations, we are led into the realm of the higher-level *page description language*. Ideally, such a language should be capable of describing the appearance of pages containing arbitrary text and graphics at a relatively high level, in terms of abstract graphical entities rather than in terms of device pixels. Such a description is economical and device-independent.

Producing printed output from an application program then becomes a two-stage process. First, the application generates a device-independent description of the desired output in the page description language. Second, a program controlling a specific raster output device interprets the description and renders it on the device. The two stages may be executed in different places and at different times; the page description language serves as an *interchange standard* for transmission and storage of printable documents.

Static versus dynamic formats

Page description languages in use today may be considered both on the basis of their *intrinsic* capabilities and on whether they are *static* or *dynamic*. Intrinsic capabilities include the built-in operations of the language, such as the ability to deal with various sorts of text and graphics. Additionally, the degree to which the built-in operations interact harmoniously is of considerable importance. For example, a page description language that offers uniform treatment of text, graphical shapes, and sampled images greatly facilitiates applications that must combine elements of all three on a single page.

A static format provides some fixed set of operations (sometimes called 'control codes') together with a syntax for specifying the operations and their arguments. Static formats have been in existence since computers first used printers; classic examples are line printer format control codes (in which the first character of each line is used to specify paper motion) and 'format effector' codes in standard character sets such as ASCII. Historically, static formats have been designed to capture the capabilities of a specific class of printing device and have subsequently evolved to include new features as they are added.

A dynamic format allows considerably more flexibility than a static format. The operator set may be extensible, and the exact meaning of an operator may not be known until it is actually encountered. A page described in a dynamic format is more appropriately thought of as a program to be executed than as data to be consumed. Dynamic page description languages contain elements of programming languages such as procedures, variables, control constructs, and so forth.

A print format that is primarily static but that purports to cover a lot of graphic and text capabilities tends to have a proliferation of special-purpose operators. A dynamic format that allows primitive operations to be combined according to the needs of the application will always be superior to a static format that tries to anticipate all possible needs.

The POSTSCRIPT design goes all the way over to the dynamic side of this classification. The language includes a set of primitive graphic operators, and it allows them to be combined in any possible manner. It not only has variables, but it allows arbitrary computations in the process of interpreting the page description. It has a rich set of programming language control structures for combining its elementary elements.

As we shall see later in this manual, for very complicated page layouts there may be situations in which a page description must depend on information about the specific output device in use, such as its page size or resolution. This information cannot be known at the time the page description is composed, but only when it is executed. Thus it is essential for a page description to be able to read information from its execution environment and to perform arbitrary computations based on that information in the process of rendering the desired image.

These considerations lead us to the POSTSCRIPT language, a dynamic print format whose page descriptions are actually programs to be executed by an interpreter. POSTSCRIPT programs can degenerate into a form that resembles a static format, i.e., an uninterrupted sequence of basic commands to image text or graphics. POSTSCRIPT programs generated by applications with simple needs will often have this boring, repetitive nature. However, when the need arises, the power is there to be exploited by the knowledgeable application designer.

2.5 USING POSTSCRIPT

Thus far we have concentrated primarily on the POSTSCRIPT graphical model and descriptive capabilities. Now let us turn to some more practical matters of how the POSTSCRIPT language is actually used.

The interpreter

We have already touched upon the most common scenario of using the POSTSCRIPT language. An application program generates a POSTSCRIPT page description of a desired document and transmits it to a POSTSCRIPT interpreter. The interpreter executes the page description and produces output on an attached printer or other raster device. The POSTSCRIPT interpreter and the output device are bundled together and treated essentially as a black box by the application; the interpreter has little or no direct interaction with the end user.

To support this model of use, the POSTSCRIPT interpreter is typically implemented on a dedicated processor that has direct control over the raster output device. One example of such a POSTSCRIPT implementation is the Apple LaserWriter. Its usual mode of operation is to consume a stream of 'print jobs' and produce the requested output.

A quite different scenario is one in which a programmer interacts with the POSTSCRIPT interpreter directly, treating it as a general-purpose programming language. Running POSTSCRIPT on a time-sharing system or personal computer is quite similar to running other interactive programming languages such as BASIC or FORTH. Dedicated POSTSCRIPT printers, such as the Apple LaserWriter, also have an interactive mode of operation that permits them to be used as if they were personal computers.

Although POSTSCRIPT is a general-purpose programming *language*, it is not a complete, self-contained programming *environment* because it lacks an editor and other tools required for program development. Interacting directly with the POSTSCRIPT interpreter is useful mainly for experimenting with its capabilities and for trying out POSTSCRIPT programs under development.

Even when a POSTSCRIPT interpreter is being used non-interactively to process documents prepared previously, there may be some dynamic interactions between the process sending the documents and the POSTSCRIPT interpreter. For example, the sender may ask the POSTSCRIPT interpreter whether certain fonts referenced by a document are already resident. This is accomplished by sending a program for the POSTSCRIPT interpreter to execute; this program reads the required information from its environment and sends it back. There is no formal distinction between a POSTSCRIPT program that is a page description and one that makes environmental queries or performs other, arbitrary computations.

Program structure

Returning to the use of POSTSCRIPT as a page description language, let us now consider how POSTSCRIPT programs are typically organized and how applications may be structured to use POSTSCRIPT effectively.

A POSTSCRIPT document generally consists of two parts: a *prologue* followed by a *script*. The prologue contains application-specific definitions that are used in the script. It is written manually by a programmer and is then included as the first part of every document generated by the application. It contains definitions that match the output functions of the application to the capabilities that POSTSCRIPT supports.

The script is generated automatically by the application program to describe the specific elements of the pages being produced. It consists of references both to POSTSCRIPT primitives and to definitions made in the prologue, interspersed with operands and data required by those operations. The script, unlike the prologue, is usually very stylized, repetitive, and simple.

An example may aid in understanding the purpose of having a separate prologue and script. POSTSCRIPT does not have a primitive to draw rectangles. To construct a rectangle, a POSTSCRIPT program must first define a rectangular *path* by specifying four invisible line segments, then *paint* the path by drawing a stroke along it or by filling it with some color. If rectangles appear commonly in output produced by an application, it may be advantageous for the prologue to define a procedure that draws a rectangle. Then, for each rectangle that is to appear in the page description, the script invokes the rectangle drawing procedure, passing it any operands it requires.

The script portion of a printable document ordinarily consists of a sequence of separate pages. The description of an individual page can stand by itself, depending only on the definitions in the prologue and not on anything in previous pages of the script. The language includes facilities (described in section 3.7) that may be used to guarantee page independence.

There is nothing in the POSTSCRIPT *language* that formally distinguishes the prologue from the script or that requires pages of the script to be independent of each other. Such structuring of POSTSCRIPT programs is merely a *convention*, but one that is quite useful and is recommended for most applications.

We have established a set of conventions by which document structure may be made explicit. These structuring conventions are documented in appendix C of this manual. The POSTSCRIPT interpreter doesn't distinguish between a page description that conforms to these conventions and one that does not. However, the structural information is of considerable importance to utility programs that operate on POSTSCRIPT page descriptions as data. Such programs may change the order of pages, extract subsets of pages, embed individual pages within other pages, and so on.

Another reason for adhering to the recommended document structure is that it serves as a good basis for organizing application programs that generate POSTSCRIPT page descriptions. An application program has its own data structure that represents the application's model of the appearance of a printable document. Some parts of this model are fixed for the entire document (or for all documents); the application should incorporate their descriptions into the prologue. Other parts vary from one page (or smaller division) to another; the application should emit the necessary descriptions of these as they appear.

While generating a printable document, an application should maintain an up-to-date version of its own model of the high-level graphical state. After it crosses a structural boundary such as a page break, it should generate descriptions that first restore the standard state defined by the prologue and then explicitly reestablish nonstandard portions of the graphical state for the next page. This technique ensures that each page is independent of any other.

The foregoing discussion has been concerned with application programs that generate POSTSCRIPT page descriptions directly. Many existing applications generate printable documents in some other print file format or in some intermediate representation. It is possible to print such documents by *translating* them into POSTSCRIPT page descriptions.[1]

---

[1]For example, the TRANSCRIPT package translates UNIX documents from a number of widely-used representations into POSTSCRIPT.

Implementing a translator is often the least expensive way to interface an existing application to a POSTSCRIPT printer. Unfortunately, while such translation is usually straightforward, a translator may not be able to generate POSTSCRIPT programs that make effective and efficient use of the POSTSCRIPT descriptive capabilities. This is because the print file being translated often describes the desired results at too low a level; any higher-level information maintained by the original application has been lost and is not available to the translator.

While direct POSTSCRIPT output from applications is most desirable, translation from another print format may be the only choice available for some applications. In any event, a translator should do the best it can to produce output that conforms to the POSTSCRIPT structuring conventions. This ensures that such output is compatible with the tools for manipulating POSTSCRIPT page descriptions.

Once again, these guidelines for program structure are not part of the POSTSCRIPT language and are not enforced by the POSTSCRIPT interpreter. In some cases, a POSTSCRIPT program may require an organization that is incompatible with the structuring conventions; this is especially true of very sophisticated page descriptions composed directly by a programmer. However, for page descriptions generated automatically by applications, adherence to the structuring conventions is strongly recommended.

CHAPTER 3

LANGUAGE

3.1 INTRODUCTION

We now shift our attention from POSTSCRIPT as a page description language to POSTSCRIPT as a general-purpose programming language. This chapter describes elements of the POSTSCRIPT language—syntax, data types, execution semantics, and so forth—that are an essential aspect of any POSTSCRIPT program, whether or not that program constitutes a page description. Later chapters will document the graphics and font capabilities that specialize POSTSCRIPT to the task of page description.

The POSTSCRIPT language borrows elements and ideas from several other programming languages with which you may be familiar. The syntax most closely resembles that of the programming language FORTH. It incorporates a *postfix* notation in which operators are preceded by their operands. The number of special characters is small and there are no reserved words. (Though the number of built-in *operators* is large, the names that represent operators are not reserved by the language.)

The data model includes elements such as numbers, strings, and arrays that are found in many modern programming languages. It also includes the ability to treat programs as data and to monitor and control many aspects of the language's execution state; these notions are derived from programming languages such as LISP.

You may wonder why a page description language should require such general-purpose programming language underpinnings. Actually, POSTSCRIPT is a relatively simple language, and the number of language features is not large. POSTSCRIPT's power derives from the ability to combine these features in unlimited ways without arbitrary restrictions. Though this power is seldom exploited fully, its availability makes it feasible to design sophisticated graphical applications that would otherwise be difficult or impossible.

Since this is a reference manual and not a tutorial, this chapter describes each aspect of the language systematically and thoroughly before moving on to the next. We begin with a brief overview of the POSTSCRIPT interpreter. The following sections cover in detail the syntax, data types, execution semantics, and memory organization of the POSTSCRIPT language. The final section is an overview of the general-purpose operators of the language, excluding the ones that deal with graphics and fonts.

3.2 INTERPRETER

The POSTSCRIPT interpreter is the process that executes the POSTSCRIPT language according to the rules given in this chapter. These rules tell us the order in which operations are carried out and how the pieces of a POSTSCRIPT program fit together to produce the desired results.

The interpreter manipulates entities called POSTSCRIPT *objects*. Some objects are ordinarily thought of as data, such as numbers, booleans, strings, and arrays. Other objects are ordinarily thought of as elements of programs to be executed, such as names, operators, and procedures. But there is not actually any formal distinction between data and programs: any POSTSCRIPT object may be treated as data or be executed as part of a program.

The interpreter operates by executing a sequence of objects. The effect of executing a particular object depends on that object's type, attributes, and value. For example, executing a number object simply causes a copy of that object to be pushed on the operand stack (to be described shortly). Executing a name object causes the name to be looked up in a dictionary and the associated value to be fetched and perhaps executed. Executing an operator object causes a built-in action to be performed such as adding two numbers together or painting characters in raster memory.

The objects to be executed by the interpreter come from two principal sources. First, objects previously stored in an array in POSTSCRIPT memory may be executed in sequence. Such an array is conventionally known as a *procedure*. Second, a character stream may be scanned according to the syntax rules of the POSTSCRIPT language, producing a sequence of new objects. As each object is scanned it is immediately executed. The character stream may come from an external source such as a file or a communication channel, or it may come from a string object previously stored in POSTSCRIPT memory.

The interpreter can switch back and forth between executing an array and scanning a character stream. For example, if it encounters a name in a character stream, it executes that name by looking it up in a dictionary and retrieving the associated value. If that value is an array (procedure) object, the interpreter suspends scanning the character stream and begins executing the objects contained in the array. When it reaches the end of the array, it resumes scanning the character stream from where it left off. The interpreter maintains an *execution stack* for remembering all of its suspended execution contexts.

It is important to understand that the sole function of the interpreter is to execute a sequence of POSTSCRIPT objects. How those objects come into existence, what their properties are, and precisely what it means to execute a particular object are the topics of the next few sections.

3.3 SYNTAX

A POSTSCRIPT program is represented externally (in a file or sent through a communication channel) as a sequence of characters conforming to syntax rules described in this section.

Interpretation of a POSTSCRIPT program creates various types of

POSTSCRIPT objects, such as numbers, strings, and procedures. This section discusses only the syntactic representation of such objects. Their internal representation and behavior are covered in section 3.4.

Scanner

POSTSCRIPT differs from most other programming languages in that it does not have any syntactic entity for a 'program'; nor is it necessary for an entire 'program' to exist in one place at one time. POSTSCRIPT has no notion of 'reading in' a program prior to executing it. Instead, the POSTSCRIPT interpreter *consumes* a program by reading and executing one syntactic entity at a time. From POSTSCRIPT's point of view, the program itself has no permanent existence. Of course, *execution* of the program may have side-effects (in POSTSCRIPT memory or elsewhere); these side-effects may include the creation of procedure objects in memory that are intended to be invoked later in the program.

It is not quite correct to think of the POSTSCRIPT interpreter 'executing' the character stream directly. What actually happens is that a *scanner* groups characters into *tokens* according to the POSTSCRIPT syntax rules. It then assembles one or more tokens to create a POSTSCRIPT *object*, i.e., a data value in POSTSCRIPT memory. Finally, the interpreter *executes* the object.

For example, when the scanner encounters a group of consecutive digits surrounded by spaces or other separators, it assembles the digits into a token and then converts the token into a number object (represented internally as a binary integer). The interpreter then executes this number object; in this case, it pushes a copy of the number object on the operand stack.

The reason we stress the separation of scanning and execution is that there are situations in which objects created by scanning are not executed immediately; their execution is *deferred* to some later time. This is explained below in the discussion of creating procedure objects.

Character set

The standard character set for POSTSCRIPT programs is the printable subset of the ASCII character set,[1] plus the characters space, tab, and newline (return or line-feed). POSTSCRIPT does not prohibit the use of characters outside this set; but such use is not recommended since it impairs portability and may make transmission and storage of POSTSCRIPT programs more difficult.

The characters space, tab, and newline are referred to as *white space* characters and are treated equivalently (except in comments and strings). White space characters serve to separate other syntactic constructs such as names and numbers from each other. Any number of consecutive white space characters are treated as if there were just one.

The characters '(', ')', '<', '>', '[', ']', '{', '}', '/', and '%' are *special*: they serve to delimit syntactic entities such as strings, procedure bodies, name literals, and comments. Any of these characters terminates the entity preceding it and is not included in it.

All characters besides the white space and special characters are referred to as *regular* characters. These include non-printing characters that are outside the recommended POSTSCRIPT character set.

Comments

Any occurrence of the character '%' not inside a string (see below) introduces a *comment*. The comment consists of all characters between the '%' and the next newline, including regular, special, space, and tab characters.

The scanner ignores comments, treating each one as if it were a single white space character. That is, a comment separates the token preceding it from the one following. Thus, the program fragment

```
abc% comment {/%) blah blah
123
```

is treated by the scanner as just two tokens, 'abc' and '123'.

---

[1] ASCII is the American Standard Code for Information Interchange, a widely-used convention for encoding characters as binary numbers.

Numbers

Numbers in POSTSCRIPT include signed integers, such as

```
123  -98  43445  0  +17
```

reals, such as

```
-.002  34.5  -3.62  123.6e10  1E-5  -1.  0.0
```

and radix numbers, such as

```
8#1777  16#FFFE  2#1000
```

An integer consists of an optional sign followed by one or more decimal digits. The number is interpreted as a signed decimal integer and is converted to a POSTSCRIPT integer object. (If it exceeds the range representable as an integer, it is instead converted to a real object.)

A real consists of an optional sign and one or more decimal digits, with an embedded period (decimal point), a trailing exponent, or both. The exponent, if present, consists of 'E' or 'e' followed by an optional sign and one or more decimal digits. The number is interpreted as a real and is converted to a POSTSCRIPT real (floating point) object.

A radix number takes the form *base#number*, where *base* is a decimal integer in the range 2 through 36. The *number* is then interpreted in this base; it must consist of digits ranging from 0 to *base*−1. Digits greater than 9 are represented by the letters 'A' through 'Z' (or 'a' through 'z'). The number is treated as an unsigned integer and is converted to a POSTSCRIPT integer object. This notation is intended for specifying integers in a nondecimal radix such as binary, octal, or hexadecimal.

Strings

A string in POSTSCRIPT is delimited by balanced parentheses. This notation is POSTSCRIPT's way of 'quoting' a literal string to make a string object. Within a string the only special characters are parentheses and the '\' (back-slash) character. The following are examples of valid strings:

```
(This is a string)
(Strings may contain newlines
and such.)
(Strings may contain special characters *-&}^% and
balanced parentheses () (and so on).)
(The following is an "empty" string.)
()
(It has 0 (zero) length.)
```

Within a string, the '\' (back-slash) character is used as an 'escape' for various purposes such as including unbalanced parentheses, non-printing characters, and the '\' character itself.[2] The character immediately following the '\' determines the precise interpretation, as follows:

\n	linefeed (newline)
\r	carriage return
\t	horizontal tab
\b	backspace
\f	form feed
\\	backslash
\(	left parenthesis
\)	right parenthesis
\ddd	character code ddd (octal)
\newline	no character — both are ignored

If the character following the '\' is not one of the above, the '\' is ignored.

The \ddd form may be used to include any 8-bit character constant in a string. One, two, or three octal digits may be specified (with high-order overflow ignored). This notation is preferred for specifying a character outside POSTSCRIPT's recommended standard character set, since the notation itself stays within the standard set and thereby avoids possible difficulties in transmitting or storing the text of the program.

The \newline form is used to break a string into a number of lines but not have the newlines be part of the string.

---

[2]The scanner does not follow the '\' escape convention when the source of the characters being scanned is itself a string. The assumption in this case is that any '\' escapes were interpreted and removed at the time the source string was originally scanned.

```
(These\
 two strings \
are the same.)
(These two strings are the same.)

(This string has a newline at the end of it.
)
(So does this one.\n)
```

A string may also be described in hexadecimal (base 16) notation by bracketing a sequence of hex characters (the digits '0' through '9' and the letters 'A' through 'F' or 'a' through 'f') with '<' and '>'. Each pair of hex digits defines one character of the string. (If the last digit is missing, it is taken to be zero.) Spaces, tabs, and newlines are ignored. For example,

```
<901fa3>
```

is a 3-character string containing the characters whose hex codes are 90, 1f, and a3. Hexadecimal strings are useful for including arbitrary binary data as literal text.

Names

Any token that consists entirely of regular characters and that cannot be interpreted as a number is treated as a POSTSCRIPT *name* object (more precisely, an *executable* name). All characters except specials and white space can appear in names, including characters ordinarily considered to be punctuation. The following are examples of valid names:

```
abc Offset $$ 23A 13-456 a.b $MyDict @pattern
```

A '/' (slash) introduces a *literal* name. The slash is not part of the name itself but is a prefix indicating that the following name is a literal.

The important properties and uses of names and the distinction between executable and literal names are described in section 3.4.

Arrays

The characters '[' and ']' are self-delimiting tokens that specify the construction of an array. The program fragment

    [123 /abc (xyz)]

results in the construction of an array object containing the integer object '123', the literal name object 'abc', and the string object 'xyz'.

However, we are jumping ahead. The behavior just described results from *executing* the program fragment and not just from *scanning* it. '[' and ']' are actually just special syntax for *names* which, when executed, invoke POSTSCRIPT operators that collect objects together and construct an array containing them. Thus, the above example really contains five tokens denoting the name object '[', the integer object '123', the literal name object 'abc', the string object 'xyz', and the name object ']'; when the example is executed, a sixth object (the array) results from executing the '[' and ']' name objects.

Procedures

The special characters '{' and '}' delimit an *executable array*, otherwise known as a *procedure*. The syntax is superficially similar to that for the array construction operators '[' and ']'; however, the semantics are entirely different and arise as a result of *scanning* the procedure, not of *executing* it.

Scanning the program fragment

    {add 2 div}

results in the production of a single procedure object that contains the name object 'add', the integer object '2', and the name object 'div'. When the scanner encounters the initial '{', it continues scanning and creating objects, but the interpreter does not execute them. When the scanner encounters the matching '}', it collects all the objects created since the initial '{' into a new executable array (procedure) object.

Furthermore (jumping ahead again), the interpreter will not execute the procedure immediately, but will just treat it as data (i.e., push it on the operand stack). Only when the procedure is explicitly invoked (by means yet to be described) will it be executed. We say that execution of the procedure (and of all objects within the procedure, including any embedded procedures) has been *deferred*.

The matter of immediate versus deferred execution is discussed further in section 3.6.

3.4 DATA TYPES AND OBJECTS

All data accessible to POSTSCRIPT programs, including procedures that are part of the programs themselves, exist in the form of *objects*. Objects are produced, manipulated, and consumed by the POSTSCRIPT operators. They are also created by the scanner and executed by the interpreter.

Each object has a *type*, some *attributes*, and a *value*. Objects contain their own dynamic types; that is, an object's type is a property of the object itself, not of where it is stored or what it is called.

The complete list of object types supported by POSTSCRIPT is:

integer	operator
real	file
boolean	mark
array	null
string	save
name	fontID
dictionary	

In this section we introduce all of these types and describe many of their important properties. For some types, however, we are interested less in the intrinsic properties of objects than in what you can do with them—execute them (section 3.6) or operate on them (section 3.8). This section concludes with a brief description of the attributes of objects. Attributes are of interest primarily when objects are *executed*; details of execution are presented in section 3.6.

Simple and composite objects

Objects of most types are simple, atomic entities. There is no visible substructure in the object; the type, attributes, and value are irrevocably bound together and cannot be changed. (But it is possible to derive a *new* object by copying an existing one, perhaps with modifications.)

Objects of types *array*, *dictionary*, and *string*, however, are *composite*, meaning that their values have internal substructure that is visible and can sometimes be selectively modified. The details of the substructure are presented below in the descriptions of these individual types.

A most important distinction between simple and composite objects has to do with the behavior of operations that *copy* objects. By 'copy' we refer to any operation that transfers the contents of an object from one place to another in POSTSCRIPT's memory; 'fetching' and 'storing' objects are both copying operations.

When a simple object is copied, all of its parts (type, attributes, and value) are copied together. But when a composite object is copied, the value is *not* copied; instead, the original and copy objects *share* the same value. Consequently, any changes made to the substructure of one object's value also appear as part of the other object's value.

The sharing of composite objects' values in POSTSCRIPT corresponds to the use of *pointers* in system programming languages such as C and Pascal. Indeed, the POSTSCRIPT interpreter actually uses pointers to implement shared values: a composite object contains a pointer to its value. However, the POSTSCRIPT language does not have any explicit notion of a pointer. It is better to think in terms of the copying and sharing notions presented here.

Integer and real

POSTSCRIPT provides two types of numeric object: *integer* and *real*. Integer objects represent mathematical integers within a certain interval centered at zero. Real objects approximate mathematical real numbers within a much larger interval but with limited precision; they are implemented as floating-point numbers.

Most POSTSCRIPT arithmetic and mathematical operators can be applied freely to numbers of both types, and the interpreter performs automatic type conversion when necessary. Some operators expect only integers (or a subrange of the integers) as operands. There exist operators to convert from one type to another explicitly. Throughout this manual, when we refer to a *number* we mean an object whose type is either integer or real.

The range and precision of numbers is limited by the internal representations used in the machine on which the POSTSCRIPT interpreter is running. Appendix B gives these limits for current POSTSCRIPT implementations. The machine representation of integers is accessible to POSTSCRIPT programs through the bitwise operators. The machine representation of reals is not accessible to POSTSCRIPT programs.

Boolean

POSTSCRIPT provides *boolean* objects with values *true* and *false* for use in conditional and logical expressions. Booleans are the results of the relational (comparison) and logical operators, and they are also returned as status from various other operators. The main use of booleans is as operands for the control operators **if** and **ifelse**. The names **true** and **false** are associated with the two values of this type.

Array

An *array* is a one-dimensional collection of objects, accessed by a numeric index. Unlike arrays in many other computer languages, POSTSCRIPT arrays may be heterogeneous; that is, an array's elements may be any combination of numbers, strings, dictionaries, other arrays, or any other POSTSCRIPT objects. A *procedure* is simply an array that may be executed by the POSTSCRIPT interpreter.

All POSTSCRIPT arrays are indexed from zero, so an array of n elements has indices from 0 through $n-1$. All accesses to POSTSCRIPT arrays are bounds checked, and a reference with an out-of-bounds index results in an error.

POSTSCRIPT directly provides only one-dimensional arrays. Arrays of higher dimension may be constructed by using arrays as elements of arrays, nested arbitrarily deeply.

As discussed earlier, an array is a composite object. When an array object is copied, the value is not copied, but instead the old and new objects share the same value. Additionally, there is an operator that creates a new array object whose value is a subinterval of an existing array; the old and new objects share the array elements in that subinterval.

String

A *string* is similar to an array, but its elements must be integers in the range 0 to 255. The string elements are not actually integer objects but are stored in a more compact format; however, the operators that access string elements accept or return ordinary integer objects (with values in the range 0 to 255).

String objects are conventionally used to hold text, one character per string element. However, POSTSCRIPT does not have a distinct 'character' syntax or data type and does not require that the integer elements of a string encode any particular character set. String objects may be used to hold arbitrary binary data.

To enhance program portability, strings appearing literally as part of a POSTSCRIPT program should be limited to characters from the POSTSCRIPT standard character set, with other characters inserted by means of the '\' octal character escape convention (see section 3.3).

Like an array, a string is a composite object. Copying a string object or creating a subinterval (substring) results in sharing the string's value.

Name

A *name* is an atomic symbol uniquely defined by a sequence of characters. Names serve the same purpose as 'identifiers' in other programming languages, i.e., as tags for variables, procedures, and so forth. However, POSTSCRIPT names are not just language artifacts but are first-class data objects, similar to 'atoms' in LISP.

A name object is ordinarily created when the scanner encounters a POSTSCRIPT token consisting entirely of regular characters, as was described in section 3.3. However, a name may also be created by explicit conversion from a string; so there is no actual restriction on the set of characters that can be included in names.

Unlike a string, a name is a *simple* object, not a composite one. Although a name is defined by a sequence of characters, those characters are in no sense 'elements' of the name.

The important property of a name is that it is *unique*. Any two name objects defined by the same sequence of characters are in fact identical copies of each other. Name equality is based on an exact match between the corresponding characters defining each name. This includes the case of letters, so the names 'A' and 'a' are different.

The interpreter can determine whether two existing name objects are equal or unequal inexpensively by a means that does not involve comparing the characters that define the names. This makes names useful as keys in dictionaries (to be described shortly).

Note that names do not *have* values in the same sense as do variable or procedure names in other programming languages. However, names can be *associated* with values in dictionaries, which we shall describe next.

Dictionary

A *dictionary* is an associative table whose elements are pairs of POSTSCRIPT objects. We call the first element of a pair the *key* and the second element the *value*. The language includes operators that insert a key-value pair into a dictionary, look up a key and fetch the associated value, and perform various other operations.

Keys are normally name objects; the POSTSCRIPT syntax and the interpreter are optimized for this most common case. However, a key may be any POSTSCRIPT object except **null** (defined below). If you attempt to use a string as a key, the POSTSCRIPT interpreter will first convert the string to a name object; thus, strings and names are interchangeable when used as keys in dictionaries.

Dictionaries ordinarily associate the names and values of a program's components, such as variables and procedures. This corresponds to the conventional use of identifiers in other programming languages. However, there are many other uses for dictionaries. For example, a POSTSCRIPT font is a dictionary that associates the names of characters with the procedures for drawing those characters' shapes (see chapter 5).

There are three main methods for accessing dictionaries. First, operators exist to access a specific dictionary supplied as an operand. Second, there is a *current dictionary* and a set of operators to access it implicitly. Third, the interpreter generally references the current dictionary when it encounters a name object in the program being executed.

More precisely, the interpreter maintains a *dictionary stack* defining the current dynamic name space. Dictionaries may be pushed on and popped off the dictionary stack at will. The topmost dictionary on the stack is the *current dictionary*.

When the interpreter looks up a key implicitly, e.g., when it executes a name object, it first searches for the key in the current dictionary. If the key is not there, the interpreter searches the next lower dictionary on the dictionary stack. This continues until either it finds the key or it exhausts the dictionary stack.

There are two built-in dictionaries called **systemdict** and **userdict**. **systemdict** associates the names of all the POSTSCRIPT operators (the ones defined in this manual) with their values (the built-in actions that implement them). **userdict** is the outermost modifiable naming environment for use by POSTSCRIPT programmers. **systemdict** and **userdict** are always the bottommost two dictionaries on the dictionary stack (with **userdict** above **systemdict**); neither of them can be popped off.

A dictionary is a composite object. Copying a dictionary object does not copy the dictionary's contents; instead, the contents are shared.

Operator

An *operator* object represents one of the POSTSCRIPT built-in actions; when the object is executed, its built-in action is invoked. Most of this manual is devoted to describing the semantics of the various operators.

Operators have names. Most operators are associated with names in **systemdict**: the names are the keys and the values are the operators themselves. When the interpreter executes one of these names, it looks up the name in the context of the dictionary stack. Unless the name has been defined in some dictionary higher on the dictionary stack, the interpreter finds its definition in **systemdict**, fetches the associated value (the operator object itself), and executes it, thus performing the built-in action.

When we speak of an operator such as **add**, it is important to understand that there is nothing special about the name 'add' that distinguishes it as an operator. Rather, the name 'add' is associated in **systemdict** with the operator for performing addition; and it is execution of the *operator* that causes the addition to occur. Thus the name 'add' is not a 'reserved word', as it might be in other programming languages; its meaning can be changed by a POSTSCRIPT program.

Throughout this manual, the notation **add** means "the operator object associated with the name 'add' in **systemdict**" (or, occasionally, in some other dictionary).[3]

File

A *file* is a readable or writable stream of characters, used to communicate data between POSTSCRIPT and its environment. For example, a file object can represent data in a disk file (perhaps accessed via operating system calls), transferred through a communication channel, and so forth.

Operators exist to open a file (thereby creating a file object) and to read and write characters and process them in various ways — as strings, as POSTSCRIPT tokens, as binary data represented in hexadecimal, and so on.

[3]POSTSCRIPT also has some internal operators, not documented in this manual or named in **systemdict**, which may be encountered if a program reads the execution stack.

POSTSCRIPT always provides standard input and output files. The standard input file is the usual source of POSTSCRIPT programs to be interpreted; the standard output file is the usual destination of such things as error and status messages.

A file object is not composite (it doesn't have components visible at the POSTSCRIPT level); but it is similar to the composite objects in that all copies of a file object share the same value, namely the underlying file. If a file operator has a side-effect on the underlying file, such as closing it or changing the current position in the stream, all file objects sharing the file are affected.

The properties of files and the operations on them are described in more detail in the presentation of file operators in section 3.8.

Mark

A *mark* is a special object used to mark a position on the operand stack. This use is described in the presentation of stack and array operators in section 3.8. There is only one value of type mark, created by invoking the operator **mark** or '['. Mark objects are not legal operands to most operators.

Null

The POSTSCRIPT interpreter uses *null* objects to fill empty or uninitialized positions in composite objects when they are created. There is only one value of type null; the name **null** is associated with a null object in **systemdict**. Null objects are not legal operands to most operators.

Save

Save objects represent snapshots of the state of POSTSCRIPT's memory. They are created and manipulated by the **save** and **restore** operators, introduced in section 3.7.

FontID

FontIDs are special objects used in the construction of POSTSCRIPT fonts; they are described in chapter 5.

Attributes of objects

In addition to type and value, each object has one or more *attributes*. These attributes affect the behavior of the object when it is executed or when certain operations are performed on it. But they do not affect its behavior when it is treated strictly as data; so, for example, two integers with the same value are considered 'equal' even if their attributes differ.

Every object is either *literal* or *executable*. This distinction comes into play when the interpreter attempts to execute the object. If the object is *literal*, the interpreter will treat it strictly as data and will push it on the operand stack for use as an operand of some subsequent operator. But if the object is *executable*, the interpreter will execute it.

What it means to execute an object depends on the object's type; this is described in section 3.6. For some types of objects, e.g., integers, execution consists of pushing the object on the operand stack; the distinction between literal and executable integers is meaningless. But for other types, such as names, operators, and arrays, execution consists of performing some quite different action. Executing an executable name causes it to be looked up in the current dictionary context and the associated value to be executed. Executing an executable operator causes some built-in action to be performed. Executing an executable array (otherwise known as a procedure) causes the elements of the array in turn to be executed.

Referring back to the POSTSCRIPT syntax described in section 3.3, we see that some tokens produce literal objects and some produce executable ones. Specifically, integer, real, and string constants are always literal objects. Names are literal if they are preceded by '/' and executable if not. The '[' and ']' operators, when executed, produce a literal array object with the enclosed objects as elements. Finally, '{' and '}' enclose an executable array or procedure.

The other attribute of an object is its *access*. Only objects of certain types have access attributes, namely arrays, strings, dictionaries, and files. Access attributes serve to restrict the set of operations that can be performed on the value of an object.

There are four values of access: *unlimited*, *read-only*, *execute-only*, and *none*, in increasing order of restriction. Normally, objects have unlimited access: all operations defined for that object are allowed. An object with read-only access may not have its value modified (or written to, in the case of files), but may still be read or executed. An object with execute-only access may not have its value either read or written, but may still be executed as a program by the POSTSCRIPT interpreter. Finally, an object with no access may not be operated on in any way by a POSTSCRIPT program. (Such objects are not of any direct use to POSTSCRIPT programs but serve certain internal purposes that are not documented in this manual.)

The literal/executable distinction and the access attribute are entirely independent, though obviously there are certain combinations that aren't of any practical use (e.g., a literal array that is execute-only).

With one exception, attributes are properties of an *object* itself and not of its *value*. Thus, two composite objects can share the same value but have different literal/executable or access attributes. The exception is the dictionary type: a dictionary's access attribute is a property of the value; so multiple dictionary objects sharing the value have the same access attribute.

3.5 STACKS

The POSTSCRIPT interpreter manages four distinct *stacks* representing the execution state of a POSTSCRIPT program. Three of them (the operand, dictionary, and execution stacks) are described here; the fourth (the graphics state stack) is presented in chapter 4.

The *operand stack* holds arbitrary POSTSCRIPT objects that are the operands and results of POSTSCRIPT operators being executed. When an operator requires one or more operands, it obtains them by popping them off the top of the operand stack. When an operator returns one or more results, it does so by pushing them on the operand stack. The interpreter itself pushes objects on the operand stack when it encounters them as literal data in a program being executed.

The *dictionary stack* holds only dictionary objects. The current set of dictionaries on the dictionary stack defines the context for all implicit name searches, such as those that occur when the interpreter encounters an executable name. The role of the dictionary stack was introduced in section 3.4 and is elaborated further in section 3.6.

The *execution stack* holds executable objects (mainly procedures and files) that are in partial stages of execution. At any point in the execution of a POSTSCRIPT program, this stack represents the *call stack* of the program. Whenever the interpreter interrupts execution of an object in order to execute some other object, it pushes the suspended object on the execution stack. When the interpreter finishes executing an object, it pops that object off the execution stack and resumes executing the suspended object beneath it.

The three stacks are entirely independent and have different means for accessing them. The operand stack is directly under control of the POSTSCRIPT program being executed; objects may be pushed and popped arbitrarily by use of any of a variety of operators. The dictionary stack is also under control of the POSTSCRIPT program being executed; but it can hold only dictionaries, and the bottommost two dictionaries on this stack (**systemdict** and **userdict**) cannot be popped off. The execution stack is entirely under the control of the interpreter; it can be read but not modified by a POSTSCRIPT program.

When an object is pushed on a stack, the *object* itself is copied from wherever it was obtained; however, in the case of a composite object (array, string, or dictionary), the object's *value* is not copied on the stack but rather is shared with the original object. Similarly, when a composite object is popped off a stack and put somewhere, it is only the object itself and not its value that is moved. Section 3.4 for an elaboration of this point.

Each of the stacks has a fixed limit on the number of objects it can contain; the limits for one implementation of the POSTSCRIPT interpreter are given in appendix B. Attempting to push an object on a stack that is full or to pop from a stack that is empty results in an error.

3.6 EXECUTION

Now that we have described POSTSCRIPT's language syntax, objects, and stacks, it is time to present its execution semantics in detail. In particular, we need to understand what it means to execute objects of each of the various types, and we need to clarify the issue of *immediate* versus *deferred* execution.

Immediate execution

Our discussion of POSTSCRIPT execution will be facilitated by several examples of POSTSCRIPT program fragments. The first example illustrates immediate execution of a few operators and operands to perform some simple arithmetic:

    40 60 add 2 div

The interpreter first encounters the literal integer object '40' and pushes it on the operand stack. Similarly, it then pushes the integer object '60' on the operand stack.

Now it encounters the executable name object 'add', which it looks up in the context of the current dictionary stack. Unless 'add' has been defined elsewhere, the interpreter finds it associated in **systemdict** with an operator object, which it executes. This invokes a built-in **add** function that pops the two integer objects off the operand stack, adds them together, and pushes the result (a new integer object whose value is 100) on the operand stack.

The rest of the program fragment is executed similarly. The interpreter pushes the integer '2' on the operand stack; then it executes the name 'div'. The **div** operator pops two operands off the stack (the integers whose values are 2 and 100), divides the second-to-top one by the top one, and pushes the integer result 50 on the stack.

We have been deliberately vague about the source of the objects being executed by the POSTSCRIPT interpreter. Did they already exist in POSTSCRIPT memory as a sequence of objects, perhaps contained within an array? Or were they produced by scanning a character stream (e.g., a file) and interpreting it as a sequence of tokens according to the POSTSCRIPT syntax? In fact, it does not matter. Executing a sequence of objects produces the same results regardless of where the objects came from.

Operand order

Before proceeding further, we need to establish a bit of terminology used throughout the remainder of this manual, namely how to refer to the operands of an operator when there are more than one of them.

In the above example, we say that '40' and '60' are the first and second operands of the **add** operator. That is, we refer to the objects according to the order in which they are pushed on the operand stack. Of course, this is the reverse of the order in which they are popped off by the **add** operator itself. Similarly, the result pushed by the **add** operator is the first operand of the **div** operator, and the '2' is its second operand.

The same terminology applies to the results of an operator. If an operator pushes more than one object on the operand stack, we say that the first object pushed is the first result.

We have adopted this terminology because it corresponds to the usual left-to-right order of appearance of operands in a POSTSCRIPT program.

Deferred execution

Now we are ready for a more interesting program fragment:

```
/average {add 2 div} def
40 60 average
```

Before going into details, we should summarize what this program does. The first line defines a procedure named 'average' that computes the average of two numbers. The second line applies that procedure to the integers '40' and '60', producing the same result as our previous example.

The interpreter first encounters the literal name 'average' (recall from section 3.3 that '/' introduces a literal name). It pushes this object on the operand stack, as it would do for any object having the literal attribute.

Next it encounters the executable array '{add 2 div}'. Recall from section 3.3 that '{' and '}' enclose an executable array or *procedure* that is produced by the scanner. This array contains three elements: the executable name 'add', the literal integer '2', and the executable name 'div'. These elements have not yet been encountered by the interpreter.

The interpreter's action upon encountering this procedure object is to push it on the operand stack. This may seem surprising given that the object has the executable attribute; we shall explain this shortly.

The interpreter now encounters the executable name 'def'. Looking up this name in the current dictionary context, it finds 'def' to be associated in **systemdict** with an operator object, which it invokes. The **def** operator pops two objects off the operand stack (the procedure '{add 2 div}' and the name 'average'). It then enters this pair into the current dictionary (most likely **userdict**), creating a new association having the name 'average' as its key and the procedure '{add 2 div}' as its value.

Stated less formally, we have defined a procedure named 'average', which in the second line of the example we proceed to call. The interpreter pushes the integer objects '40' and '60' on the operand stack as before, then encounters the executable name 'average'. It looks up 'average' in the current dictionary context, finds it to be associated with the procedure '{add 2 div}', and *executes* that procedure. In this case, execution of the array object consist of executing the elements of the array in sequence, namely the objects 'add', '2', and 'div'. This has the same effect as executing those objects directly (as in the first example); it produces the same result, namely the integer object 50.

Now, why did the interpreter treat the procedure as data in the first line of the example but execute it in the second, despite the procedure having the executable attribute in both cases? There is a special rule that determines this behavior: an executable array encountered directly by the interpreter is treated as data (i.e., pushed on the operand stack); but an executable array encountered *indirectly* (i.e., as a result of executing some other object such as a name or an operator) is invoked as a procedure.

This exception to the usual literal/executable semantics is made for pragmatic reasons having to do with the ways in which procedures are ordinarily used. Procedures appearing directly (either as part of a program being read from a stream or as part of some larger procedure in memory) are usually part of a definition or of a construct such as a conditional that operates on the procedure explicitly. But procedures obtained indirectly, e.g., as a result of looking up a name, are usually intended to be called. Of course, means exist to override these semantics when necessary.

Control constructs

In POSTSCRIPT, control constructs such as conditionals and iterations are specified by means of operators that take procedures as operands. The program fragment

    a b gt {a} {b} ifelse

computes the maximum of the values associated with the names 'a' and 'b', as follows. The interpreter encounters the executable names 'a' and 'b' in turn and looks them up. Let's assume both names are both associated with numbers. Executing the numbers causes them to be pushed on the operand stack. The **gt** operator removes two operands from the stack and compares them. If the first operand is greater than the second operand, it pushes the boolean value *true*; otherwise it pushes *false*.

The interpreter now encounters the procedure objects '{a}' and '{b}', which it pushes on the operand stack. Then it encounters the name 'ifelse', which it finds to be associated with a POSTSCRIPT operator. The **ifelse** operator takes three operands: a boolean and two procedures. If the boolean's value is *true*, **ifelse** causes the first procedure to be executed; otherwise it causes the second procedure to be executed. All three operands are removed from the operand stack before the selected procedure is executed.

The procedure in this case consists of a single element which is an executable name (either 'a' or 'b'). The interpreter looks up this name and, since it is associated with a number, pushes that number on the operand stack. So the result of executing the entire program fragment is to push on the operand stack the maximum of the values associated with 'a' and 'b'.

Execution of specific types

This section describes the precise effects of executing objects of each specific type. Remember that objects with the literal attribute are *always* treated as data (i.e., pushed on the operand stack by the interpreter), regardless of their type. Even POSTSCRIPT operator objects are treated this way if they have the literal attribute. The following descriptions apply only to objects having the executable attribute.

For many objects, executing them has the same effect as treating them as data. This is true of integer, real, boolean, dictionary, mark, save, and fontID objects. So the distinction between literal and executable objects of these types is meaningless.

An executable array (procedure) object is pushed on the operand stack if it is encountered directly by the interpreter. But if it is invoked *indirectly* as a result of executing some other object (a name or an operator), it is *called* instead. The interpreter calls a procedure by pushing it on the execution stack and then beginning to execute the array elements in turn. When it reaches the end of the procedure, it pops the procedure object off the execution stack.[4]

An executable string object is pushed on the execution stack. The interpreter then uses the string as a source of characters to be converted to tokens and interpreted according to the POSTSCRIPT syntax rules. This continues until the interpreter reaches the end of the string, at which point it pops the string object from the execution stack.

An executable file object is treated very much the same as a string: the interpreter pushes it on the execution stack. It then

---

[4]Actually, it pops the procedure object when there is one element remaining and then pushes that element. This is to permit unlimited depth of 'tail recursion' without overflowing the execution stack.

reads the characters of the file and interprets them as POSTSCRIPT tokens until it encounters end-of-file. Then it closes the file and pops the file object from the execution stack.

An executable name object is looked up in the context of the current dictionary stack and its associated value is executed. Precisely, the interpreter looks first in the topmost dictionary on the dictionary stack and then in other dictionaries successively lower on the stack. If it finds the name as a key in some dictionary, it executes the associated value. To do that, it examines the value's type and executable attribute and performs the appropriate action described in this section; note that if the value is a procedure, the interpreter calls it (see above). If the interpreter fails to find the name in any dictionary on the dictionary stack, it executes an **undefined** error (see below).

An executable operator object causes the interpreter to perform one of the built-in operations described in this manual.

An executable null object causes the interpreter to perform no action (in particular, it does not push the object on the operand stack).

Errors

Various sorts of errors can occur during execution of a POSTSCRIPT program. Some errors are detected by the interpreter itself, such as overflow of one of the POSTSCRIPT stacks. Others are detected during execution of the built-in operators, such as an operand of the wrong type.

Errors are handled in a uniform fashion that is under the control of the POSTSCRIPT program itself. Each distinct error is associated with a name, such as **stackoverflow** or **typecheck**. Each error name appears as a key in a special dictionary named **errordict** and is associated with a value that is the handler for that error. The complete set of error names appears in chapter 6.

When an error occurs, the interpreter first restores the operand stack to the state it was in at the beginning of executing the current object. Next, it pushes that object on the operand stack. Finally, it looks up the error's name in **errordict** and executes the associated value, which is the *error handler* for that error.

Those actions are everything that the interpreter itself does in response to an error. All other actions are the responsibility of the error handler that is found in **errordict**. The default error handlers do something reasonable, such as print an error message and terminate the POSTSCRIPT program being executed; this is discussed in section 3.8. However, a POSTSCRIPT program can modify error behavior by defining its own error handling procedures and associating them with the names in **errordict**.

3.7 VIRTUAL MEMORY

We have made occasional reference to 'POSTSCRIPT memory' without saying anything about what that really is. We now describe the *virtual memory*, or 'VM' for short, as it is viewed by POSTSCRIPT programs. (The adjective 'virtual' emphasizes that we are describing its abstract behavior at the POSTSCRIPT level as opposed to its actual implementation in computer storage.)

For the most part, VM is the place in which the *values* of all *composite* objects are stored. Recall from section 3.4 that the value of a composite object (array, dictionary, or string) is separate from the object itself and that several objects may share the same value. Viewed slightly differently, composite objects are ones whose values are collections of other objects; those collections are stored in VM.

POSTSCRIPT's operand, dictionary, and execution stacks are *not* part of the VM. The stacks should be thought of as temporary working storage for objects being manipulated by POSTSCRIPT programs and by the interpreter itself. However, the VM contains all the values and objects that can be *reached*, directly or indirectly, from objects in any of the three stacks.

The reason for distinguishing between what is in VM and what is not is that POSTSCRIPT provides several useful facilities that operate on the VM as a whole.

In versions of POSTSCRIPT running on computers with an operating system and a file system, POSTSCRIPT can store its VM in a file at the end of a session and recover it from the file at the beginning of the next. This is convenient for using POSTSCRIPT in an interactive environment, since user definitions can be preserved from one session to another. This VM file contains only definitions in **systemdict** and **userdict** (and in dictionaries and other composite objects reachable from those dictionaries); it does not preserve the contents of the operand, dictionary, and execution stacks.

All versions of POSTSCRIPT (with or without a file system) include **save** and **restore** operators that enable a running program to save a snapshot of the state of the VM and to restore the VM to that saved state. **restore** effectively undoes all changes that have been made to the values of composite objects since the corresponding **save**.[5] It does not affect the contents of the stacks, nor does it undo side-effects such as writing to files or to raster memory.

save/restore pairs can be nested to a limited depth; the limit is given in appendix B. See the descriptions of the **save** and **restore** operators in chapter 6 for complete information on their use.

The save/restore facility is of particular value in POSTSCRIPT programs that are page descriptions, for several reasons. First, a page description is ordinarily executed solely for its side-effect of causing output to be produced on a raster device. It is undesirable for a page description to leave a permanent side-effect in POSTSCRIPT memory, since that might influence the behavior of the next page description to be executed. For this reason, POSTSCRIPT processors that are dedicated to executing page descriptions and driving printers usually save a VM snapshot before receiving each page description and restore it afterward.

Second, page descriptions typically have internal structure, such as separate pages or separate major elements within a page. Within each section, it may be desirable to make wholesale changes to the contents of dictionaries and other data structures for some special purpose that is local to that section. The save/restore facility is used to encapsulate that section of the page description, thereby restoring the correct initial conditions for the next section. This is much simpler (and more efficient) than reestablishing all the initial conditions explicitly.

---

[5]In the current POSTSCRIPT design, **restore** actually does not undo changes made to the elements of strings. We consider this behavior to be a defect, and we do not recommend that POSTSCRIPT programs take advantage of it.

Third, the save/restore facility recovers the VM resources consumed in the course of executing a POSTSCRIPT program. There is a large but fixed limit on the size of the VM. As new composite objects are created (either by reading POSTSCRIPT tokens from a character stream or by executing operators that allocate them explicitly), their values accumulate in VM. Even when the objects are consumed or discarded, their values are not removed but continue to occupy VM resources. The only way to destroy those values and free the VM resources is to restore the VM to a previous snapshot.

This point is sufficiently important that it is worth elaborating. The POSTSCRIPT language has no operators that explicitly discard individual objects and their values; nor does the interpreter have a 'garbage collector' to discard values that are no longer accessible from any object.[6] Each string, array, or procedure value encountered in a POSTSCRIPT program (bracketed by '(...)', '<...>', '[...]', or '{...}') occupies VM resources, even if it is used only temporarily (e.g., as text to be printed by **show** or as a section of code to be executed conditionally by **ifelse**). The only way to get rid of accumulated composite objects is to execute a **restore**.

A common and recommended style for use of the save/restore facility is to issue a **save** at the beginning of the description of each page and a **restore** at the end. Each page thus stands by itself, without interference from other pages. And when the *script* of all the pages is preceded by the application-specific *prologue* (as discussed in section 2.5), each page is executed with the initial conditions established by the prologue; there are no unwanted legacies from previous pages.

3.8 OPERATOR OVERVIEW

We now present an overview of the general-purpose POSTSCRIPT operators, excluding all operators that deal with graphics and fonts (which are described in later chapters). The organization of this section roughly parallels that of the operator summary at the

---

[6]Some POSTSCRIPT implementations *may* include such facilities, but POSTSCRIPT programs that are page descriptions should not depend on their existence, since that would impair portability.

beginning of chapter 6. The information here is insufficient for actual programming; it is intended only to acquaint you with the available facilities. For complete information about any particular operator, you should refer to the operator's detailed description in chapter 6.

Stack operators

The operand stack is the POSTSCRIPT interpreter's mechanism for passing arguments to operators and for gathering results from operators; it was introduced in section 3.5.

There exist various operators that rearrange or otherwise manipulate the objects on the operand stack. Such rearrangement is often required when the results of some operators are to be used as arguments to other operators that require their operands in a different order. Simple stack operations include ones to duplicate (**dup**), exchange (**exch**), or discard (**pop**) the top elements of the stack. Other operators duplicate portions of the operand stack (**copy**), treat a portion of the stack as a circular queue (**roll**), and access the stack as if it were an indexable array (**index**).

There is a facility to *mark* a position on the stack (**mark**) and to count the elements above the highest mark (**counttomark**). This is used primarily for array construction (described below), but has other applications as well.

Arithmetic and mathematical operators

The POSTSCRIPT language includes a conventional complement of arithmetic and mathematical operators. In general, these operators accept either integer or real number objects as operands; they produce either integer or real numbers as results depending on the types of the operands and the magnitude of the results. If the result of an operation is mathematically meaningless or cannot be represented as a real, the error operator **undefinedresult** is executed.

Arithmetic operators of two arguments are **add**, **sub**, **mul**, **div**, **idiv**, and **mod**; those of one argument are **abs**, **neg**, **ceiling**, **floor**, **round**, and **truncate**. Mathematical and trigonometric functions include **sqrt**, **exp**, **ln**, **log**, **sin**, **cos**, and **atan**. A pseudo-random number generator is accessed by **rand**, **srand**, and **rrand**.

Array, dictionary, and string operators

A number of operators are *polymorphic*, meaning that they may be applied to operands of several different types and that their precise functions depend on the types of the operands. In particular, there are various operators that perform similar operations on all types of composite objects—arrays, dictionaries, and strings.

The **get** operator takes a composite object and an index (or key, in the case of a dictionary) and returns a single element of the object; **put** stores an element into a composite object analogously.

copy copies the *value* of a composite object to another composite object of the same type, replacing the second object's former value. (This is different from merely copying the object; see the discussion of simple versus composite objects in section 3.4.)

The **length** operator returns the number of elements in a composite object. **forall** accesses all of the elements of a composite object in sequence, calling a POSTSCRIPT procedure for each one.

getinterval creates a new object that shares a subinterval of an array or string; **putinterval** overwrites a subinterval of one array or string with the contents of another. (These operators do not apply to dictionaries.)

In addition to the polymorphic operators, there are operators that apply to only one of the array, dictionary, and string types. For each type, there is an operator (**array**, **dict**, **string**) that creates a new object of that type and a specified length. These three operators explicitly create new composite object values, thereby consuming VM resources (see section 3.7). Most other operators read and write the values of composite objects but do not create new ones. Operators that return composite results usually require an operand that is the composite object into which the result values are to be stored. (The operators are organized this way so as to afford maximum programmer control over consumption of VM.)

The special array operators **aload** and **astore** transfer all the elements of an array to or from the operand stack in a single operation.

As mentioned in section 3.3, the array construction operators '[' and ']' combine to produce a new array object whose elements are (more or less) the objects appearing between the brackets in a POSTSCRIPT program. The '[' operator (which is a synonym for **mark**) pushes a mark object on the operand stack. Execution of the program fragment between the '[' and the ']' causes one or more objects to be pushed on the operand stack. Finally, the ']' operator counts the number of objects above the mark on the stack, creates an array of that length, stores the elements from the stack into the array, removes the mark from the stack, and pushes the array.

Dictionary operators include ones to push new dictionaries on the dictionary stack and pop them off (**begin** and **end**), to search for keys in the context of the current dictionary stack (**load** and **where**), to associate keys with values (**def** and **store**), and to read the dictionary stack (**countdictstack** and **dictstack**). There is no way to explicitly remove individual keys from a dictionary; however, **restore** removes any definitions made since the corresponding **save**.

String operators exist to perform textual string searching and matching (**search**, **anchorsearch**) and to scan the characters of a string according to the POSTSCRIPT syntax rules (**token**).

Relational, boolean, and bitwise operators

The relational operators compare two operands and produce a boolean result indicating whether the relation holds. Any two objects may be compared for equality (**eq** and **ne**); numbers and strings may be compared by the inequality operators (**gt**, **ge**, **le**, and **lt**).

The boolean and bitwise operators (**and**, **or**, **xor**, and **not**) compute logical combinations of boolean operands or bitwise combinations of integer operands. The bitwise shift operator **bitshift** applies only to integers.

Control operators

The control operators modify the interpreter's usual sequential execution of objects. Most of them take a procedure operand which they execute conditionally or repeatedly.

if and **ifelse** execute a procedure conditionally depending on the value of a boolean operand (**ifelse** was introduced in section 3.6). **exec** executes an arbitrary object unconditionally. **for**, **repeat**, **loop**, **forall**, and **pathforall** execute a procedure repeatedly; **exit** transfers control out of the scope of any of these looping operators.

A POSTSCRIPT program may terminate prematurely by executing the **stop** operator. This occurs most commonly as a result of an error; i.e., the default error handlers (in **errordict**) all execute **stop**.

The **stopped** operator establishes an execution context that encapsulates the effect of a **stop**. That is, **stopped** executes a procedure given as an operand, just the same as **exec**. If the interpreter executes **stop** during that procedure, it terminates the procedure and resumes execution at the object immediately after the **stopped** operator. (The interpreter itself invokes a user's POSTSCRIPT program with the **stopped** operator so that it can regain control and perform proper error recovery if the program stops prematurely.)

When the POSTSCRIPT interpreter is first started up, it begins by executing the procedure named **start**. The operator **quit** terminates the interpreter. The precise actions of **start** and **quit** are installation-dependent; ordinary POSTSCRIPT programs should not concern themselves with them.

Type, attribute, and conversion operators

These operators deal with the details of POSTSCRIPT types, attributes, and values, which were introduced in section 3.4. The **type** operator returns the type of any operand as a name object ('integertype', 'realtype', etc.) The operators **xcheck**, **rcheck**, and **wcheck** query the literal/executable and access attributes of an object.

The operators **cvlit** and **cvx** change the literal/executable attribute of an object. **readonly**, **executeonly**, and **noaccess** reduce an object's access attribute (access can only be reduced by this means, never increased).

Several operators convert from one type to another; that is, they create a new object derived from the value of an existing one. **cvi** and **cvr** convert between integer and real types and interpret a numeric string as an integer or real number. **cvn** converts a string to a name object defined by the characters of the string. **cvs** and **cvrs** convert objects of several types to a printable string representation.

File operators

A file is a finite sequence of characters bounded by an end-of-file indication. These characters may be stored permanently in some place (e.g., a disk file) or they may be generated on the fly and transmitted over some communication channel. Files are the means by which the POSTSCRIPT interpreter receives executable programs and exchanges data with the external environment.

There are two kinds of files: *input* and *output*. An input file is a source from which a POSTSCRIPT program can read a sequence of characters. An output file is a destination to which a POSTSCRIPT program can write characters.

A POSTSCRIPT file object represents a file. The file operators take a file object as an operand in order to read or write characters. Ignoring for a moment how a file object comes into existence, the most basic file operators are **read**, which reads the next character from an input file, and **write**, which appends a character to an output file. Higher-level operations include ones that transfer POSTSCRIPT strings to and from files (**readstring**, **readline**, and **writestring**), that read and write binary data represented in the file by hexadecimal notation (**readhexstring** and **writehexstring**), and that scan the characters from an input file according to the POSTSCRIPT syntax rules (**token**).

The operators that write to a file do not necessarily deliver the characters to their destination immediately; they may leave some characters in buffers for reasons of implementation or efficiency.

The **flush** and **flushfile** operators deliver these buffered characters immediately; they are useful in certain situations, such as during two-way interactions with another computer or with a human user, when it is important that such data be transmitted immediately.

At the end of reading or writing a file, a program should *close* the file so as to break the association between the POSTSCRIPT file object and the actual file. The file operators close a file automatically if end-of-file is encountered during reading (see below). The **closefile** operator closes a file explicitly.

End-of-file and exception conditions are treated uniformly by all operators that access files. During reading, if an end-of-file indication is encountered before the requested item can be read, the file is closed and the operation returns an explicit end-of-file result. (This also occurs if the file has already been closed when the operator is executed.) All other exceptions during reading and any exceptions during writing result in execution of the error **ioerror**.

File objects are created by the **file** operator. This operator takes two strings: the first identifies the file and the second specifies whether input or output is desired. **file** returns a new file object associated with that file.

Details of file naming are dependent on the operating system and runtime environment in which the POSTSCRIPT interpreter is embedded. In general, POSTSCRIPT file names follow the standard conventions for that environment; but it is inappropriate to describe those conventions in this manual.

All POSTSCRIPT interpreters, however, define several special file names that are built-in and are not dependent on the operating system environment. These names all have to do with the *standard input* and *standard output* files, which usually represent a real-time communication channel to and from another computer or user terminal.

The POSTSCRIPT interpreter ordinarily reads and interprets the standard input file as POSTSCRIPT program text. It ordinarily sends error and status messages to the standard output file. Additionally, a POSTSCRIPT program may execute the **print** operator to send arbitrary data to the standard output file. Note that **print** is a *file* operator; it has nothing to do with placing text on a page or causing pages to emerge from a printer.

It is not often necessary for a POSTSCRIPT program to deal explicitly with file objects for the standard files, since the POSTSCRIPT interpreter reads the standard input file by default and the **print** operator references the standard output file implicitly. However, when necessary, a program may apply the **file** operator to the identifying strings '%stdin' or '%stdout' in order to obtain file objects for the standard input and output files.[7]

When the POSTSCRIPT interpreter is used interactively, it treats the standard input and output files somewhat differently. Instead of simply reading and executing the standard input file, it obtains an entire statement entered by the user, executes that statement, and prompts for another statement. In this context, a 'statement' consists of one or more lines (terminated by newline) that together constitute one or more complete POSTSCRIPT tokens, with no '{' or '(' left unmatched. The interpreter 'echoes' characters from the standard input file to the standard output file. It provides some simple control character functions for making corrections: backspace character (BS), erase line (control-U), and retype line (control-R).

An edited input statement, with all corrections processed, is available to POSTSCRIPT programs via a special kind of file.[8] Applying the **file** operator to the identifying string '%statementedit' causes an edited statement to be obtained from the standard input file. The characters of that statement may then be read from the file returned by the **file** operator. (Another special file, identified by the string '%lineedit', consists of just one line of edited input, without regard to whether it constitutes a complete POSTSCRIPT statement.)

There are miscellaneous other file operators. **status** and

---

[7]Another file, the *standard error* file, is identified to the **file** operator by the string '%stderr'. This is intended for reporting low-level errors. In many configurations, it is the same as the standard output file.

[8]In fact, the interactive mode of operation is implemented entirely by a built-in POSTSCRIPT procedure, named **executive**, that uses the file facilities described here. Appendix D describes the operation of **executive** in a particular POSTSCRIPT implementation, the Apple LaserWriter.

bytesavailable return status information about a file. **currentfile** returns the file object from which the interpreter is currently reading. **run** is a convenience operator that combines the functions of **file** and **exec**. **prompt** and **echo** control details of the interactive mode of operation.

Several built-in procedures print the values of objects on the operand stack, sending a readable representation of those values to the standard output file. The name '=' is associated with a procedure that pops one object from the operand stack and writes a text representation of its value to the standard output file, followed by a newline. '==' is similar to '=' but produces results closer to full POSTSCRIPT syntax and expands the values of arrays. **stack** prints the entire contents of the operand stack with '=', but leaves the stack unchanged. **pstack** performs the analogous operation using '=='.

Virtual memory operators

The POSTSCRIPT virtual memory (VM) was introduced in section 3.7, as were the principal VM operators **save** and **restore**. Additionally, the **vmstatus** operator returns information about the current state of the VM.

Errors

As discussed in section 3.6, when the POSTSCRIPT interpreter detects an error condition, it executes a name object that identifies the error. It looks up this name in the special dictionary **errordict** rather than in **systemdict**, **userdict**, or other dictionaries on the dictionary stack. The values associated with these names are typically not operators but are procedures. For convenience of presentation, however, errors are grouped with the operators in chapter 6.

The default error handler procedures all operate in a standard way: they record information about the error in a special dictionary named **$error** and then execute **stop**. They do not print anything.

Execution of **stop** exits the innermost enclosing context established by **stopped**. Assuming the user program has not invoked **stopped** itself, interpretation continues in an outer control program (which invoked the user program with **stopped**). This program executes the name **handleerror** from **errordict**. The default **handleerror** procedure accesses the error information in the **$error** dictionary and writes a text message to the standard output file.

After an error occurs, **$error** will contain the following key-value entries:

Name	Type	Value
newerror	boolean	set to *true* to indicate that an error has occurred (**handleerror** sets it to *false*).
errorname	name	the name of the error that was invoked.
command	any	the operator or other object being executed by the interpreter at the time the error occurred.
ostack	array	a snapshot of the entire operand stack immediately before the error, stored as if by **astore**.
estack	array	a snapshot of the execution stack, stored as if by **execstack**.
dstack	array	a snapshot of the dictionary stack, stored as if by **dictstack**.

A program that wishes to modify the behavior of error handling can do so in one of two ways. First, it can change the way in which errors are *reported* simply by redefining **handleerror** in **errordict**. For example, a revised error handler might report more information about the context of the error, or it might produce a printed page containing the error information instead of reporting it to the standard output file.

Second, a program can change the way in which errors are *invoked* by redefining the error names themselves. There is no restriction on what an error handling procedure can do. For example, in an interactive environment, an error handler might invoke a debugging facility that would enable the user to examine or alter the execution environment and perhaps resume execution.

CHAPTER 4

GRAPHICS

4.1 INTRODUCTION

Now we turn from the general programming language aspects of POSTSCRIPT to the language extensions that deal with describing pages to be rendered on a raster output device. These extensions consist of some additional data structures and a considerable number of special operators. The facilities described here are intended for both display and printer applications.

The POSTSCRIPT graphics operators form six major groups:

- *Graphics state operators*. This group contains operators that manipulate a data structure called the *graphics state*, which defines the context in which the other graphics operators execute.

- *Coordinate system and matrix operators*. The graphics state includes a *current transformation matrix* (CTM) that maps coordinates specified by the POSTSCRIPT program into output device coordinates. The operators in this group manipulate the CTM to achieve any combination of translation, scaling, rotation, reflection, and skewing of user coordinates onto device coordinates.

- *Path construction operators*. The graphics state includes a *current path* that defines shapes and line trajectories. The operators in this group begin a new path, add straight and curved line segments to the current path; and close the current path. All of these operators implicitly reference CTM parameter in the graphics state.

- *Painting operators.* These operators cause shapes and paths to be scan converted and rendered in raster memory. After a path is constructed and colors, images, character fonts, line widths, and other parameters are set in the graphics state, the painting operators 'push' images or color through the shape defined by the current path or render line trajectories along that path. POSTSCRIPT programs may use a variety of color models to specify output color, halftone screens, and sampled images.

- *Character and font operators.* These operators allow the specification, selection, and modification of fonts (descriptions of typefaces) and provide the means to render characters from those fonts onto the page. POSTSCRIPT treats characters as general graphical shapes, so strictly speaking many of the font operators should be grouped with the path construction or painting operators. However, the data structures and mechanisms for dealing with character and font descriptions are sufficiently specialized that we defer all discussion of fonts until chapter 5.

- *Device setup and output operators.* Device setup operators establish the association between raster memory and a physical output device. Once a page has been completely described in raster memory, executing an output operator causes the page to be transmitted to the device.

In this chapter, we present general information about graphics in POSTSCRIPT: the imaging model, coordinate system, and data structures. We then introduce the principal operators for path construction, painting, and image rendering. Details of specific graphics operators are presented in chapter 6.

4.2 IMAGING MODEL

The POSTSCRIPT imaging model is a simple and unified view of two-dimensional graphics borrowed from the graphic arts industry. An image is built up by placing 'paint' on a page in selected areas. The paint may be in the form of letter shapes, general filled shapes, lines, or halftone representations of photographs. The paint itself may be in color or in black, white, or any shade of gray. Any of these elements may be cropped to within any shape as they are placed onto the page. Once a page has been built up to the desired form, it may be printed on an output device.[1]

POSTSCRIPT maintains an implicit *current page* that accumulates the marks made by the POSTSCRIPT *painting operators*. When a program begins, the current page is completely white. As each painting operator executes, it places marks on the current page. Each new mark completely obscures any marks that it may overlay. This method is known as a *painting model*: no matter what color a mark has—white, black, gray, or color—it is put onto the current page as if it were applied with opaque paint. Once the page has been completely composed, the **showpage** operator may be invoked to render the accumulated marks on the output media and then clear the current page to white again.

The principal painting operators are **fill**, **stroke**, **image**, and **show**. **fill** marks an area, **stroke** marks lines, **image** paints a sampled image, and **show** paints character shapes onto the current page. Each of these operators requires several arguments, some explicit and some implicit.

Chief among the implicit arguments is the *current path* (used by **fill**, **stroke**, and **show**.) A path consists of an arbitrary sequence of connected and disconnected points, lines, and curves that together describe shapes and their positions. It is built up through the sequential application of the *path construction operators*, each of which modifies the current path in some way (usually by appending one new element to the current path).

Path construction operators include **newpath**, **moveto**, **lineto**, **curveto**, **arc**, **closepath**, and many others. None of these operators places marks on the current page; that is left to the painting operators.

Other implicit arguments to the painting operators include the

---

[1] A detailed, technical description of a similar imaging model has appeared in a paper by John Warnock and Douglas Wyatt, "A Device Independent Graphics Imaging Model for Use with Raster Devices," *Computer Graphics*, Vol. 16, No. 3, July 1982, pp. 313-320. The description given here is in terms that a POSTSCRIPT programmer should understand before using POSTSCRIPT to prepare printed pages.

current color, current line thickness, current font (typeface-size-rotation combination), etc. Operators exist to examine and set each implicit argument. The values held in the implicit arguments at the time a painting operator is executed will affect the behavior of that operator.

POSTSCRIPT programs that make printed pages will contain many instances of the following pattern: build a path using path construction operators; set any implicit arguments (if their values need to change); perform a painting operation.

There is one additional implicit element in the POSTSCRIPT imaging model that modifies the foregoing description: a *current clipping path* that outlines the area of the current page upon which paint may be placed. Initially, this clipping path outlines the entire imageable area of the current page; parts of the page description which lie off of the page (outside the clipping path) are discarded. By using the **clip** operator, a POSTSCRIPT program can shrink the current clipping path to any shape desired. It is quite normal for a painting operator to attempt to place marks outside of the current clipping path. Those marks falling within the clipping area will affect the current page; those marks falling outside will not.

4.3 GRAPHICS STATE

The POSTSCRIPT interpreter maintains a data structure called the *graphics state* that holds current graphics control parameters. These parameters define the context in which the graphics operators execute. For example, the **show** operator implicitly uses the *current font* parameter in the graphics state, and the **fill** operator implicitly uses the *current color* parameter.

The graphics state is not itself an object and cannot be accessed directly. However, it consists of many objects, nearly all of which can be both read and altered by graphics state operators.

Graphics states are maintained in a stack. A POSTSCRIPT program may preserve the current graphics state by pushing it on the graphics state stack with the **gsave** operator. It may then modify the current graphics state to have many different characteristics, such as a different font, transformation matrix, line style, and so forth. After executing any desired graphics operators in the new context, the program may restore the original graphics state by popping the stack (with **grestore**). This facility permits elements of a page description to be encapsulated: they may make local changes for their own purposes, but such changes are not permanent.

The complete set of graphics state parameters is summarized below. More details are given in the descriptions of the operators for accessing these parameters (see chapter 6).

Parameter	Type	Value
CTM	array	The current transformation matrix: a matrix that maps positions from user coordinates to device coordinates. This matrix is modified by each application of the coordinate system operators. (Initial value: a straightforward matrix transforming default user coordinates to device coordinates.)
color	(internal)	The color to use during painting operations. This may be specified and read according to any of several different color models; the actual internal representation is not accessible. (Initial value: black.)
position	2 numbers	Current position in user space, also known as the current *point*. (Initial value: undefined.)
path	(internal)	The current path as built up by the path construction operators. The current path is an implicit argument to the **fill**, **stroke**, and **clip** operators. (Initial value: empty.)
clipping path	(internal)	A path defining the current boundary against which all output is cropped. (Initial value: the entire imageable portion of the output device.)
font	dictionary	Set of graphic shapes (characters) that define the current typeface. (Initial value: installation dependent.)
line width	number	The thickness (in user coordinate units) of lines to be drawn by the **stroke** operator. (Initial value: 1.)
line cap	integer	A code that defines the shape of the endpoints of any open path that is stroked. (Initial value: 0, for a square butt end.)
line join	integer	A code that defines the shape of joints between connected segments of a stroked line. (Initial value: 0, for mitered joins.)

halftone screen	(several)	A collection of POSTSCRIPT objects that define the current halftone screen pattern for gray and color output. (Initial value: installation dependent.)
transfer	array	A procedure that maps user gray levels into device gray levels. (Initial value: installation dependent.)
flatness	number	The accuracy (or smoothness) with which curves are to be rendered on the output device. This number gives the maximum error tolerance (in output device pixels) of a straight line segment approximation of any portion of a curve. Smaller numbers give smoother curves at the expense of more computation. (Initial value: 1.0.)
miter limit	number	The maximum length of mitered line joins for the **stroke** operator. This limits the length of 'spikes' produced when line segments join at sharp angles. (Initial value: 10, for a miter cutoff below 11 degrees.)
dash pattern	(several)	A description of the dash pattern to be used when lines are rendered by the **stroke** operator. (Initial value: a normal solid line.)
device	(internal)	An internal data structure representing the current output device, along with a set of internal primitives for rendering graphical objects in the raster memory associated with that device. (Initial value: installation dependent.)

4.4 COORDINATE SYSTEMS AND TRANSFORMATIONS

User space and device space

Paths and shapes are defined in terms of points on the current page (or outside the page) specified as coordinates. A *coordinate* is a pair of real numbers x and y that locate a point within a Cartesian coordinate system superimposed on the current page. The POSTSCRIPT language defines a standard, default coordinate system that POSTSCRIPT programs may depend on for locating any point on the page.

Output devices vary greatly in the built-in coordinate systems they use to address actual pixels within their imageable area. We refer to a particular device's coordinate system as *device space*. Device space origins can be anywhere on the output page; the paper moves through different printers in different directions; different devices have different resolutions; and some devices even have resolutions that are different in the x and y directions.

Coordinates specified in a POSTSCRIPT program, however, refer to locations within an ideal coordinate system that always bears the same relationship to the current page regardless of the output device on which printing will be done. We call this coordinate system *user space*, as it is the coordinate system that programs use to specify points.

The POSTSCRIPT interpreter automatically transforms points specified in user space into the device space of the actual raster device being used. For the most part, this transformation is hidden from the POSTSCRIPT program; a program needs to consider device space only rarely for certain special effects. This independence of user space from device space is a major contributor to the device independent nature of POSTSCRIPT page descriptions.

To specify a coordinate system with respect to the current page, we must know the location of the origin, the orientation of the x and y axes, and the lengths of the units along each axis. Initially, the user space origin is located at the lower left corner of the output page, with the positive x axis extending horizontally to the right and the positive y axis extending vertically upward (as in standard mathematical practice.) The length of a unit along the x axis and along the y axis is 1/72 of an inch. We call this coordinate system *default user space*.

These features of default user space are chosen for their mathematical simplicity and convenience. The location and orientation of the axes follow common mathematical practice and cause all points within the current page to have positive x and y coordinate values. The unit size, 1/72 of an inch, is very close to the size of a printer's point (1/72.27 inch), which is a standard measuring unit used in the printing industry.

It is important to understand that coordinates in user space are specified as arbitrary POSTSCRIPT numbers, i.e., either integers or reals. Therefore, the unit size in default user space does not constrain points to any arbitrary grid; the resolution of coordinates in user space is not related in any way to the resolution of pixels in device space.

Although the choices made for default user space are arbitrary, they provide a consistent, dependable starting place for POSTSCRIPT programs regardless of the output device being used. The POSTSCRIPT program may then modify its user space into one more suitable for its needs (if necessary) by applying *coordinate transformation operators*, such as **translate**, **rotate**, and **scale**.

Thus, what may appear to be absolute coordinates in a POSTSCRIPT program are actually quite changeable with respect to the current page, since they are described in a coordinate system that may slide around and shrink or expand. Coordinate system transformation not only enhances device independence but is a useful tool in its own right. For example, a page description originally composed to occupy an entire page may be incorporated without change into another page description that uses it as just one element of a page.

Transformations

Transformation of coordinates from one space to another is specified by means of a *transformation matrix*. Such a matrix specifies how the *x* and *y* values of a point in one coordinate space are transformed into the *x* and *y* values of the corresponding point in another coordinate space. Included in the graphics state is a *current transformation matrix* (CTM) describing the transformation from user space to device space.

The elements of a matrix actually specify the coefficients of a pair of linear equations in *x* and *y* that generate a transformed *x* and *y*. However, in graphical applications, matrices are not often thought of in this abstract mathematical way. Instead, a matrix is considered to capture some sequence of geometric manipulations: translation, rotation, scaling, reflection, etc. Most of the POSTSCRIPT matrix operators are organized according to this model.

The matrix operators most commonly used are the ones that *modify* the current transformation matrix (CTM) in the graphics state. That is, they change the mapping between user space and device space that will be used during subsequent graphical operations. These operators do not create a new transformation matrix from nothing; instead, they change the existing transformation matrix in some specific way. It is usually convenient to visualize these operators as modifying user space itself, e.g., moving the origin (translation) or changing the length of a unit (scaling).

translate moves the user space origin to a new position with respect to the current page while leaving the orientation of the axes and the unit sizes unchanged. **rotate** turns the user space axes about the current user space origin by some angle, leaving the unit lengths unchanged in their current directions. **scale** modifies the unit lengths independently along the current x and y axes, leaving the origin location and the orientation of the axes unchanged.

Such modifications have a variety of uses. The simplest is changing the user coordinate system conventions for an entire page. For example, in some application it might be convenient for user coordinates to be expressed in centimeters rather than points; or it might be convenient to have the origin in the center of the page rather than the lower left corner.

A more interesting and powerful use of coordinate system modification is to define each graphical element of a page in its *own* coordinate system, independent of any other element. Each element may then be positioned, oriented, and scaled to the desired location on the page by temporarily modifying the user coordinate system. This permits the description of an element to be decoupled from the description of how it is to be placed on the page.

A simple example may aid in understanding this concept. This example uses graphics operators that we haven't formally introduced yet, but the comments in the example should make it clear what they do.

```
/box {newpath       % Define a procedure to construct a unit square
    0 0 moveto      % path in the current user coordinate system,
    0 1 lineto      % with its lower left corner at the origin.
    1 1 lineto
    1 0 lineto
    closepath
    } def

gsave               % Save the current graphics state and create a
                    % new one which we shall then modify.
```

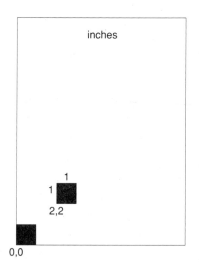

72 72 scale	% Modify the current transform matrix so that % everything subsequently drawn will be 72 times % larger; that is, each unit will represent an inch % instead of a point.
box fill	% Draw a unit square with its lower left corner at % the origin, and fill it with black. Since the unit size % is now one inch, this box is one inch on a side.
2 2 translate	% Change the transformation matrix again so that % the origin is at 2″, 2″ (displaced two inches % in from the left and bottom edges of the page).
box fill	% Draw the box again. This box has its lower % left corner two inches up from and two inches % to the right of the lower left corner of the page, % and it is one inch square.
grestore	% Restore the saved graphics state. % Now we are back to default user space.

This example shows how coordinates such as the ones given to the **moveto** and **lineto** graphics operators are transformed by the current transformation matrix. By combining translation, scaling, and rotation, one may use very simple prototype graphics procedures, such as **box** in the example, to generate an infinite variety of instances.

Matrix representation and manipulation

Understanding the descriptions of the coordinate system and matrix operators in chapter 6 requires some knowledge of the representation and manipulation of matrices. We now present a brief introduction to this topic.[2] It is not essential that you understand the details of matrix arithmetic on first reading, but only that you obtain a clear geometrical model of the effects of the various transformations.

A two-dimensional transformation is described mathematically by a 3×3 matrix:

[2]For a complete mathematical explanation of matrix operations and their uses in describing geometrical transformations, see the book by W. M. Newman and R. F. Sproull, *Principles of Interactive Computer Graphics*, McGraw-Hill, 1979.

$$
\begin{matrix}
a & b & 0 \\
c & d & 0 \\
t_x & t_y & 1
\end{matrix}
$$

In the POSTSCRIPT language, this matrix is represented as a six-element array object:

$$[a \ b \ c \ d \ t_x \ t_y]$$

(omitting the matrix elements in the third column, which always have constant values.)

This matrix transforms a coordinate (x, y) into another coordinate (x', y') according to the linear equations:

$$x' = ax + cy + t_x$$
$$y' = bx + dy + t_y$$

The common transformations are easily described in this matrix notation. Translation by a specified displacement (t_x, t_y) is described by the matrix:

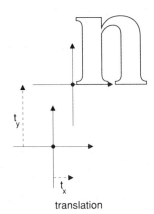

translation

$$
\begin{matrix}
1 & 0 & 0 \\
0 & 1 & 0 \\
t_x & t_y & 1
\end{matrix}
$$

Scaling by the factor s_x in the x dimension and s_y in the y dimension is accomplished by:

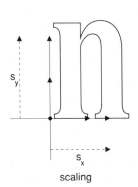

scaling

$$
\begin{matrix}
s_x & 0 & 0 \\
0 & s_y & 0 \\
0 & 0 & 1
\end{matrix}
$$

Rotation counterclockwise about the origin by an angle θ is described by the matrix:

$$
\begin{matrix}
\cos\theta & \sin\theta & 0 \\
-\sin\theta & \cos\theta & 0 \\
0 & 0 & 1
\end{matrix}
$$

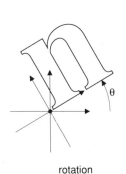

rotation

Any desired transformation can be described as a sequence of these and other operations performed in some order. An important property of the matrix notation is that a sequence of operations can be *concatenated* to form a single matrix that embodies all of those operations in combination.[3] That is, transforming any coordinate by the single concatenated matrix produces the same result as transforming it by all of the original matrices in sequence. Consequently, any linear transformation from user space to device space can be described by a single matrix, the CTM.

The POSTSCRIPT operators **translate**, **scale**, and **rotate** each concatenate the CTM with a matrix describing the desired transformation, producing a new matrix that describes the combination of the original and additional transformations. This matrix is then established as the new CTM.

It is sometimes necessary to perform the *inverse* of a transformation, e.g., to find the coordinate in user space that corresponds to a specific device space coordinate. (This is only occasionally done explicitly by POSTSCRIPT programs but occurs fairly commonly in the POSTSCRIPT graphics machinery.) Not all transformations are invertible in this way; for example, if a matrix contains a, b, c, and d elements that are all zero, all user coordinates map to the same device coordinate and there is no unique inverse transformation. Occurrence of this state of affairs gives rise to the error **undefinedresult**. Non-invertible transformations aren't very useful and generally arise only from unintentional operations such as scaling by zero.

4.5 PATH CONSTRUCTION

The POSTSCRIPT *path* is the means for defining shapes, trajectories, and regions of all sorts. Paths are used to draw lines, to specify boundaries of filled areas, and to define templates for clipping other graphics.

A path is composed of straight and curved line segments. These segments may connect to one another or they may be disconnected. The topology of a path is unrestricted: it may be concave or convex, it may contain multiple closed subpaths, thus representing several areas, and it may intersect itself in arbitrary ways.

---

[3]Concatenation is performed by matrix multiplication. The requirement that matrices conform during multiplication is what leads to the use of 3×3 matrices; otherwise, 2×3 matrices would suffice to describe transformations.

Paths are represented by data structures internal to the POSTSCRIPT graphics machinery. Though a path is not directly accessible as a POSTSCRIPT object, its construction and use are entirely under the control of the POSTSCRIPT program. A path is constructed by sequential application of one or more *path construction operators*. At any time, the path may be read out or (more commonly) used to control the application of one of the painting operators described in section 4.6.

There is a *current path* which is part of the graphics state. The path construction operators modify the current path (usually by appending to it), and the painting operators refer to the current path. Like all components of the graphics state, the current path is saved and restored by **gsave** and **grestore**.

The order of segments defining a path is significant. A pair of line segments is said to *connect* only if they are defined consecutively, with the second segment starting where the first one ends. Non-consecutive segments that meet or intersect fortuitously are not considered to connect.

A *subpath* of a path is a sequence of connected segments; a path is made up of one or more disconnected subpaths. An operator exists to explicitly connect the end of a subpath back to its starting point; such a subpath is said to be *closed*. A subpath that has not been closed explicitly is said to be *open*.

A path is begun by executing the **newpath** operator, which initializes the current path to be empty. (Some of the painting operators also initialize the path at the end of their execution.) The path is then built up by executing one or more of the operators for adding segments to the current path in any sequence (however, a **moveto** must usually come first).

All the points used to describe the path are coordinates in user space. Each coordinate is transformed by the CTM into device space at the time the point is entered into the current path; changing the CTM does not cause existing points to move in device space.

The trailing endpoint of the segment most recently entered is referred to as the *current point*. If the current path is empty, the current point is undefined. Most operators that add a segment to the current path start at the current point; if the current point is undefined, they will execute the error **nocurrentpoint**.

- **moveto** establishes a new current point without adding a segment to the path. This begins a new subpath of the current path.

- **lineto** adds a straight line segment to the path, connecting the previous current point to the new one.

- **arc**, **arcn**, and **arcto** add an arc of a circle to the current path.

- **curveto** adds a section of a Bézier cubic curve to the current path.

- **rmoveto**, **rlineto**, and **rcurveto** perform the **moveto**, **lineto**, and **curveto** operations but specify new points as displacements (in user space) relative to the current point.

- **closepath** adds a straight line segment connecting the current point to the starting point of the current subpath (usually the point most recently specified by **moveto**), thereby *closing* the current subpath.

There are several other path construction operators; complete details are presented in chapter 6.

The graphics state also contains a *clipping path* that defines the regions of the page that may be affected by the painting operators. Marks falling inside the area defined by the closed subpaths of this path will be applied to the page; marks falling outside will not. (Precisely what is considered to be 'inside' a path is discussed in section 4.6.) The **clip** operator computes a new clipping path from the intersection of the current path with the existing clipping path.

Remember that the path construction operators do not place any marks on the page; that is done only by the painting operators. The usual procedure for rendering a graphic element on the page is to define that element as a path and then invoke one of the painting operators. This is repeated for each element on the page.

A path that is to be used more than once in a page description should be defined by a POSTSCRIPT procedure that invokes the operators for constructing the path. Each instance of the path may then be constructed and rendered on the page by a three-step sequence. First, modify the CTM by invoking coordinate transformation operators to properly locate, orient, and scale the path to the desired place on the page. Second, call the procedure to construct the path. Finally, execute a painting operator to render the path on the page in the desired manner. The entire sequence may be encapsulated by surrounding it with **gsave** and **grestore**. A simple illustration of this style of use appeared in the 'box' example of section 4.4.

We stated previously that a POSTSCRIPT path is unrestricted in its topology. However, since the entire set of points defining a path must exist as data simultaneously, there is a limit to the number of segments a path may have. Since several paths may exist simultaneously (current path, clipping path, and paths saved by **gsave**), this limit actually applies to the total amount of storage occupied by all paths. The value of the limit is given in appendix B.

As a practical matter, the limits on path storage are sufficiently large that they do not impose an unreasonable restriction. It is important, however, that separate elements of a page be constructed as separate paths that are each painted and then discarded. An attempt to describe an entire page as a single path is likely to exceed the path storage limit.

4.6 PAINTING

The painting operators scan convert graphical shapes into raster memory to represent marks on the current page. The principal general-purpose painting operators are **stroke** and **fill**, described below. More specialized operators are **image**, described in section 4.7, and the character and font operators, described in chapter 5.

The **stroke** operator draws a line of some thickness along the current path. For each straight or curved segment in the path, **stroke** draws a line that is centered on the segment and whose sides are parallel to the segment.

The results produced by **stroke** are controlled by a number of parameters in the graphics state: color, line width, line cap, line join, flatness, miter limit, and dash. These were summarized in section 4.3; details appear in chapter 6.

stroke treats each subpath of a path separately. Wherever two consecutive segments are connected, the joint between them is treated with the current *line join*, which may be mitered, rounded, or beveled (see the description of the **setlinejoin** operator). If the subpath is open, the unconnected ends are treated with the current *line cap*, which may be butt, rounded, or square (see **setlinecap**). Points at which unconnected segments happen to meet or intersect receive no special treatment. (In particular, 'closing' a subpath with an explicit **lineto** rather than with **closepath** may result in a messy corner, since line caps rather than a line join are applied in that case.)

A stroke may be drawn either with a solid line or with a user-specified dash pattern (see **setdash**). The color of the line is determined by the current color in the graphics state (see **setgray**, **sethsbcolor**, and **setrgbcolor**). The accuracy and smoothness with which curves are rendered is controlled by the 'flatness' parameter (see **setflat**).

The **fill** operator paints the entire region enclosed by the current path with the current color. If the path consists of several disconnected subpaths, **fill** paints the insides of all subpaths, considered together. Any subpaths of the path that are open are implicitly closed before being filled.

For a simple path, it is intuitively clear what region lies 'inside'. However, for a more complex path (e.g., a path that intersects itself or has one subpath that encloses another), the interpretation of 'inside' is not so obvious. The POSTSCRIPT path machinery uses one of two rules for determining which points lie inside a path.

The *non-zero winding number rule* determines whether a given point is inside a path by (conceptually) drawing a ray from that point to infinity in any direction and then examining the places where a segment of the path crosses the ray. Starting with a count of zero, we add one each time a path segment crosses the ray from left to right and subtract one each time a path segment crosses the ray from right to left.[4] After counting all the cross-ings, if the result is zero then the point is outside the path, other-wise it is inside.

With this rule, a simple convex path yields inside and outside as we would expect. Now consider a five pointed star, drawn with five connected straight line segments intersecting each other. The entire area enclosed by the star, including the pentagon in the center, is considered inside by the non-zero winding number rule. For a path composed of two concentric circles, if they are both drawn in the same direction, the areas enclosed by both circles are inside according to the rule. If they are drawn in op-posite directions, only the 'doughnut' shape between the two circles is inside according to the rule; the 'hole' is outside.

An alternative to the non-zero winding number rule is the *even-odd rule*. This rule determines the 'insideness' of a point by drawing a ray from that point in any direction and counting the number of path segments that the ray crosses. If this number is odd, the point is inside; if even, the point is outside.

The even-odd rule yields the same results as the non-zero wind-ing number rule for paths with simple shapes, but different results for more complex ones. For the five pointed star drawn with five intersecting lines, the even-odd rule considers the tri-angular points to be inside but the pentagon in the center to be outside. For the two concentric circles, only the 'doughnut' shape between the two circles is inside according to the even-odd rule, regardless of whether the circles are drawn in the same or opposite directions.

The non-zero winding number rule is more versatile than the even-odd rule and is the default rule used by the POSTSCRIPT **fill** and **clip** operators. The even-odd rule is occasionally useful for special effects or for compatibility with other graphics systems; the **eofill** and **eoclip** operators invoke this rule.

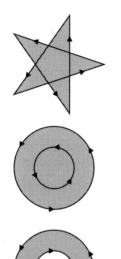

Non-zero winding number rule

Even-odd rule

---

[4]The rule does not specify what to do if a path segment coincides with or is tangent to the ray. Since any ray will do, one may simply choose a different ray that does not encounter such problem intersections.

4.7 IMAGES

The POSTSCRIPT painting operators include general facilities for dealing with sampled images and rendering them on a page. These facilities are sufficiently different from the other painting operators that we deal with them separately.

A *sampled image* (or just 'image' for short) is a rectangular array of sample values, each of which represents some color. This image may approximate the appearance of some natural scene (much the same as a television picture) or it may be generated synthetically.

A POSTSCRIPT image is defined by a sequence of gray-level values obtained by scanning the image rectangle in row or column order. There are no constraints on the number of rows or columns in the array. Each value consists of a 1, 2, 4, or 8 bit integer, permitting the representation of 2, 4, 16, or 256 different gray level values for each sample.[5]

The operators that render an image on a page are **image** and **imagemask**. The details of these operators may be found in the operator descriptions in chapter 6, along with an example of using each one. However, some general information about the rendering of images is presented here.

Image parameters

The properties of an image (resolution, orientation, scanning order, etc.) are entirely independent of the properties of the raster output device on which the image is to be rendered. The POSTSCRIPT graphics machinery usually renders an image by a sampling and halftoning technique that attempts to approximate the gray values of the source as accurately as possible. The accuracy depends on the resolution and other properties of the raster output device.

In order to paint an image on a page, a POSTSCRIPT program must specify four interrelated items:

[5]At present, the POSTSCRIPT language does not provide a way to represent full color in a single image. However, under suitable conditions, full color can be represented as three color separations each defined by a gray-scale image. Such image processing is beyond the scope of this manual.

- The format of the source image: number of columns (width), number of rows (height), and number of bits per sample.

- The image data itself, consisting of *height* × *width* × *bits/sample* bits of information.

- The correspondence between coordinates in user space and coordinates in the source image space, defining the region of user space that will receive the image.

- The mapping from gray-level values in the source image to apparent gray values in the printed result.

These four aspects of image rendering are entirely under the control of the POSTSCRIPT program.

Sample data representation

The source format is specified straightforwardly as three integers: *width*, *height*, and *bits/sample*.

The image data is represented as a stream of characters, i.e., 8-bit integers in the range 0 to 255. Each character contains one or more sample values (depending on *bits/sample*); the first sample value in a character consists of the most significant *bits/sample* bits of the character.

The image operators obtain source data by repeatedly calling a POSTSCRIPT procedure passed as an operand. This procedure must return a POSTSCRIPT string object containing any number of characters of sample data. (The number of characters is arbitrary and need bear no relation to the dimensions of the source image.)

This technique for supplying samples to the image operators provides a flexible means of dealing with a variety of image formats. There is no requirement that all the samples of the source image reside in POSTSCRIPT memory at the same time. The procedure may obtain the data from some external file (perhaps the primary input file), which it reads a piece at a time into a temporary string using the **readstring** or **readhexstring** operator. It may derive the data from some compressed representation, decompressing it incrementally. It may even generate the data itself according to some algorithm, producing a synthetic image.

The image operators impose a coordinate system on the source image: it is considered to be a rectangle that is *height* units high and *width* units wide; each sample occupies one square unit. The origin (0, 0) is in the lower left corner; *x* values range from 0 to *width* inclusive; and *y* values range from 0 to *height* inclusive.

Additionally, the image operators assume that they receive sample data from their procedure operand in *x*-axis major indexing order. The coordinate of the lower left corner of the first sample is (0, 0), of the second is (1, 0), and so on through the last sample of the first row, whose lower left corner is at (*width*−1, 0) and whose lower right corner is at (*width*, 0). The next samples after that are at coordinates (0, 1), (1, 1), etc., until the final sample of the image, whose lower left corner is at (*width*−1, *height*−1) and whose upper right corner is at (*width*, *height*).[6]

The source coordinate system and scanning order imposed by the POSTSCRIPT image operators do not preclude the use of different conventions in the actual source image. Other conventions can be mapped into the POSTSCRIPT convention by coordinate transformation.

The correspondence between this source image coordinate system (or *image space*) and user space is specified by a matrix operand. For reasons that will become apparent in a moment, this matrix defines a mapping from user space to image space; that is, a user space coordinate transformed by the matrix yields an image space coordinate. There exist four points in user space that map to the coordinates of the four corners of the image in image space. This is a fully general linear transformation that can include translation, rotation, reflection, and skewing (see section 4.4).

Though it is possible to map directly between current user space and image space by appropriate definition of the image matrix,

[6] If *bits/sample* is less than 8 and *width* is not a multiple of the number of samples per character, there must be extra samples at the end of each row to fill up the last character. The values of the extra samples are not used; they are present only in order to align the data so that each row starts on a character boundary.

the transformation is easier to think about if it is divided into two steps. The first step maps the unit square of user space (bounded by (0, 0) and (1, 1) in user space) to the boundary of the source image in image space. The second step maps the unit square of user space to the rectangle (or parallelogram) in current user space that is to receive the image. This is just a convention, but a useful one that is recommended.

With this convention, the image matrix is used solely to describe the image itself, independent of how it is to be positioned, oriented, and scaled on a particular page. That is, it serves to map between the actual image space and an idealized one corresponding to the POSTSCRIPT standard coordinate system and scanning order.

Thus, an image that happens to use POSTSCRIPT's conventions (scanning left-to-right, bottom-to-top) can be described by the image matrix

[*width* 0 0 *height* 0 0].

An image that is scanned left-to-right, top-to-bottom (a very commonly used order) is described by the image matrix

[*width* 0 0 *–height* 0 *height*].

Images scanned in other common orders can be described by other image matrices that are translated reflections or multiples of 90-degree rotations from these.

An image that has been mapped into the unit square in this manner may then be placed on the output page in the desired position, orientation, and size by invoking the POSTSCRIPT operators that transform user space, namely **translate**, **rotate**, and **scale**. For example, to map such an image into a rectangle whose lower left corner is at (100, 200), is rotated 45 degrees counterclockwise, and is 150 units wide and 80 high, one would execute

100 200 translate 45 rotate 150 80 scale

prior to invoking the **image** or **imagemask** operator. This works for *any* image that has been mapped into the unit square by an appropriate image matrix. Of course, if the aspect ratio (width to height) of the source image in this example were different from the ratio 150:80 then the result would be distorted.

Note that if only part of an image is desired, one should establish a clipping path (using the **clip** operator) before invoking **image** or **imagemask**. Only the portions of the image that fall within the clipping path will actually produce marks on the page.

Gray-scale rendering

Sample values in the source image are integers in the range 0 to 2^n-1 inclusive, where n is the number of bits per sample. The default interpretation of these values is that the lowest value represents black (minimum intensity), the highest value represents white (maximum intensity), and intermediate values represent intermediate shades of gray. However, this correspondence can be modified by changing the output *transfer function* using the **settransfer** operator.

Details of the halftoning process are also under program control. The frequency, angle, and spot shape used for the halftone screen may all be set by means of the **setscreen** operator. Both **settransfer** and **setscreen** are described in section 4.8.

Device-resolution images

A special case of a sampled image is a *binary image* that uses one bit per sample. Under certain circumstances, the POSTSCRIPT image operators will transfer samples directly from a binary image to the raster output device rather than using the more general sampling and halftoning technique. This produces results that are precisely predictable down to the pixel level; it is also a great deal faster than general imaging.

The conditions under which samples are transferred directly from an image to a device are as follows:

- The image is one bit per sample.
- The combination of the image matrix and the current transformation matrix is such that one unit in image space corresponds to one unit in device space. (In other words, the image and device resolutions are the same.)
- The image coordinate system's x and y axes are parallel to the corresponding axes of device space, and the x coordinate values increase in the same direction.

Device-resolution binary images are used by applications that wish to control printed results down to the pixel level. A situation in which this is useful is the printing of characters that are represented as bitmaps (i.e., binary pixel arrays) rather than as outlines. (Such bitmaps are usually printed using the mask facility, described below.) While no standard POSTSCRIPT fonts are represented as bitmaps, there are many bitmap fonts available from other sources.

Use of device-resolution images might seem to violate the device independence of a POSTSCRIPT page description. However, this is not so. If such a page description is printed on an output device different from the one for which it was intended (or the page is transformed in some other way), the special conditions will not apply and the bitmap will be treated as a general image; that is, it will be rendered by the sampling and halftoning technique described earlier in this chapter. This may take longer than expected, but the results will still be correct.

Masks

Normal images are consistent with the POSTSCRIPT imaging model (section 4.2) in that all areas of a page affected by an image are marked as if with opaque paint. Any portion of an image, whether black, white, or halftone gray, completely obscures any marks that previously existed in the same place on the page.

There is a special variant of a binary image, called a *mask*, whose properties are quite different: whereas an image is opaque, a mask is partially transparent. The **imagemask** operator applies masks.

The samples of a mask do not represent colors; instead, they designate places on the page that should be marked (with some separately specified color) or not marked at all. The places that are not marked retain their former color values. One should think of pouring paint 'through' a mask, where a '1' sample permits the paint to reach the page but a '0' blocks it (or vice versa).

Masks are most often useful for painting characters represented as bitmaps, as discussed in the previous section. Ordinarily when printing such characters, one wants the 'black' bits of the character to be transferred to the page but the 'white' bits (which are really just background) to be left alone. For reasons discussed in section 5.6, **imagemask** rather than **image** should almost always be used to paint bitmap characters.

4.8 COLORS AND HALFTONES

The POSTSCRIPT graphics machinery includes facilities for controlling quite precisely how marks having a given abstract color are actually rendered in raster memory. In this section, we introduce the POSTSCRIPT color models and describe the aspects of the halftoning process that are accessible to POSTSCRIPT programs. Understanding this information is not essential to basic use of POSTSCRIPT graphics; you may wish to skip this section on first reading.

Though the number of operators for controlling color rendition and halftoning is fairly small, their detailed behavior is complex. Furthermore, some aspects of color rendition and halftoning depend on physical properties of the raster output device. The device setup procedure for each device establishes default settings that are appropriate for that device. The defaults are suitable for rendering most page descriptions; only in very unusual situations is it appropriate for a POSTSCRIPT program to change them.

Color models

As described in section 4.6, marks placed on the page have a color that is determined by the *current color* parameter in the graphics state. The POSTSCRIPT language allows specification of any color; black, white, and gray shades are special cases of full color. Due to the importance and predominance of black-and-white binary and gray-scale output devices, however, we shall mention full color only briefly and then concentrate on black-and-white and gray-scale rendition.

Colors may be specified according to either of two POSTSCRIPT color models, called the *hue-saturation-brightness* (HSB) and *red-green-blue* (RGB) models. Each of these models can specify any color by three numeric parameters, but the numbers mean different things in the two models.[7]

In the RGB model, a color is described as a combination of the three primary colors of light (red, green, and blue) in particular concentrations. The intensity of each primary color is specified by a number in the range 0 to 1, where 0 indicates no contribution at all and 1 indicates maximum intensity of that color. If all three colors have equal intensity, the perceived result is a pure gray on the scale from black to white. If the intensities are not all equal, the result is some color that is a function of the relative intensities of the primary colors. Note that this convention parallels the mixing of colored light; the presence of all primary colors in equal measure yields white light.

In the HSB model, a color is described as a combination of three parameters called hue, saturation, and brightness. There exists a convention for arranging colors around a 'color circle'. The hue parameter specifies the position of a color on this circle: 0 corresponds to pure red, 1/3 to pure green, 2/3 to pure blue, and 1 to red again; intermediate values correspond to mixtures of the adjacent colors. The saturation component refers to the concentration of the selected hue with respect to the overall intensity: 0 corresponds to no color (only a shade of gray), 1 corresponds to maximum concentration (no white light mixed in). The brightness component refers to the overall intensity of light: 0 is black and 1 is maximum intensity.

Color may be specified according to either model by the **setrgbcolor** and **sethsbcolor** operators. The current color may be read according to either model (**currentrgbcolor** and **currenthsbcolor**); these operators convert between color models if necessary according to the NTSC video standard (a discussion of which is beyond the scope of this manual).

Black, white, and intermediate shades of gray are special cases of full color. A gray-scale value is described by a single number in the range 0 to 1: 0 corresponds to black, 1 to white, and intermediate values to different gray levels. The **setgray** operator sets

---

[7]For a complete explanation of these color models and the conversions between them, see the article by Alvy Ray Smith, "Color gamut transform pairs," *Computer Graphics*, Vol. 12, No. 3, August 1978. In that article, the HSB model is referred to as the hue-saturation-value model.

the current color in the graphics state to be a specified gray level. When an arbitrary color is to be rendered on a black-and-white or gray-scale device, the gray level used is the brightness component according to the HSB model. This is also the result that is returned by the **currentgray** operator.

Halftone screens

When an intermediate shade of gray is to be rendered on a raster output device whose pixels can be only black or white, the POSTSCRIPT graphics machinery employs a *halftoning* technique to approximate the desired results.[8] The halftone pattern (or *screen*) is under the control of the POSTSCRIPT program, which may execute the **setscreen** operator to establish a new screen.

All parameters of a screen are interpreted in *device space*, unaffected by the current transformation matrix (CTM). For correct results, a POSTSCRIPT program that defines a new screen must know the resolution and orientation of device space. Furthermore, the best choice of screen parameters is often dependent on specific physical properties of the output device itself (e.g., pixel shape, overlap between pixels, and effects of electronic or mechanical noise).

A screen is defined by laying a uniform square grid of *halftone cells* over the device pixel array. Each pixel belongs to one cell of the grid; a cell may (and typically does) contain many device pixels. The grid has a *frequency* (number of cells per inch) and *angle* (orientation of the grid lines relative to the device coordinate system). The **setscreen** operator may make slight adjustments to the requested frequency and angle so as to ensure that the patterns of enclosed pixels remain constant as the screen cells are replicated over the entire page. The screen grid is defined entirely in device space, unchanged by modifications to the CTM; this property is essential for ensuring that adjacent areas colored by halftones are properly stitched together without 'seams'.

Each cell of a screen can be made to approximate a shade of gray by painting some of the cell's pixels black and some pixels

---

[8]A similar technique is used for rendering full color on a device whose pixels consist of primary colors that are either completely on or completely off.

white. Numerically, the gray level produced within a cell is the ratio of the cell's pixels that are white to the total number of pixels in that cell. If a cell contains n pixels then it is capable of rendering $n+1$ different gray levels: all pixels black, one pixel white, two pixels white, ..., $n-1$ pixels white, all n pixels white. A particular desired gray value g in the range 0 to 1 is produced by making i pixels white, where $i = \text{floor}(g \times n)$.

As a cell's desired gray value varies from black to white, individual pixels in the cell change from black to white in a well-defined sequence. If a particular gray includes certain white pixels, lighter grays will include the same white pixels as well as some additional ones. The order in which pixels change from black to white for increasing gray levels is specified by a *spot function*, which is defined as a POSTSCRIPT procedure.

The spot function describes the order of pixel whitening in an indirect way that minimizes interactions with screen frequency and angle. Consider a halftone cell to have its own coordinate system: the center of the square is the origin and the corners are at ± 1 in x and y. In this system, each pixel in the cell is centered at x and y coordinates that are both between -1 and 1. For each pixel, **setscreen** pushes the pixel's coordinates on the operand stack and calls the spot function procedure; the procedure must return a single number between -1 and 1 that defines the pixel's position in the ordering.

The actual values returned by the spot function are not significant; all that matters is the *relative* spot function values for different pixels. As a cell's gray value varies from black to white, the first pixel whitened is the one whose spot function has the lowest value, the next pixel is the one with the next higher spot function value, and so on. (If two pixels have the same spot function value, **setscreen** chooses their relative order arbitrarily.)

There are relatively simple spot functions that define common halftone patterns. A spot function whose value is inversely related to the distance from the center of the cell produces a 'dot screen' in which the black pixels are clustered within a circle whose area is inversely proportional to the gray level. An example of such a spot function is:

```
{dup mul exch dup mul add 1 exch sub}
```

(This is not actually the inverse distance function but a simpler one that produces values in the same order.) A spot function whose value is the distance from a line through the center of the cell produces a 'line screen' in which the white pixels grow away from that line. More complex patterns are occasionally useful, including those based on an externally-supplied mask (see the POSTSCRIPT *Language Tutorial and Cookbook* for some examples). Remember, though, that screens are defined in *device* space; page descriptions that use screens for special purposes are therefore tied to a particular device.

In principle, the POSTSCRIPT language permits defining screens with arbitrarily large cells (i.e., arbitrarily low frequencies). However, cells that are very large (relative to device resolution) or are at unfavorable angles may exceed screen storage in some POSTSCRIPT configurations; if this occurs, **setscreen** executes a **limitcheck** error.

Transfer function

The POSTSCRIPT *transfer function* permits correction of gray values to compensate for nonlinear gray-level response in an output device and in the human eye. A halftone gray produced by making n percent of the pixels white is typically not perceived as n percent gray by the viewer. The transfer function enables 'user gray' values to be mapped to arbitrary 'device gray' values that actually determine the percentage of whitened pixels per halftone cell.

Gray levels supplied to the **setgray** operator by a POSTSCRIPT program or appearing as data values in a sampled image are not used directly but are mapped through the current transfer function. This is a POSTSCRIPT procedure that takes a numeric operand in the range 0 to 1 and returns a result in the same range. The **settransfer** operator may be used to establish a new transfer function.

The transfer function may also be redefined to produce specific effects. For example, the transfer function

```
{1 exch sub}
```

will invert the output image; this is useful for producing photographic negatives. Other transfer functions may be used to enhance or reduce contrast in a sampled image.

4.9 DEVICE SETUP AND OUTPUT

The POSTSCRIPT graphics machinery requires information about the parameters and properties of the raster output device before it can perform scan conversion for that device. This information includes page dimensions, resolution, orientation, preferred halftone screen, etc. This information is kept in the graphics state and is established by the POSTSCRIPT device setup operators.

The setup for a particular device is usually defined as a single POSTSCRIPT procedure that establishes all the parameters for that device. It is unusual for a POSTSCRIPT program other than this procedure to execute lower-level setup operators such as **framedevice**, **setmatrix**, **setscreen**, **settransfer**, etc.

In an implementation of the POSTSCRIPT interpreter dedicated to driving a single device, the necessary device setup is performed automatically; in an implementation that supports several devices, the desired device must be specified explicitly. Even in the case of a single device, however, there are sometimes variations in device parameters (e.g., to print on different sizes of paper).

The general strategy is that some appropriate default device is set up automatically, but when a POSTSCRIPT program has special needs, it can perform special device setup explicitly. Preferably, composition programs should not embed such device setup in page descriptions they produce, since doing so ties the page description to a specific device. Instead, special device setup should be added to a page description at the moment printing is requested, at which time the identity of the specific device is known.

A special 'null device', established by the **nulldevice** operator, exists in all implementations to permit execution of a POSTSCRIPT page description without generating any actual output. This is useful for various purposes such as preloading the font cache, determining character bounding boxes, or simply verifying that a POSTSCRIPT program runs to completion without error.

When a POSTSCRIPT program has completed painting all desired marks on the current page, it must execute an output operator to cause the contents of raster memory to be transmitted to the output device. No output is ever produced unless an output operator is executed. The usual output operator is **showpage**, which transmits the page to the output device, resets the current page to all white, and partially resets the graphics state in preparation for the next page. Another operator, **copypage**, transmits the current page but does not reset it, so any marks subsequently placed on the page will be added to the ones that are already there.

CHAPTER 5

FONTS

5.1 INTRODUCTION

In this chapter, we describe the special POSTSCRIPT facilities that deal with text (more generally, with characters from fonts). As mentioned previously, a character is defined as a general graphical shape and is subject to all graphical manipulations such as coordinate transformation. However, due to the importance of text in most page descriptions, the POSTSCRIPT language provides higher-level facilities that permit characters to be described, selected, and rendered conveniently and efficiently.

We begin by giving a general description of how fonts are organized and accessed. This description covers all normal uses of the standard fonts.

The information in subsequent sections is somewhat more complex, but it is needed only by programs with sophisticated needs. We discuss in detail the organization of *font dictionaries*, the *encoding* scheme used to map characters to descriptions, the *metric* information available for fonts, and the operation of the *font cache*. Finally, we describe how user-defined fonts may be constructed.

As usual, details of the individual POSTSCRIPT operators are not presented here but are deferred to chapter 6.

5.2 ORGANIZATION AND USE OF FONTS

A font, in the POSTSCRIPT context, is a dictionary through which the POSTSCRIPT interpreter obtains definitions that generate character shapes. The interpreter uses a character's code to select the definition that represents the character.

A character's definition is a procedure body that executes graphics operations to produce the character's shape. To print a character, the POSTSCRIPT interpreter executes this procedure.

If you have experience with scan conversion of general shapes, you may be concerned over the amount of computation the above description seems to imply. However, we have described only the abstract behavior of character shapes and fonts, not how they are actually implemented. In fact, the POSTSCRIPT font machinery works very efficiently in normal situations.

A simple example should help to illustrate the most straightforward uses of fonts. Suppose we wish to print the text 'ABC' 10 inches from the bottom of the page and 4 inches from the left edge, using the Helvetica typeface in a 12 point size. This may be accomplished by the following program:

```
/Helvetica findfont
12 scalefont setfont
288 720 moveto
(ABC) show
```

The first step selects the font to be used. Each POSTSCRIPT implementation includes a collection of built-in standard fonts; additional fonts may be downloaded or defined by the POSTSCRIPT program itself. There is a dictionary that associates the names of fonts (POSTSCRIPT name objects) with their definitions (font dictionaries).

The **findfont** operator takes the font name and returns (on the operand stack) a dictionary containing all the information that the POSTSCRIPT interpreter needs to generate any of that font's characters.

A font specifies the shape of its characters for one standard size. This standard is arranged so that the height of a singly spaced line of text is 1 unit. In the default user coordinate system, this means that the standard font size is one point. Since nobody can read one point type, the font must be *scaled* to be usable. (We could scale the user coordinate system with the coordinate system operators, but it is usually more convenient to encapsulate the desired size in the definition of the font itself.)

The **scalefont** operator scales fonts without affecting the user coordinate system. **scalefont** takes two operands: the nominal font dictionary and the desired scale factor. It returns a new font dictionary that renders character shapes in the desired size. (Another operator, **makefont**, applies more complicated general transformations to a font.)

In the above example, the **scalefont** operator scales the Helvetica font (obtained previously) to a 12 point size and returns it on the operand stack. Then the **setfont** operator establishes that font as the *current font* in the graphics state.

What we have produced is not actually a 12 *point* font but a 12 *unit* font, where the unit size is that of the user space at the time the characters are rendered on the page. If the user space is later scaled to make the unit size be one centimeter, printing characters from the same 12 unit font will generate results that are 12 centimeters high.

Now that we have selected a font, we may print characters from it. The **moveto** operator (already mentioned in chapter 4) sets the current position to the specified *x* and *y* coordinates; these are in points (1/72 inch units) since we are using the default user coordinate system. This determines the position on the page at which to begin printing characters.

The **show** operator takes a POSTSCRIPT string from the operand stack and prints it using the current font. More precisely, it treats each element of the string (an integer in the range 0 to 255) as a character code. Each code selects a character description in the font dictionary, which is executed to render the desired character on the page.

The above example uses POSTSCRIPT operators in a direct way. However, it is usually desirable to define procedures to help the application generating the text. To illustrate this point, assume that an application is printing many independently-positioned text strings and requires switching frequently between three fonts: Helvetica, Helvetica-Oblique, and Helvetica-Bold, all in a 10 point size.

```
% Start the prologue section.
% First make some font definitions.

% define "fnr" to be 10 pt Helvetica.
/fnr /Helvetica findfont 10 scalefont def

% define "fni" to be 10 pt Helvetica-Oblique.
/fni /Helvetica-Oblique findfont 10 scalefont def

% define "fnb" to be 10 pt Helvetica-Bold.
/fnb /Helvetica-Bold findfont 10 scalefont def

% Define some procedures to move to a given position,
% switch fonts, and show the given character string.

/shwr {moveto fnr setfont show} def
/shwi {moveto fni setfont show} def
/shwb {moveto fnb setfont show} def

% Start the script section.
```

This is in Helvetica.
This is in Helvetica-Oblique.
This is in Helvetica-Bold.
And more in Helvetica.

```
(This is in Helvetica.) 45 292 shwr
(This is in Helvetica-Oblique.) 45 280 shwi
(This is in Helvetica-Bold.) 45 268 shwb
(And more in Helvetica.) 45 256 shwr

        ...
```

This example shows several things. First, it scales the required fonts and associates them with the names 'fnr', 'fni', and 'fnb'. Next, it defines three procedures, each of which moves the current point to a given position, switches to a particular font, and shows the given string. Finally, it sets text using the procedures defined earlier.

There are some extra facts to know about fonts. Associated with each character is its width, the amount of space it occupies when it appears in a line of text. In some fonts this spacing is constant, i.e., it does not vary from character to character. These fonts are called *fixed pitch* or *monospaced* fonts; they are used mainly for typewriter-style printing. Most fonts used for high quality typography, however, associate a different width with each character. Such fonts are called *variable pitch* fonts. In either case, POSTSCRIPT's **show** operator positions consecutive characters of a string according to their widths.

The width information for each character is stored in the POSTSCRIPT dictionary that represents the font. A POSTSCRIPT program may access this information to obtain a character's width, and the program may use any of several character printing operators (**show**, **widthshow**, **ashow**, **awidthshow**, and **kshow**) to obtain a variety of width modification effects. These facilities are sufficiently powerful that a POSTSCRIPT program should rarely need to resort to positioning each character individually.

Normal use of **show** and other character printing operators causes black filled characters to be placed on the page. By combining font operators with general graphics operators, one may obtain other effects.

The color used for painting characters is actually determined by the current color in the graphics state. The default color is black; but other colors may be obtained by executing **setgray** (or some other color setting operator) prior to printing characters. Thus,

```
newpath 60 280 moveto
.5 setgray (ABC) show
```

will print characters in 50 percent gray rather than in black. (This example and the ones below assume that an appropriate sequence of **findfont**, **scalefont**, and **setfont** has been executed previously.)

More general graphical manipulations can be performed by treating the character outline as a path instead of immediately printing it. **charpath** is a path construction operator that appends the outlines of one or more characters to the current path in the graphics state.[1]

---

[1]This works only for characters that are defined as outlines. Obtaining a path for characters defined as strokes (e.g., the Courier font) is more difficult; and obtaining a path for characters defined as images (or bitmaps) is not possible. Also, a path consisting of the outlines of more than a few characters is likely to exceed the limit on number of path elements (see appendix B); if possible, it is best to deal with only one character's path at a time.

For example,

    newpath 60 566 moveto (ABC) false charpath
    2 setlinewidth stroke

obtains the outlines for the string of characters 'ABC' in the current font and makes them be the current path in the graphics state. (The *false* argument to **charpath** is explained in the description of **charpath** in chapter 6.) It then strokes this path with a line 2 points thick, thereby rendering the characters' outlines on the page.

Finally,

    newpath 60 420 moveto (ABC) false charpath clip

obtains the characters' path as before, then establishes it as the current clipping path. All subsequent painting operations will actually mark the page only within this path. This state persists until some other clipping path is established (e.g., by **grestore**).

5.3 FONT DICTIONARIES

The remainder of this chapter presents more detailed information about font definitions. You may wish to skip this material on first reading.

Font dictionaries are ordinary POSTSCRIPT dictionary objects, but with certain special key-value pairs. POSTSCRIPT has several operators that deal with font dictionaries (see chapter 6). Some of the contents of a font dictionary are optional and user-definable, while other key-value pairs *must* be present and have the correct semantics for the POSTSCRIPT font machinery to operate properly.

POSTSCRIPT requires that the following key-value pairs exist in each font dictionary:

Key	Type	Semantics
FontMatrix	array	transforms character coordinates system into the user coordinate system. The fonts returned by **findfont** are assumed to be one unit high. The actual characters may be defined in some other coordinate system (the *character coordinate system*) and the **FontMatrix** maps that system into one unit in the user coordinate system. For example, built-in POSTSCRIPT fonts are usually defined in terms of a 1000 unit character coordinate system, and their initial **FontMatrix** is [0.001 0 0 0.001 0 0]. When a font is modified by the **scalefont** or **makefont** operator, the new matrix is concatenated with the **FontMatrix** to yield a transformed font.
FontType	integer	indicates where the information for the character descriptions is to be found and how it is represented. User-defined fonts should have a **FontType** whose value is the integer 3. See section 5.7 on user-defined fonts.
FontBBox	array	an array of four numbers in the character coordinate system giving lower left *x*, lower left *y*, upper right *x*, and upper right *y* of the font bounding box. The font bounding box is the smallest rectangle enclosing the shape that would result if all of the characters of the font were placed with their origins coincident and painted. This information is used in making decisions about character caching and clipping. If all four values are zero, the POSTSCRIPT font machinery makes no assumptions based on the font bounding box. If any value is non-zero, it is essential that the font bounding box be accurate; if any character's marks fall outside this bounding box, incorrect behavior may result.
Encoding	array	an array of 256 names that maps character codes (the array indices in the range 0 to 255) to character names (the values in the array). This is described in section 5.4.

A font dictionary is created as a POSTSCRIPT object by ordinary means and then is made known to the font machinery by execution of the **definefont** operator. **definefont** takes a name and a dictionary, checks that the dictionary is a well-formed font dictionary, makes the dictionary's access read-only, and associates the font name with the dictionary in the global dictionary **FontDirectory**. (It also inserts an additional entry whose name is **FID** and whose value is an object of type fontID; this entry serves internal purposes in the font machinery. For this reason, a font dictionary presented to **definefont** must have room for at least one additional key-value pair.)

POSTSCRIPT's built-in fonts contain the following additional entries:

Key	Type	Semantics
FontName	name	the font's name. This entry is for information only; it is not actually used by the font machinery.
PaintType	integer	a code indicating how the characters of the font are to be painted:

0   The character descriptions are filled.
1   The character descriptions are stroked.
2   The character descriptions (designed to be filled) are outlined.
3   The character descriptions are responsible for filling or stroking (or some combination of those operations) themselves.

Arbitrarily changing a font's **PaintType** will most likely have disastrous effects. The only reasonable change is from 0 (filled) to 2 (outlined).

Key	Type	Semantics
Metrics	dictionary	width and side bearing information. This entry is not normally present in built-in fonts. Adding a **Metrics** entry to a font overrides the widths and side bearings encoded in the character descriptions themselves (see sections 5.5 and 5.7).
StrokeWidth	number	stroke width (in units of the character coordinate system) for outline fonts (**PaintType** 2). This field is not initially present in filled font descriptions; it must be added when creating an outline font from an existing filled font.
FontInfo	dictionary	(see below)
UniqueID	integer	an integer in the range 0 to 16777215 ($2^{24}-1$) that uniquely identifies this font. That is, every different font (or different version of the same font, regardless of how small the difference is) should have a different value of the **UniqueID** entry. This entry is not necessarily present in all fonts; but if present, it may enable the font cache to operate more efficiently. Each **FontType** has its own independent space of **UniqueID** values.
CharStrings	dictionary	associates character names (keys) with shape descriptions (values, stored in a protected, proprietary format).
Private	dictionary	contains other protected information about the font.

The **FontInfo** dictionary may contain the following information. This information is entirely for the benefit of POSTSCRIPT programs making use of the font; it is not accessed by the POSTSCRIPT font machinery.

Key	Type	Semantics
Notice	string	trademark or copyright notice (if applicable).
FullName	string	full text name of the font. (This and the next three entries are primarily for documentation purposes. Font names are not organized in any systematic way, nor do they have anything to do with the font keys specified to **definefont** and **findfont**.)
FamilyName	string	name of the 'font family' to which it belongs.
Weight	string	'weight' of the font (e.g., Bold, Medium, Light, Ultra, Heavy).
version	string	font version number.
ItalicAngle	number	angle in degrees counter-clockwise from the vertical of the dominant vertical strokes of the font.
isFixedPitch	boolean	if *true*, indicates that the font is a fixed pitch (monospaced) font.
UnderlinePosition	number	distance from the baseline for positioning underlining strokes. This number is in units of the character coordinate system.
UnderlineThickness	number	stroke width for underlining. This number is in units of the character coordinate system.

5.4 CHARACTER ENCODING

The standard POSTSCRIPT fonts use a flexible *encoding* scheme by which character codes select character descriptions. (User-defined fonts are encouraged but not required to employ this scheme as well.) The association between character codes and descriptions is not directly part of the font itself but instead is described by a separate *encoding vector*. A POSTSCRIPT page description may change a font's encoding vector to match the requirements of the application generating the description.

In a font dictionary, the descriptions of the individual characters (in the **CharStrings** dictionary) are keyed by character *names*, not by character *codes*. Character names are ordinary POSTSCRIPT name objects. Alphabetic characters are normally associated with names consisting of single letters such as 'A' or 'a'. Other characters are associated with names composed of words such as 'three', 'ampersand', or 'parenleft'.

The encoding vector is defined by a 256-element POSTSCRIPT array object. The array is indexed by character code (an integer in the range 0 to 255). The elements of the array are character names.

The operand to the **show** operator is a POSTSCRIPT string object. Each element of the string is treated as a character code. When **show** prints a character, it first uses the character code as an index into the current font's encoding vector to obtain a character name. Then it looks up the name in the font's **CharStrings** dictionary to obtain a character description, which it proceeds to execute.

For example, in the standard encoding vector (used by built-in text fonts such as Helvetica), the element at index 97 is the POSTSCRIPT name object 'a'. When **show** encounters the value 97 (the ASCII character code for 'a') as an element of a string it is printing, it fetches the encoding vector entry at index 97, obtaining the name object 'a'. It then uses 'a' as a key in the current font's **CharStrings** dictionary and executes the associated description, which produces a rendition of the 'a' letterform.

Changing an existing font's encoding simply involves creating a new font dictionary which is a copy of the existing one except for its **Encoding** entry. (The embedded dictionaries, such as **CharStrings** and **FontInfo**, continue to be shared with the original font.) Of course, a new user-defined font may be created with any desired encoding vector.

This flexibility in character encoding is valuable for two reasons. First, it permits printing text encoded in character sets other than ASCII (e.g., EBCDIC). Second, it allows applications to specify how characters outside a standard character set are to be encoded. Some fonts contain more than 256 characters: they include ligatures, accented characters, and other symbols required for high-quality typesetting or foreign languages. There is no existing standard that specifies how to encode such characters; the POSTSCRIPT language leaves this choice to be made by the programmer.[2]

The encoding vector used by most standard text fonts is associated with the name **StandardEncoding** in **systemdict**. Complete details of the standard encoding and of the characters present in standard fonts appear in appendix A.

All unused positions in an encoding vector must be filled with the name '.notdef'. Printing one of these unused characters produces no marks on the page and no side-effects.

5.5 FONT METRIC INFORMATION

The *character coordinate system* is the system in which an individual character shape is defined. The *origin* (or *reference point*) of the character is the point (0, 0) in the character coordinate system. **show** and other character printing operators position the origin of the first character shown at the current point in user space. For example, in the POSTSCRIPT sequence

40 50 moveto (ABC) show

the origin of the 'A' is placed at coordinate (40, 50) in the user coordinate system.

bounding box

character origin

next character origin

left side bearing

character width

The *width* of a character is the distance from the character's origin at which the origin of the next character should normally be placed when printing consecutive characters of a word. This distance is a vector in the character coordinate system: it has x and y components. (Most Indo-European alphabets, including Roman, have a positive x width and a zero y width; Semitic alphabets have a negative x width; some Oriental alphabets have a non-zero y width.)

The *bounding box* of a character is the smallest rectangle

---

[2]Many of the accented characters are *composite*, meaning that they are composed of two or more other characters (e.g., a letter and an accent) defined in the same font. If an encoding vector includes the name of a composite character, it must also include the names of the components of that character.

(oriented with the coordinate system axes) that will just enclose the entire character's shape. The bounding box is expressed in terms of its lower left corner and upper right corner relative to the character origin in the character coordinate system.

The *left side bearing* of a character is the distance from the character's origin to the left edge of the character bounding box. Note that this distance may be negative for characters that extend to the left of their origin. Built-in fonts are defined in such a way that a character's left side bearing can be adjusted; that is, the character bounding box can be shifted around relative to the origin (see section 5.7).

Character metric information for built-in fonts may be accessed procedurally by a POSTSCRIPT program. The **stringwidth** operator may be used to obtain character widths. The sequence

charpath flattenpath pathbbox

may be used to determine character bounding boxes and side bearings. The font bounding box appears in the font dictionary as an array of four numbers associated with the key **FontBBox**.

Character width information is also available separately in the form of *font metrics files*. These files are for use by application programs that generate POSTSCRIPT page descriptions and that must make formatting decisions based on the widths (and other metrics) of characters. Kerning information is also available separately.

A POSTSCRIPT program may change the metrics of the fonts it uses by means that are described in section 5.7.

5.6 FONT CACHE

The POSTSCRIPT font machinery includes a data structure called the *font cache* whose purpose is to make the process of printing characters very efficient. For the most part, operation of the font cache is automatic. However, there exist several operators that control the behavior of the font cache. Additionally, user-defined fonts must adhere to certain conventions in order to take advantage of the font cache.

As mentioned in section 5.2, rendering a character from an outline (or other high-level description) is a relatively costly operation, since it involves performing scan conversion of arbitrary shapes. This presents special problems for printing text, since it is common for several thousand characters to appear on a single page.

However, a page description that includes large amounts of text normally has many repetitions of the same character in a given font, size, and orientation. The number of distinct characters is very much smaller than the total number of characters.

The font cache operates by saving the results of character scan conversions (including metric information and device pixel arrays) in temporary storage and using those saved results when the same character is requested again. The font cache is large enough to accomodate all the distinct characters in most page descriptions. Printing a character that is already in the font cache is typically a thousand times faster than scan converting it from the character description in the font.

The font cache does not retain color information; it remembers only which pixels were painted and which pixels were left unchanged within the character's bounding box. For this reason, there are a few restrictions on the set of graphical operators that may be executed as part of character descriptions that are to be cached. In particular, the **image** operator is not permitted; however, **imagemask** may be used to define a character according to a bitmap representation (see section 4.7).

The principal manifestation of font caching visible to the POSTSCRIPT programmer is that printing a character does not necessarily result in the character's description being executed. This means that user-defined fonts must interact with the font cache machinery so that the results of their execution are properly saved. This is described in the next section.

5.7 USER-DEFINED FONTS

User-defined fonts are created in two ways: by copying an existing font and modifying certain things in it or by defining a new font from scratch.

Changing things

The most common modification to an existing font consists of installing a different encoding vector, as discussed in section 5.4. The way to make this change is as follows.[3]

First, make a copy of the font dictionary including all entries except the one whose name is **FID**. In this example, we copy the Helvetica font dictionary and temporarily associate it with the name 'newdict':

```
/Helvetica findfont
dup length dict /newdict exch def
  {1 index /FID ne
    {newdict 3 1 roll put}
    {pop pop}
    ifelse
  } forall
```

Second, install the the desired changes. Suppose we wish to install an entirely new encoding vector for the EBCDIC character set. Assuming that the name 'EbcdicEncoding' is already associated with such an encoding vector (a 256-element array), we simply say:

```
newdict /Encoding EbcdicEncoding put
```

Finally, register this modified font under some new name, for example, 'E-Helvetica':

```
/E-Helvetica newdict definefont pop
```

It is possible to change a built-in font's metric information (character widths and side bearings) on a per-character basis. However, some words of caution are in order. Determining

---

[3]See the *POSTSCRIPT Language Tutorial and Cookbook* for some fully worked out examples.

pleasing and correct character spacing is a difficult and laborious art that requires considerable skill. A font's character shapes have been designed with certain metrics in mind; changing those metrics haphazardly will almost certainly produce poor results.

The procedure for changing a built-in font's metrics is to add a **Metrics** entry to the font dictionary; the value of this entry should be another dictionary containing new metric information.

The **Metrics** dictionary consists of entries in which the keys are character names (as they appear in the **CharStrings** dictionary and **Encoding** array); the values of these entries take various forms. Entries in the **Metrics** dictionary override the normal metrics for the corresponding characters. An entry's value may be one of the following:

- a single number, indicating a new x width only (the y value is zero);

- an array of two numbers, indicating new left side bearing and new x width (the y values are zero);

- an array of four numbers, indicating true vectors (both x and y components) for left side bearing and width.

All of these values are in the character coordinate system of the font.

In the following example, we make a copy of the Helvetica font and then change the widths of the digits '0' through '9'. First, we copy the existing font dictionary except for the **FID** entry, just as in the preceding example; however, we must also leave room in the new dictionary for the **Metrics** entry that we are adding:

```
/Helvetica findfont
dup length 1 add dict /newdict exch def
  {1 index /FID ne
    {newdict 3 1 roll put}
    {pop pop}
    ifelse
  } forall
```

Next, we create the **Metrics** dictionary, insert the desired values into it, and insert it into the font dictionary. Here, we set the x width of all digits to 700 (remember we are in the character coordinate system, which for built-in fonts is usually on a 1000-unit scale).

```
10 dict begin
  [/zero /one /two /three /four
   /five /six /seven /eight /nine]
  {700 def} forall
newdict /Metrics currentdict put
end
```

Finally, we register the modified font under some new name, for example, 'My-Helvetica':

```
/My-Helvetica newdict definefont pop
```

Building a new font

User-defined fonts must be carefully constructed; POSTSCRIPT assumes that such fonts will be reasonably well-behaved. As mentioned above, a user-defined font must contain the mandatory entries described in section 5.3 and must have a **FontType** value of 3. Additionally, it must contain a procedure named **BuildChar**.

When a POSTSCRIPT program tries to print a character of a user-defined font and the character is not already present in the font cache, the font machinery pushes the current font dictionary and the character's code (an integer) on the operand stack and executes the font's **BuildChar** procedure. **BuildChar** must use the information at hand to construct the requested character. This typically involves determining the character definition needed, supplying character metric information, constructing the character shape, and painting it.

BuildChar is called within the confines of a **gsave** and a **grestore**, so any changes **BuildChar** makes to the graphics state do not persist after it finishes. Each call to **BuildChar** is independent of any other call. Because of the effects of font caching, no assumptions may be made about the order in which character descriptions will be executed.

When **BuildChar** gets control, the current transformation matrix (CTM) is the concatenation of the font matrix (**FontMatrix** in the current font dictionary) and the CTM that was in effect at the time the font machinery was invoked (the user coordinate system). This means that shapes described in the character coordinate system will be transformed into the user coordinate system and will appear in the appropriate size and orientation on the page. **BuildChar** should describe the character in terms of absolute coordinates in the character coordinate system, placing the character origin at (0, 0) in this space; in particular, it should make no assumptions about the initial value of the current point parameter.

Before executing the graphics operators that describe the character, **BuildChar** *must* execute either the **setcachedevice** or the **setcharwidth** operator. These operators pass width and bounding box information to POSTSCRIPT's font machinery, and **setcachedevice** additionally requests POSTSCRIPT to save the result in the font cache if possible. (See the descriptions of **setcachedevice** and **setcharwidth** in chapter 6 for more information.)

After executing one of these operators, **BuildChar** should execute a sequence of graphics operators, ordinarily path construction and painting operators. The POSTSCRIPT font machinery transfers the results both into the font cache (if appropriate) and onto the page at the correct position. It also uses the width information to control the spacing between this character and the next. (Note that the final position of the current point in character space has no bearing on character spacing.)

Here is a small example of a user-defined font with only two characters, a filled square and a filled triangle, selected by the characters 'a' and 'b'. The character coordinate system is on a 1000 unit scale. This is not a realistic example, but it does illustrate all the elements of a user-defined font, including a **BuildChar** procedure, an encoding vector, and a subsidiary dictionary for the individual character definitions.

```
/newfont 10 dict def
newfont begin

/FontType 3 def                    % Required elements of font
/FontMatrix [.001 0 0 .001 0 0] def
/FontBBox [0 0 1000 1000] def
```

```
/Encoding 256 array def              % Trivial encoding vector
0 1 255 {Encoding exch /.notdef put} for
Encoding 97 /square put              % ASCII 'a' = 97
Encoding 98 /triangle put            % ASCII 'b' = 98

/CharProcs 3 dict def                % Subsidiary dictionary for
CharProcs begin                      % individual character definitions
/.notdef {} def
/square
  {0 0 moveto 750 0 lineto 750 750 lineto
   0 750 lineto closepath fill} def
/triangle
  {0 0 moveto 375 750 lineto 750 0 lineto
   closepath fill} def
end                                  % of CharProcs

/BuildChar                           % Stack contains: font char
  {1000 0                            % Width
   0 0 750 750                       % Bounding box
   setcachedevice
   exch begin                        % i.e., font begin
   Encoding exch get                 % Index by char in Encoding
   CharProcs exch get                % Look up name in CharProcs
   end
   exec                              % Execute character procedure
  }def
end                                  % of newfont

/ExampleFont newfont definefont pop

% Now show some characters in a 12 point size
/ExampleFont findfont 12 scalefont setfont
74 240 moveto (ababab) show
```

CHAPTER 6

OPERATORS

6.1 INTRODUCTION

This chapter contains detailed information about all the standard operators in the POSTSCRIPT language. It is divided into two parts.

First, there is a summary of the operators, organized into groups of related functions. The summary is intended to assist in locating the operators needed to perform specific tasks.

Second, there are detailed descriptions of all the operators, organized alphabetically by operator name. Each operator description is presented in the following format:

operator   operand$_1$ operand$_2$ ... operand$_n$ **operator** result$_1$ ... result$_m$

Detailed explanation of the operator

EXAMPLE:
>An example of the use of this operator. The symbol '$\Rightarrow$' designates values left on the operand stack by the example.

ERRORS:
A list of the errors that this operator might execute

SEE ALSO:
A list of related operator names

At the head of an operator description, *operand*$_1$ through *operand*$_n$ are the operands that the operator requires, with *operand*$_n$ being the topmost element on the operand stack. The operator pops these objects from the operand stack and consumes them. After executing, the operator leaves the objects *result*$_1$ through *result*$_m$ on the stack, with *result*$_m$ being the topmost element.

Normally the operand and result names suggest their types. For example, *num* indicates that the operand or result is a number, *int* indicates an integer number, *any* indicates a value of any type, and *proc* indicates a POSTSCRIPT procedure (i.e., an executable array). The notation '*bool|int*' indicates a value that is either a boolean or an integer. Names representing numbers sometimes suggest their purpose, e.g., *x*, *y*, or *angle*. A *matrix* is an array of six numbers describing a transformation matrix (see section 4.4). A *font* is a dictionary constructed according to the rules for font dictionaries (see section 5.3).

The notation '⊢' indicates the bottom of the stack. The notation '–' in the operand position indicates that the operator expects no operands, and a '–' in the result position indicates that the operator returns no results.

The documented effects on the operand stack and the possible errors are those produced directly by the operator itself. Many operators cause arbitrary POSTSCRIPT procedures to be invoked. Obviously, such procedures can have arbitrary effects that are not mentioned in the operator descriptions.

6.2 OPERATOR SUMMARY

Operand stack manipulation operators

operands	operator	results	description
any	**pop**	–	discard top element *193*
any$_1$ any$_2$	**exch**	any$_2$ any$_1$	exchange top two elements *151*
any	**dup**	any any	duplicate top element *148*
any$_1$..any$_n$ n	**copy**	any$_1$..any$_n$ any$_1$..any$_n$	duplicate top *n* elements *131*
any$_n$..any$_0$ n	**index**	any$_n$..any$_0$ any$_n$	duplicate arbitrary element *172*
a$_{n-1}$..a$_0$ n j	**roll**	a$_{(j-1) \bmod n}$..a$_0$ a$_{n-1}$..a$_{j \bmod n}$	roll *n* elements up *j* times *205*
⊢ any$_1$..any$_n$	**clear**	⊢	discard all elements *127*
⊢ any$_1$..any$_n$	**count**	⊢ any$_1$..any$_n$ n	count elements on stack *132*
–	**mark**	mark	push mark on stack *184*

mark obj$_1$..obj$_n$	**cleartomark**	–	discard elements down through *mark* *127*
mark obj$_1$..obj$_n$	**counttomark**	mark obj$_1$..obj$_n$ n	count elements down to mark *133*

Arithmetic and math operators

num$_1$ num$_2$	**add**	sum	*num$_1$* plus *num$_2$* *115*
num$_1$ num$_2$	**div**	quotient	*num$_1$* divided by *num$_2$* *148*
int$_1$ int$_2$	**idiv**	quotient	integer divide *168*
int$_1$ int$_2$	**mod**	remainder	*int$_1$* mod *int$_2$* *185*
num$_1$ num$_2$	**mul**	product	*num$_1$* times *num$_2$* *186*
num$_1$ num$_2$	**sub**	difference	*num$_1$* minus *num$_2$* *230*
num$_1$	**abs**	num$_2$	absolute value of *num$_1$* *115*
num$_1$	**neg**	num$_2$	negative of *num$_1$* *187*
num$_1$	**ceiling**	num$_2$	ceiling of *num$_1$* *126*
num$_1$	**floor**	num$_2$	floor of *num$_1$* *157*
num$_1$	**round**	num$_2$	round *num$_1$* to nearest integer *206*
num$_1$	**truncate**	num$_2$	remove fractional part of *num$_1$* *234*
num	**sqrt**	real	square root of *num* *224*
num den	**atan**	angle	arctangent of *num/den* in degrees *121*
angle	**cos**	real	cosine of *angle* (degrees) *132*
angle	**sin**	real	sine of *angle* (degrees) *223*
base exponent	**exp**	real	raise *base* to *exponent* power *154*
num	**ln**	real	natural logarithm (base *e*) *180*
num	**log**	real	logarithm (base 10) *181*
–	**rand**	int	generate pseudo-random integer *197*
int	**srand**	–	set random number seed *224*
–	**rrand**	int	return random number seed *207*

Array operators

int	**array**	array	create array of length *int* *120*
–	**[**	mark	start array construction *113*
mark obj$_0$..obj$_{n-1}$	**]**	array	end array construction *113*
array	**length**	int	number of elements in *array* *179*
array index	**get**	any	get array element indexed by *index* *164*
array index any	**put**	–	put *any* into *array* at *index* *195*
array index count	**getinterval**	subarray	subarray of *array* starting at *index* for *count* elements *165*
array$_1$ index array$_2$	**putinterval**	–	replace subarray of *array$_1$* starting at *index* by *array$_2$* *196*
array	**aload**	a$_0$..a$_{n-1}$ array	push all elements of *array* on stack *115*
any$_0$..any$_{n-1}$ array	**astore**	array	pop elements from stack into *array* *121*
array$_1$ array$_2$	**copy**	subarray$_2$	copy elements of *array$_1$* to initial subarray of *array$_2$* *131*
array proc	**forall**	–	execute *proc* for each element of *array* *161*

Dictionary operators

int	**dict**	dict	create dictionary with capacity for *int* elements *146*
dict	**length**	int	number of key-value pairs in *dict* *179*
dict	**maxlength**	int	capacity of *dict* *185*
dict	**begin**	–	push *dict* on dict stack *124*
–	**end**	–	pop dict stack *149*
key value	**def**	–	associate *key* and *value* in current dict *145*
key	**load**	value	search dict stack for *key* and return associated *value* *181*
key value	**store**	–	replace topmost definition of *key* *227*
dict key	**get**	any	get value associated with *key* in *dict* *164*
dict key value	**put**	–	associate *key* with *value* in *dict* *195*
dict key	**known**	bool	test whether *key* is in *dict* *177*
key	**where**	dict true	
		or false	find dict in which *key* is defined *238*
dict₁ dict₂	**copy**	dict₂	copy contents of *dict₁* to *dict₂* *131*
dict proc	**forall**	–	execute *proc* for each element of *dict* *161*
–	**errordict**	dict	push **errordict** on operand stack *151*
–	**systemdict**	dict	push **systemdict** on operand stack *231*
–	**userdict**	dict	push **userdict** on operand stack *236*
–	**currentdict**	dict	push current dict on operand stack *134*
–	**countdictstack**	int	count elements on dict stack *133*
array	**dictstack**	subarray	copy dict stack into *array* *147*

String operators

int	**string**	string	create string of length *int* *228*
string	**length**	int	number of elements in *string* *179*
string index	**get**	int	get string element indexed by *index* *164*
string index int	**put**	–	put *int* into *string* at *index* *195*
string index count	**getinterval**	substring	substring of *string* starting at *index* for *count* elements *165*
string₁ index string₂	**putinterval**	–	replace substring of *string₁* starting at *index* by *string₂* *196*
string₁ string₂	**copy**	substring₂	copy elements of *string₁* to initial substring of *string₂* *131*
string proc	**forall**	–	execute *proc* for each element of *string* *161*
string seek	**anchorsearch**	post match true	
		or string false	determine if *seek* is initial substring of *string* *116*
string seek	**search**	post match pre true	
		or string false	search for *seek* in *string* *211*
string	**token**	post token true	
		or false	read token from start of *string* *232*

Relational, boolean, and bitwise operators

any_1 any_2	**eq**	bool	test equal *150*
any_1 any_2	**ne**	bool	test not equal *186*
$num_1\|str_1$ $num_2\|str_2$	**ge**	bool	test greater or equal *163*
$num_1\|str_1$ $num_2\|str_2$	**gt**	bool	test greater than *167*
$num_1\|str_1$ $num_2\|str_2$	**le**	bool	test less or equal *179*
$num_1\|str_1$ $num_2\|str_2$	**lt**	bool	test less than *182*
$bool_1\|int_1$ $bool_2\|int_2$	**and**	$bool_3\|int_3$	logical | bitwise and *116*
$bool_1\|int_1$	**not**	$bool_2\|int_2$	logical | bitwise not *189*
$bool_1\|int_1$ $bool_2\|int_2$	**or**	$bool_3\|int_3$	logical | bitwise inclusive or *191*
$bool_1\|int_1$ $bool_2\|int_2$	**xor**	$bool_3\|int_3$	logical | bitwise exclusive or *241*
–	**true**	true	push boolean value *true* *234*
–	**false**	false	push boolean value *false* *155*
int_1 shift	**bitshift**	int_2	bitwise shift of int_1 (positive is left) *125*

Control operators

any	**exec**	–	execute arbitrary object *152*
bool proc	**if**	–	execute *proc* if *bool* is true *169*
bool $proc_1$ $proc_2$	**ifelse**	–	execute $proc_1$ if *bool* is true, $proc_2$ if *bool* is false *169*
init incr limit proc	**for**	–	execute *proc* with values from *init* by steps of *incr* to *limit* *160*
int proc	**repeat**	–	execute *proc int* times *202*
proc	**loop**	–	execute *proc* an indefinite number of times *182*
–	**exit**	–	exit innermost active loop *154*
–	**stop**	–	terminate **stopped** context *226*
any	**stopped**	bool	establish context for catching **stop** *227*
–	**countexecstack**	int	count elements on exec stack *133*
array	**execstack**	subarray	copy exec stack into *array* *152*
–	**quit**	–	terminate interpreter *197*
–	**start**	–	executed at interpreter startup *225*

Type, attribute, and conversion operators

any	**type**	name	return name identifying *any*'s type *235*
any	**cvlit**	any	make object be literal *141*
any	**cvx**	any	make object be executable *144*
any	**xcheck**	bool	test executable attribute *240*
array|file|string	**executeonly**	array|file|string	reduce access to execute-only *153*
array|dict|file|string	**noaccess**	array|dict|file|string	disallow any access *188*
array|dict|file|string	**readonly**	array|dict|file|string	reduce access to read-only *200*
array|dict|file|string	**rcheck**	bool	test read access *198*
array|dict|file|string	**wcheck**	bool	test write access *238*
num|string	**cvi**	int	convert to integer *141*
string	**cvn**	name	convert to name *142*
num|string	**cvr**	real	convert to real *142*
num radix string	**cvrs**	substring	convert to string with radix *143*

any string	**cvs**	substring	convert to string *144*

File operators

string$_1$ string$_2$	**file**	file	open file identified by *string$_1$* with access *string$_2$* *155*
file	**closefile**	–	close file *129*
file	**read**	int true	
		or false	read one character from *file* *198*
file int	**write**	–	write one character to *file* *239*
file string	**readhexstring**	substring bool	read hex from *file* into *string* *199*
file string	**writehexstring**	–	write *string* to *file* as hex *240*
file string	**readstring**	substring bool	read string from *file* *201*
file string	**writestring**	–	write characters of *string* to *file* *240*
file string	**readline**	substring bool	read line from *file* into *string* *200*
file	**token**	token true	
		or false	read token from *file* *232*
file	**bytesavailable**	int	number of bytes available to read *125*
–	**flush**	–	send buffered data to standard output file *158*
file	**flushfile**	–	send buffered data or read to EOF *158*
file	**resetfile**	–	discard buffered characters *202*
file	**status**	bool	return status of *file* *226*
string	**run**	–	execute contents of named file *207*
–	**currentfile**	file	return file currently being executed *135*
string	**print**	–	write characters of *string* to standard output file *193*
any	**=**	–	write text representation of *any* to standard output file *114*
⊢ any$_1$ .. any$_n$	**stack**	⊢ any$_1$ .. any$_n$	print stack nondestructively using = *224*
any	**==**	–	write syntactic representation of *any* to standard output file *114*
⊢ any$_1$ .. any$_n$	**pstack**	⊢ any$_1$ .. any$_n$	print stack nondestructively using == *194*
–	**prompt**	–	executed when ready for interactive input *194*
bool	**echo**	–	turn on/off echoing *149*

Virtual memory operators

–	**save**	save	create VM snapshot *208*
save	**restore**	–	restore VM snapshot *203*
–	**vmstatus**	level used maximum	report VM status *238*

Miscellaneous operators

proc	**bind**	proc	replace operator names in *proc* by operators *124*
–	**null**	null	push null on operand stack *189*
–	**usertime**	int	return time in milliseconds *237*
–	**version**	string	interpreter version *237*

Graphics state operators

–	**gsave** –	save graphics state *166*
–	**grestore** –	restore graphics state *165*
–	**grestoreall** –	restore to bottommost graphics state *166*
–	**initgraphics** –	reset graphics state parameters *173*
num	**setlinewidth** –	set line width *219*
–	**currentlinewidth** num	return current line width *137*
int	**setlinecap** –	set shape of line ends for stroke (0=butt, 1=round, 2=square) *217*
–	**currentlinecap** int	return current line cap *136*
int	**setlinejoin** –	set shape of corners for stroke (0=miter, 1=round, 2=bevel) *218*
–	**currentlinejoin** int	return current line join *137*
num	**setmiterlimit** –	set miter length limit *220*
–	**currentmiterlimit** num	return current miter limit *137*
array offset	**setdash** –	set dash pattern for stroking *214*
–	**currentdash** array offset	return current dash pattern *134*
num	**setflat** –	set flatness tolerance *215*
–	**currentflat** num	return current flatness *135*
num	**setgray** –	set color to gray value from 0 (black) to 1 (white) *216*
–	**currentgray** num	return current gray *136*
hue sat brt	**sethsbcolor** –	set color given hue, saturation, brightness *216*
–	**currenthsbcolor** hue sat brt	return current color hue, saturation, brightness *136*
red green blue	**setrgbcolor** –	set color given red, green, blue *221*
–	**currentrgbcolor** red green blue	return current color red, green, blue *138*
freq angle proc	**setscreen** –	set halftone screen *221*
–	**currentscreen** freq angle proc	return current halftone screen *139*
proc	**settransfer** –	set gray transfer function *222*
–	**currenttransfer** proc	return current transfer function *139*

Coordinate system and matrix operators

–	**matrix** matrix	create identity matrix *184*
–	**initmatrix** –	set CTM to device default *174*
matrix	**identmatrix** matrix	fill *matrix* with identity transform *167*
matrix	**defaultmatrix** matrix	fill *matrix* with device default matrix *145*
matrix	**currentmatrix** matrix	fill *matrix* with CTM *137*
matrix	**setmatrix** –	replace CTM by *matrix* *219*
t_x t_y	**translate** –	translate user space by (t_x, t_y) *233*
t_x t_y matrix	**translate** matrix	define translation by (t_x, t_y) *233*
s_x s_y	**scale** –	scale user space by s_x and s_y *209*
s_x s_y matrix	**scale** matrix	define scaling by s_x and s_y *209*
angle	**rotate** –	rotate user space by *angle* degrees *206*
angle matrix	**rotate** matrix	define rotation by *angle* degrees *206*
matrix	**concat** –	replace CTM by *matrix* × CTM *130*

matrix$_1$ matrix$_2$ matrix$_3$	**concatmatrix**	matrix$_3$	fill *matrix$_3$* with *matrix$_1$* × *matrix$_2$* *130*
x y	**transform**	x' y'	transform (*x*, *y*) by CTM *233*
x y matrix	**transform**	x' y'	transform (*x*, *y*) by *matrix* *233*
dx dy	**dtransform**	dx' dy'	transform distance (*dx*, *dy*) by CTM *148*
dx dy matrix	**dtransform**	dx' dy'	transform distance (*dx*, *dy*) by *matrix* *148*
x' y'	**itransform**	x y	inverse transform (*x'*, *y'*) by CTM *176*
x' y' matrix	**itransform**	x y	inverse transform (*x'*, *y'*) by *matrix* *176*
dx' dy'	**idtransform**	dx dy	inverse transform distance (*dx'*, *dy'*) by CTM *168*
dx' dy' matrix	**idtransform**	dx dy	inverse transform distance (*dx'*, *dy'*) by *matrix* *168*
matrix$_1$ matrix$_2$	**invertmatrix**	matrix$_2$	fill *matrix$_2$* with inverse of *matrix$_1$* *175*

Path construction operators

–	**newpath**	–	initialize current path to be empty *187*
–	**currentpoint**	x y	return current point coordinate *138*
x y	**moveto**	–	set current point to (*x*, *y*) *186*
dx dy	**rmoveto**	–	relative moveto *204*
x y	**lineto**	–	append straight line to (*x*, *y*) *180*
dx dy	**rlineto**	–	relative lineto *204*
x y r ang$_1$ ang$_2$	**arc**	–	append counterclockwise arc *117*
x y r ang$_1$ ang$_2$	**arcn**	–	append clockwise arc *118*
x$_1$ y$_1$ x$_2$ y$_2$ r	**arcto**	xt$_1$ yt$_1$ xt$_2$ yt$_2$	append tangent arc *119*
x$_1$ y$_1$ x$_2$ y$_2$ x$_3$ y$_3$	**curveto**	–	append Bezier cubic section *140*
dx$_1$ dy$_1$ dx$_2$ dy$_2$ dx$_3$ dy$_3$	**rcurveto**	–	relative curveto *198*
–	**closepath**	–	connect subpath back to its starting point *130*
–	**flattenpath**	–	convert curves to sequences of straight lines *157*
–	**reversepath**	–	reverse direction of current path *203*
–	**strokepath**	–	compute outline of stroked path *229*
string bool	**charpath**	–	append character outline to current path *127*
–	**clippath**	–	set current path to clipping path *129*
–	**pathbbox**	ll$_x$ ll$_y$ ur$_x$ ur$_y$	return bounding box of current path *191*
move line curve close	**pathforall**	–	enumerate current path *192*
–	**initclip**	–	set clip path to device default *172*
–	**clip**	–	establish new clipping path *128*
–	**eoclip**	–	clip using even-odd inside rule *149*

Painting operators

–	**erasepage**	–	paint current page white *151*
–	**fill**	–	fill current path with current color *156*
–	**eofill**	–	fill using even-odd rule *150*
–	**stroke**	–	draw line along current path *229*
width height bits/sample matrix proc	**image**	–	render sampled image onto current page *170*

width height invert matrix proc **imagemask** – render mask onto current page *171*

Device setup and output operators

–	**showpage**	–	output and reset current page *223*
–	**copypage**	–	output current page *132*
matrix width height proc	**banddevice**	–	install band buffer device *123*
matrix width height proc	**framedevice**	–	install frame buffer device *162*
–	**nulldevice**	–	install no-output device *190*
proc	**renderbands**	–	enumerate bands for output to device *201*

Character and font operators

key font	**definefont**	font	register *font* as a font dictionary *146*
key	**findfont**	font	return font dict identified by *key* *156*
font scale	**scalefont**	font′	scale *font* by *scale* to produce new font′ *210*
font matrix	**makefont**	font′	transform *font* by *matrix* to produce new font′ *183*
font	**setfont**	–	set font dictionary *215*
–	**currentfont**	font	return current font dictionary *136*
string	**show**	–	print characters of *string* on page *222*
a_x a_y string	**ashow**	–	add (a_x, a_y) to width of each char while showing *string* *120*
c_x c_y char string	**widthshow**	–	add (c_x, c_y) to width of *char* while showing *string* *239*
c_x c_y char a_x a_y string	**awidthshow**	–	combined effects of ashow and widthshow *122*
proc string	**kshow**	–	execute *proc* between characters shown from *string* *178*
string	**stringwidth**	w_x w_y	width of *string* in current font *228*
–	**FontDirectory**	dict	dictionary of font dictionaries *159*
–	**StandardEncoding**	array	standard font encoding vector *225*

Font cache operators

–	**cachestatus**	bsize bmax msize mmax csize cmax blimit	return cache status and parameters *126*
w_x w_y ll_x ll_y ur_x ur_y	**setcachedevice**	–	declare cached character metrics *212*
w_x w_y	**setcharwidth**	–	declare uncached character metrics *213*
num	**setcachelimit**	–	set max bytes in cached character *213*

Errors

dictfull	no more room in dictionary *146*
dictstackoverflow	too many begins *147*
dictstackunderflow	too many ends *147*
execstackoverflow	exec nesting too deep *153*
handleerror	called to report error information *167*

interrupt	external interrupt request (e.g., control-C) *174*
invalidaccess	attempt to violate access attribute *174*
invalidexit	exit not in loop *175*
invalidfileaccess	unacceptable access string *175*
invalidfont	invalid font name or dict *175*
invalidrestore	improper restore *175*
ioerror	input/output error occurred *176*
limitcheck	implementation limit exceeded *180*
nocurrentpoint	current point is undefined *188*
rangecheck	operand out of bounds *197*
stackoverflow	operand stack overflow *224*
stackunderflow	operand stack underflow *225*
syntaxerror	syntax error in PostScript program text *230*
timeout	time limit exceeded *231*
typecheck	operand of wrong type *235*
undefined	name not known *235*
undefinedfilename	file not found *236*
undefinedresult	over/underflow or meaningless result *236*
unmatchedmark	expected mark not on stack *236*
unregistered	internal error *236*
VMerror	VM exhausted *237*

6.3 OPERATOR DETAILS

[– **[** mark

pushes a mark object on the operand stack (see **mark**). The customary use of the '**[**' operator is to mark the beginning of an indefinitely long sequence of objects that will eventually be formed into a new array object by the '**]**' operator. (See the discussion of the '**[**' syntax in section 3.3 and of array construction in section 3.8.)

ERRORS:
stackoverflow

SEE ALSO:
], mark, array, astore

]   mark obj_0 ... obj_{n-1} **]** array

creates a new array of n elements, where n is the number of elements above the topmost mark on the operand stack, stores those elements into the array, and returns the array on the operand stack. The '**]**' operator stores the topmost object from the stack into element $n-1$ of *array* and the bottommost one (the one immediately above the mark) into element 0 of *array*. It removes all the array elements from the stack, as well as the mark object.

EXAMPLE:
```
[5 4 3] ⇒ % a 3-element array, with elements 5, 4, 3
mark 5 4 3 counttomark array astore exch pop ⇒ [5 4 3]
[1 2 add] ⇒ % a 1-element array, with element 3
```

The second line of the example has precisely the same effect as the first but uses lower-level array and stack manipulation primitives instead of '**[**' and '**]**'.

In the last line of the example, note that the POSTSCRIPT interpreter acts on all the array elements as it encounters them (unlike its behavior with the '{...}' syntax for executable array construction), so the **add** operator is executed before the array is constructed.

ERRORS:
unmatchedmark, VMerror

SEE ALSO:
[, mark, array, astore

=   any = –

pops an object from the operand stack, produces a text representation of that object's value, and writes the result to the standard output file. The text is that produced by the **cvs** operator; thus, '=' prints the value of a number, boolean, string, name, or operator object and prints '--nostringval--' for an object of any other type.

The name '=' is in no way special; thus, in POSTSCRIPT programs it must be delimited by white space or special characters just the same as names composed of alphabetics. The value of '=' is not actually an operator but a built-in POSTSCRIPT procedure.

ERRORS:
stackunderflow

SEE ALSO:
==, stack, cvs, print

==   any == –

pops an object from the operand stack, produces a text representation of that object, and writes the result to the standard output file. '==' attempts to produce a result that resembles the POSTSCRIPT syntax for creating the object. Thus, it precedes literal names by '/', brackets strings with '(...)', and expands the values of arrays and brackets them with '[...]' or '{...}'. For an object with no printable representation, '==' produces the name of its type in the form '-marktype-' or '-dicttype-'. For an operator object, it produces the operator's name in the form '--add--'.

The name '==' is in no way special; thus, in POSTSCRIPT programs it must be delimited by white space or special characters just the same as names composed of alphabetics. The value of '==' is not actually an operator but a built-in POSTSCRIPT procedure.

ERRORS:
stackunderflow

SEE ALSO:
=, print, pstack

abs num_1 **abs** num_2

returns the absolute value of num_1. The type of the result is the same as the type of num_1 (unless num_1 is the most negative integer, in which case the result is a real).

EXAMPLE:
        4.5 abs $\Rightarrow$ 4.5
        –3 abs $\Rightarrow$ 3
        0 abs $\Rightarrow$ 0

ERRORS:
stackunderflow, typecheck

SEE ALSO:
neg

add num_1 num_2 **add** sum

returns the sum of num_1 and num_2. If both operands are integers and the result is within integer range, the result is an integer; otherwise, the result is a real.

EXAMPLE:
        3 4 add $\Rightarrow$ 7
        9.9 1.1 add $\Rightarrow$ 11.0

ERRORS:
stackunderflow, typecheck, undefinedresult

SEE ALSO:
div, mul, sub, idiv, mod

aload   array **aload** $array_0$ ... $array_{n-1}$ array

successively pushes all n elements of *array* on the operand stack (where n is the length of *array*), and finally pushes *array* itself.

EXAMPLE:
        [23 (ab) –6] aload $\Rightarrow$ 23 (ab) –6 [23 (ab) –6]

ERRORS:
invalidaccess, stackoverflow, stackunderflow, typecheck

SEE ALSO:
astore, get, getinterval

anchorsearch   string seek **anchorsearch**   *if found*: post match true
                                              if not found: string false

determines whether the string *seek* matches the initial substring of *string* (that is, *string* is at least as long as *seek* and the corresponding characters are equal). If so, **anchorsearch** splits *string* into two segments: *match*, the portion of *string* that matches *seek*, and *post*, the remainder of *string*; it then pushes the string objects *post* and *match* and the boolean *true*. If not, it pushes the original *string* and the boolean *false*. **anchorsearch** is a special case of the **search** operator.

EXAMPLE:
        (abbc) (ab) anchorsearch ⇒ (bc) (ab) true
        (abbc) (bb) anchorsearch ⇒ (abbc) false
        (abbc) (bc) anchorsearch ⇒ (abbc) false
        (abbc) (B) anchorsearch ⇒ (abbc) false

ERRORS:
invalidaccess, stackoverflow, stackunderflow, typecheck

SEE ALSO:
search, token

and $bool_1$ $bool_2$ **and** $bool_3$
          int_1 int_2 **and** int_3

If the operands are booleans, **and** returns their logical conjunction. If the operands are integers, **and** returns the bitwise 'and' of their binary representations.

EXAMPLE:
        true true and ⇒ true   % a complete truth table
        true false and ⇒ false
        false true and ⇒ false
        false false and ⇒ false

        99 1 and ⇒ 1
        52 7 and ⇒ 4

ERRORS:
stackunderflow, typecheck

SEE ALSO:
or, xor, not, true, false

arc   x y r ang₁ ang₂ **arc** –

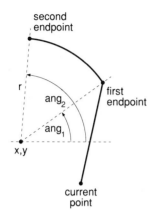

second
endpoint

first
endpoint

r

ang_2

ang_1

x,y

current
point

appends a counterclockwise arc of a circle to the current path, possibly preceded by a straight line segment. The arc has (x, y) as center, r as radius, ang_1 the angle of a vector from (x, y) of length r to the first endpoint of the arc, and ang_2 the angle of a vector from (x, y) of length r to the second endpoint of the arc.

If there is a current point, the **arc** operator includes a straight line segment from the current point to the first endpoint of this arc and then adds the arc itself into the current path. If the current path is empty, the **arc** operator does not produce the initial straight line segment. In any event, the second endpoint of the arc becomes the new current point.

Angles are measured in degrees counterclockwise from the positive x-axis of the current user coordinate system. The curve produced is circular in user space. If user space is scaled non-uniformly (i.e., differently in x and y), **arc** will produce elliptical curves on the output device.

The operators that produce arcs (**arc**, **arcn**, and **arcto**) represent them internally as one or more Bézier cubic curves (see **curveto**) that approximate the required shape. This is done with sufficient accuracy that a faithful rendition of an arc is produced. However, a program that reads the constructed path (using **pathforall**) will encounter **curveto** segments where arcs were specified originally.

EXAMPLE:
    newpath 0 0 moveto 0 0 1 0 45 arc closepath

This constructs a unit radius 45 degree 'pie slice'.

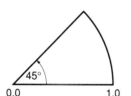

45°

0,0   1,0

ERRORS:
limitcheck, rangecheck, stackunderflow, typecheck

SEE ALSO:
arcn, arcto, curveto

arcn   x y r ang₁ ang₂ **arcn** –

(arc negative) behaves like **arc**, but **arcn** builds its arc segment in a clockwise direction (in user space).

EXAMPLE:
    newpath 0 0 2 0 90 arc 0 0 1 90 0 arcn closepath

This constructs a 2 unit radius, 1 unit wide, 90 degree 'windshield wiper swath'.

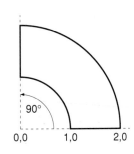

ERRORS:
limitcheck, rangecheck, stackunderflow, typecheck

SEE ALSO:
arc, arcto, curveto

arcto $x_1 \; y_1 \; x_2 \; y_2 \; r$ **arcto** $xt_1 \; yt_1 \; xt_2 \; yt_2$

appends an arc of a circle to the current path, possibly preceded by a straight line segment. The arc is defined by a radius r and two tangent lines. The tangent lines are those drawn from the current point, here called (x_0, y_0), to (x_1, y_1) and from (x_1, y_1) to (x_2, y_2). (If the current point is undefined, **arcto** executes the error **nocurrentpoint**.)

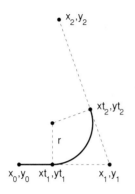

The center of the arc is located within the inner angle between the tangent lines; it is the only point located at distance r in a direction perpendicular to both lines. The arc begins at the first tangent point (xt_1, yt_1) on the first tangent line, passes between its center and the point (x_1, y_1), and ends at the second tangent point (xt_2, yt_2) on the second tangent line.

Before constructing the arc, **arcto** adds a straight line segment from the current point (x_0, y_0) to (xt_1, yt_1), unless those points are the same. In any event, (xt_2, yt_2) becomes the new current point.

The curve produced is circular in user space. If user space is scaled non-uniformly (i.e., differently in x and y), **arcto** will produce elliptical curves on the output device.

If the two tangent lines are collinear, **arcto** merely appends a straight line segment from (x_0, y_0) to (x_1, y_1), considering the arc to be part of a degenerate circle (with radius 0) at that point.

The values returned by **arcto** are for information only; they are the two tangent points in user space.

EXAMPLE:
    newpath 0 0 moveto
    0 4 4 4 1 arcto
    4 {pop} repeat
    4 4 lineto

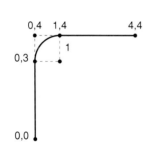

This constructs a 4 unit wide, 4 unit high right angle with a 1 unit radius 'rounded corner.'

ERRORS:
limitcheck, nocurrentpoint, stackunderflow, typecheck, undefinedresult

SEE ALSO:
arc, arcn, curveto

array   int **array** array

creates an array of length *int*, each of whose elements is initialized with a null object, and pushes this array on the operand stack. The *int* operand must be a non-negative integer not greater than the maximum allowable array length (see appendix B).

EXAMPLE:
    3 array $\Rightarrow$ [null null null]

ERRORS:
rangecheck, stackunderflow, typecheck, VMerror

SEE ALSO:
[,], aload, astore

ashow a_x a_y string **ashow** –

prints the characters of *string* in a manner similar to **show**. But while doing so, **ashow** adjusts the width of each character shown by adding a_x to its *x* width and a_y to its *y* width, thus modifying the spacing between characters. a_x and a_y are *x* and *y* displacements in the user coordinate system (not in the character coordinate system).

This operator enables fitting a string of text to a specific width by adjusting all the spaces between characters by a uniform amount. For a discussion about character widths, see section 5.5.

EXAMPLE:

Normal spacing
W i d e   s p a c i n g

    /Helvetica findfont 12 scalefont setfont
    45 270 moveto (Normal spacing) show
    45 256 moveto 4 0 (Wide spacing) ashow

ERRORS:
invalidaccess, invalidfont, nocurrentpoint, stackunderflow, typecheck

SEE ALSO:
show, awidthshow, widthshow, kshow

astore any_0 ... any_{n-1} array **astore** array

stores the objects any_0 through any_{n-1} from the operand stack into *array*, where *n* is the length of *array*. The **astore** operator first removes the *array* operand from the stack and determines its length. It then removes that number of objects from the stack, storing the topmost one into element $n-1$ of *array* and the bottommost one into element 0 of *array*. Finally, it pushes *array* back on the stack.

EXAMPLE:
        (a) (bcd) (ef) 3 array astore $\Rightarrow$ [(a) (bcd) (ef)]

This creates a three element array, stores the strings 'a', 'bcd', and 'ef' into it as elements 0, 1, and 2, and leaves the array object on the operand stack.

ERRORS:
invalidaccess, stackunderflow, typecheck

SEE ALSO:
aload, put, putinterval

atan   num den **atan** angle

returns the angle (in degrees between 0 and 360) whose tangent is *num/den*. Either *num* or *den* may be zero, but not both. The signs of *num* and *den* determine the quadrant in which the result will lie: a positive *num* yields a result in the positive *y* plane; a positive *den* yields a result in the positive *x* plane. The result is a real.

EXAMPLE:
        0 1 atan $\Rightarrow$ 0.0
        1 0 atan $\Rightarrow$ 90.0
        −100 0 atan $\Rightarrow$ 270.0
        4 4 atan $\Rightarrow$ 45.0

ERRORS:
stackunderflow, typecheck, undefinedresult

SEE ALSO:
cos, sin

awidthshow c_x c_y char a_x a_y string **awidthshow** –

prints the characters of *string* in a manner similar to **show**, but combines the special effects of **ashow** and **widthshow**. **awidthshow** adjusts the width of each character shown by adding a_x to its *x* width and a_y to its *y* width, thus modifying the spacing between characters. Furthermore, **awidthshow** modifies the width of each occurrence of the character *char* by an additional amount (c_x, c_y). *char* is an integer in the range 0 to 255 used as a character code.

This operator enables fitting a string of text to a specific width by adjusting all the spaces between characters by a uniform amount, while independently controlling the width of some specific character (such as the space character). For a discussion about character widths, see section 5.5.

EXAMPLE:

Normal spacing
Wide spacing

```
/Helvetica findfont 12 scalefont setfont
45 402 moveto (Normal spacing) show
45 388 moveto 6 0 8#040 .5 0 (Wide spacing) awidthshow
```

ERRORS:
invalidaccess, invalidfont, nocurrentpoint, stackunderflow, typecheck

SEE ALSO:
show, ashow, widthshow, kshow

banddevice   matrix width height proc **banddevice** –

installs a band buffer as the raster memory for an output device and establishes some of the properties of that device. When a band device is being used, the current page is not represented as a full array of pixels. Instead, operations that place marks on the page accumulate information in a *display list*. When it comes time to render the page on the output device (during **showpage**), the display list is read and used to construct a sequence of rectangular *bands* of pixels, each of which is immediately transmitted to the device.

The **banddevice** operator defines a full page to be 8 × *width* pixels wide by *height* pixels high; the width and height should be consistent with the physical properties of the raster output device. **banddevice** derives a clipping path from the *width*, *height*, and *matrix* information and establishes it as the current clip path in the graphics state.

The *matrix* operand is used as the default transformation matrix for the device. It should map default user coordinates into the device coordinate system. **banddevice** establishes this matrix as the current transformation matrix (CTM) in the graphics state.

The *proc* operand is a procedure that will be executed as part of the execution of the **showpage** and **copypage** operators. This procedure's task is to cause the contents of the display list to be converted to bands and transmitted to the physical output device. As part of this process, the procedure must invoke the **renderbands** operator (see the description of **renderbands** for details). For most devices, *proc* is also responsible for implementing the **#copies** convention described under **showpage**.

banddevice is ordinarily invoked by higher-level procedures for setting up specific raster output devices; it is not usually executed directly by user programs (see section 4.9). Only certain devices use band buffers, so the **banddevice** operator may not be defined in some POSTSCRIPT implementations.

ERRORS:
stackunderflow, typecheck

SEE ALSO:
framedevice, nulldevice, renderbands, showpage

begin dict **begin** –

pushes *dict* on the dictionary stack, making it the current dictionary and installing it as the first of the dictionaries defining the current naming context.

ERRORS:
dictstackoverflow, invalidaccess, stackunderflow, typecheck

SEE ALSO:
end, countdictstack, dictstack

bind proc **bind** proc

replaces executable operator names in *proc* by their values. For each element of *proc* that is an executable name, **bind** looks up the name in the context of the current dictionary stack (as if by **load**). If the name is found and its value is an operator object, **bind** replaces the name by the operator in *proc*. If the name is not found or its value is not an operator, **bind** makes no change.

Additionally, for each procedure object in *proc* whose access is unrestricted (that is, each element that is itself an executable array that is not read-only or execute-only), **bind** applies itself recursively to that procedure, makes the procedure read-only, and stores it back into *proc*.

The effect of **bind** is that all operator names in *proc* (and in procedures nested in *proc* to any depth) become 'tightly bound' to the operators themselves. Thus, during subsequent execution of *proc*, the interpreter encounters the operators themselves rather than the names of operators.

There are two main benefits of using **bind**. First, a procedure that has been bound will execute the sequence of operators that were intended when the procedure was defined, even if one or more of the operator names have been redefined in the meantime. Second, a bound procedure executes somewhat faster than one that has not been bound, since the interpreter need not look up the operator names each time but can just execute the operators directly. These benefits are of interest primarily in procedures that are part of the POSTSCRIPT system itself, such as **findfont** and '**=**', which are expected to behave correctly regardless of how a user program has altered its name environment.

ERRORS:
typecheck

SEE ALSO:
load

bitshift int_1 shift **bitshift** int_2

shifts the binary representation of int_1 left by *shift* bits and returns the result. Bits shifted out are lost; bits shifted in are zero. If *shift* is negative then a right shift by $-shift$ bits is performed (this produces an arithmetically correct result only for positive values of int_1). Both int_1 and *shift* must be integers.

EXAMPLE:
    7 3 bitshift $\Rightarrow$ 56
    142 –3 bitshift $\Rightarrow$ 17

ERRORS:
stackunderflow, typecheck

SEE ALSO:
and, or, xor, not

bytesavailable   file **bytesavailable** int

returns the number of bytes that are immediately available for reading from *file* without waiting. The result is −1 if end-of-file has been encountered or if the number of bytes available cannot be determined for other reasons.

ERRORS:
ioerror, stackunderflow, typecheck

SEE ALSO:
read, readhexstring, readline, readstring

cachestatus   – **cachestatus** bsize bmax msize mmax csize cmax blimit

returns measurements of several aspects of the font cache (see section 5.6). **cachestatus** reports the current consumption and limit for each of three font cache resources: bytes of bitmap storage (*bsize* and *bmax*), font/matrix combinations (*msize* and *mmax*), and total number of cached characters (*csize* and *cmax*). It also reports the limit on the number of bytes occupied by a single cached character (*blimit*) — characters whose bitmaps are larger than this are not cached. All **cachestatus** results except *blimit* are for information only; a POSTSCRIPT program can change *blimit* (see **setcachelimit**).

ERRORS:
stackoverflow

SEE ALSO:
setcachelimit

ceiling num_1 **ceiling** num_2

returns the least integer value greater than or equal to num_1. The type of the result is the same as the type of the operand.

EXAMPLE:
    3.2 ceiling $\Rightarrow$ 4.0
    −4.8 ceiling $\Rightarrow$ −4.0
    99 ceiling $\Rightarrow$ 99

ERRORS:
stackunderflow, typecheck

SEE ALSO:
floor, round, truncate, cvi

charpath   string bool **charpath** –

obtains the character path outlines that would result if *string* were shown (at the current point) using **show**. Instead of painting the path, however, **charpath** appends the path to the current path. This yields a result suitable for general filling, stroking, or clipping (see sections 4.5, 4.6, and 5.2).

The *bool* operand determines what happens if the character path is designed to be stroked (**PaintType** 1) rather than filled or outlined (**PaintType** 0 or 2). If *bool* is *false*, **charpath** adds the path to the current path unchanged; the result is suitable only for stroking. If *bool* is *true*, **charpath** applies the **strokepath** operator to the path; the result is suitable for filling or clipping, but not for stroking.

charpath produces no results for portions of a character defined as images or masks rather than as paths.

Note: as long as output from the **charpath** operator remains in the current path, the **pathforall** operator is disabled.

ERRORS:
limitcheck, nocurrentpoint, stackunderflow, typecheck

SEE ALSO:
show, flattenpath, pathbbox, clip

clear   ⊢ any$_1$ ... any$_n$ **clear** ⊢

pops all objects from the operand stack and discards them.

ERRORS: (none)

SEE ALSO:
count, cleartomark, pop

cleartomark   mark obj$_1$ ... obj$_n$ **cleartomark** –

pops the operand stack repeatedly until it encounters a mark, which it also pops from the stack (*obj$_1$* through *obj$_n$* are any objects other than marks).

ERRORS:
unmatchedmark

SEE ALSO:
clear, mark, counttomark, pop

intersects the inside of the current clipping path with the inside of the current path to produce a new (smaller) current clipping path. The inside of the current path is determined by the normal POSTSCRIPT non-zero winding number rule (see section 4.6), while the inside of the current clipping path is determined by whatever rule was used at the time that path was created. Before computing the intersection, the **clip** operator implicitly closes any open subpaths of the current path.

In general, **clip** produces a new path whose inside (according to the non-zero winding number rule) consists of all areas that are inside both of the original paths. The manner in which this new path is constructed (order of its segments, whether or not it self-intersects, etc.) is not specified.

There is no way to enlarge the current clipping path (other than by **initclip** or **initgraphics**) or to set a new path without reference to the current one. The recommended way of using **clip** is to bracket the **clip** and the sequence of graphics to be clipped with **gsave** and **grestore**. The **grestore** will restore the clipping path that was in effect before the **gsave**.

Unlike **fill** and **stroke**, **clip** does not implicitly perform a **newpath** after it has finished using the current path. Any subsequent path construction operators will append to the current path unless **newpath** is executed explicitly. This can be a source of unexpected behavior.

ERRORS:
limitcheck

SEE ALSO:
eoclip, clippath, initclip

clippath   – **clippath** –

sets the current path to one that describes the current clipping path. This operator is useful for determining the exact extent of the imaging area on the current output device.

If the current clipping path is the result of application of the **clip** or **eoclip** operator, the path set by **clippath** is generally suitable only for filling or clipping. It is not suitable for stroking because it may contain interior segments or disconnected subpaths produced by the clipping process.

EXAMPLE:
    clippath 1 setgray fill

This erases (fills with white) the interior of the current clipping path.

ERRORS: (none)

SEE ALSO:
clip, eoclip, initclip

closefile   file **closefile** –

closes *file*, i.e., breaks the association between the file object and the underlying file. For an output file, **closefile** first performs a **flushfile**; it may also take device-dependent actions such as truncating a disk file to the current position or transmitting an end-of-file indication. (See section 3.8.)

ERRORS:
ioerror, stackunderflow, typecheck

SEE ALSO:
file, status, read

closepath   – closepath –

closes the current subpath by appending a straight line segment connecting the current point to the subpath's starting point (generally the point most recently specified by **moveto**). If the current subpath is already closed or the current path is empty, **closepath** does nothing. (See section 4.5.)

closepath terminates the current subpath. Appending another segment to the current path will begin a new subpath, even if it is drawn from the endpoint reached by the **closepath**.

ERRORS:
limitcheck

SEE ALSO:
fill, stroke

concat   matrix **concat** –

concatenates *matrix* with the current transformation matrix (CTM). Precisely, **concat** replaces the CTM by *matrix* × CTM (see section 4.4). The effect of this is to define a new user space whose coordinates are transformed into the former user space according to *matrix*.

EXAMPLE:
    [72 0 0 72 0 0] concat
    72 72 scale

The two examples have the same effect on the current transformation.

ERRORS:
stackunderflow, typecheck

SEE ALSO:
concatmatrix, matrix, rotate, scale, setmatrix, translate

concatmatrix   matrix$_1$ matrix$_2$ matrix$_3$ **concatmatrix** matrix$_3$

replaces the value of *matrix$_3$* by the result of multiplying *matrix$_1$* × *matrix$_2$* and pushes the modified *matrix$_3$* back on the operand stack. This operator does not affect the CTM.

ERRORS:
stackunderflow, typecheck

SEE ALSO:
concat, matrix, rotate, scale, setmatrix, translate

copy any_1 ... any_n n **copy** any_1 ... any_n any_1 ... any_n

> $array_1$ $array_2$ **copy** $subarray_2$
> $dict_1$ $dict_2$ **copy** $dict_2$
> $string_1$ $string_2$ **copy** $substring_2$

In the first instance, where the top element on the operand stack is a non-negative integer *n*, **copy** pops *n* from the stack and then duplicates the top *n* elements on the operand stack as shown above.

In the other instances, **copy** copies all the elements of the first composite object into the second. The composite object operands must be of the same type. In the case of arrays or strings, the length of the second object must be at least as great as the first; **copy** returns the initial *subarray* or *substring* of the second operand into which the elements were copied. (Any remaining elements of $array_2$ or $string_2$ are unaffected by the **copy**.) In the case of dictionaries, $dict_2$ must have a **length** of zero and a **maxlength** at least as great as the length of $dict_1$.

The attributes (literal/executable and access) of the result are the same as those of the second operand except in the case of dictionaries, where the access attribute of the result is the same as that of the first operand.

copy copies the *value* of a composite object. In this respect, it is quite different from **dup** and other operators that copy only the objects themselves (see the discussion of simple versus composite objects in section 3.4). However, **copy** performs only one level of copying: it does not apply recursively to elements that are themselves composite objects; instead, the values of those elements become shared.

EXAMPLE:
```
1 2 3 2 copy ⇒ 1 2 3 2 3
1 2 3 0 copy ⇒ 1 2 3

/a1 [1 2 3] def
a1 dup length array copy ⇒ [1 2 3]
```

ERRORS:
invalidaccess, rangecheck, stackunderflow, stackoverflow, typecheck

SEE ALSO:
dup, get, put, putinterval

copypage   – copypage –

outputs one copy of the current page on the current output device, without erasing the current page or changing the graphics state. This is in contrast to **showpage**, which performs an **erasepage** and an **initgraphics**.

copypage is intended primarily as a debugging aid or as a means for printing successive pages with incrementally accumulated contents. To print multiple copies of the same page, use the **#copies** implicit parameter of **showpage**.

ERRORS: (none)

SEE ALSO:
showpage, erasepage

cos   angle **cos** real

returns the cosine of *angle*, which is interpreted as an angle in degrees. The result is a real.

EXAMPLE:
    0 cos ⇒ 1.0
    90 cos ⇒ 0.0

ERRORS:
stackunderflow, typecheck

SEE ALSO:
atan, sin

count   ⊢ any_1 ... any_n **count** ⊢ any_1 ... any_n n

counts the number of items on the operand stack and pushes this count on the operand stack.

EXAMPLE:
    clear count ⇒ 0
    clear 1 2 3 count ⇒ 1 2 3 3

ERRORS:
stackoverflow

SEE ALSO:
counttomark

countdictstack   – **countdictstack** int

counts the number of dictionaries currently on the dictionary stack and pushes this count on the operand stack.

ERRORS:
stackoverflow

SEE ALSO:
dictstack, begin, end

countexecstack   – **countexecstack** int

counts the number of objects on the execution stack and pushes this count on the operand stack.

ERRORS:
stackoverflow

SEE ALSO:
execstack

counttomark   mark obj_1 ... obj_n **counttomark** mark obj_1 ... obj_n n

counts the number of objects on the operand stack starting with the top element and continuing down to but not including the first mark encountered (obj_1 through obj_n are any objects other than marks).

EXAMPLE:
    1 mark 2 3 counttomark $\Rightarrow$ 1 mark 2 3 2
    1 mark counttomark $\Rightarrow$ 1 mark 0

ERRORS:
stackoverflow, unmatchedmark

SEE ALSO:
mark, count

currentdash   – **currentdash** array offset

returns the current dash array and offset in the graphics state (see **setdash**).

ERRORS:
stackoverflow

SEE ALSO:
setdash, stroke

currentdict   – **currentdict** dict

pushes the current dictionary (the dictionary on top of the dictionary stack) on the operand stack. **currentdict** does not pop the dictionary stack; it just pushes a duplicate of its top element on the operand stack.

ERRORS:
stackoverflow

SEE ALSO:
begin, dictstack

currentfile   – **currentfile** file

returns the file object from which the POSTSCRIPT interpreter is currently or was most recently reading program input. Precisely, **currentfile** returns the topmost file object on the execution stack. If there isn't one, it returns an invalid file object not corresponding to any file (this never occurs during execution of ordinary user programs).

The file returned by **currentfile** is usually but not always the standard input file. An important exception occurs during interactive mode operation (see section 3.8). In this case, the interpreter does not read directly from the standard input file; instead, it reads from a file representing an edited statement (each statement is represented by a different file).

The **currentfile** operator is useful for obtaining images or other data residing in the program file itself (see the example below). At any given time, this file is positioned at the end of the last POSTSCRIPT token read from the file by the interpreter. If that token was a number or a name immediately followed by a white space character, the file is positioned after the white space character (the first, if there are several); otherwise it is positioned after the last character of the token.

EXAMPLE:
```
/str 100 string def
currentfile str readline
here is a line of text
pop /textline exch def
```

After execution of this example, the name 'textline' is associated with the string 'here is a line of text'.

ERRORS:
stackoverflow

SEE ALSO:
exec, run

currentflat   – **currentflat** num

returns the current value of the flatness parameter in the graphics state (see **setflat**).

ERRORS:
stackoverflow

SEE ALSO:
setflat, flattenpath, stroke, fill

currentfont　　– **currentfont** font

returns the current font dictionary in the graphics state (see **setfont**).

ERRORS:
stackoverflow

SEE ALSO:
setfont

currentgray　　– **currentgray** num

returns the gray value of the current color parameter in the graphics state (see **setgray**). If the current color is not a pure gray but has some color hue, **currentgray** returns the brightness component of the current color.

ERRORS:
stackoverflow

SEE ALSO:
setgray, currenthsbcolor, currentrbgcolor

currenthsbcolor　　– **currenthsbcolor** hue saturation brightness

returns the three components of the current color parameter in the graphics state according to the hue-saturation-brightness model (see **sethsbcolor**).

ERRORS:
stackoverflow

SEE ALSO:
sethsbcolor, currentgray, currentrgbcolor

currentlinecap　　– **currentlinecap** int

returns the current value of the line cap parameter in the graphics state (see **setlinecap**).

ERRORS:
stackoverflow

SEE ALSO:
setlinecap, stroke, currentlinejoin

currentlinejoin   – **currentlinejoin** int

returns the current value of the line join parameter in the graphics state (see **setlinejoin**).

ERRORS:
stackoverflow

SEE ALSO:
setlinejoin, stroke, currentlinecap

currentlinewidth   – **currentlinewidth** num

returns the current value of the line width parameter in the graphics state (see **setlinewidth**).

ERRORS:
stackoverflow

SEE ALSO:
setlinewidth, stroke

currentmatrix   matrix **currentmatrix** matrix

replaces the value of *matrix* with the value of the current transformation matrix (CTM) in the graphics state, and pushes the modified matrix back on the operand stack (see section 4.4).

ERRORS:
rangecheck, stackunderflow, typecheck

SEE ALSO:
setmatrix, defaultmatrix, initmatrix, rotate, scale, translate

currentmiterlimit   – **currentmiterlimit** num

returns the current value of the miter limit parameter in the graphics state (see **setmiterlimit**).

ERRORS:
stackoverflow

SEE ALSO:
setmiterlimit, stroke

currentpoint – **currentpoint** x y

returns the x and y coordinates of the current point in the graphics state (i.e., the trailing endpoint of the current path). If the current point is undefined (because the current path is empty), **currentpoint** executes the **nocurrentpoint** error.

The current point is reported in the user coordinate system. As discussed in section 4.5, points entered into a path are immediately converted to device coordinates by the current transformation matrix (CTM); existing points are not changed by subsequent modifications to the CTM. **currentpoint** computes the user space coordinate that corresponds to the current point according to the current value of the CTM. If a current point is set and then the CTM is changed, **currentpoint** will report a different position in user space than it did before.

ERRORS:
nocurrentpoint, stackoverflow, undefinedresult

SEE ALSO:
moveto, lineto, curveto, arc

currentrgbcolor – **currentrgbcolor** red green blue

returns the three components of the current color in the graphics state according to the red-green-blue color model.

ERRORS:
stackoverflow

SEE ALSO:
setrgbcolor, currentgray, currenthsbcolor

currentscreen   – **currentscreen** frequency angle proc

returns all the current halftone screen parameters in the graphics state (see **setscreen**).

ERRORS:
stackoverflow

SEE ALSO:
setscreen, currenttransfer

currenttransfer   – **currenttransfer** proc

returns the current transfer function in the graphics state (see **settransfer**).

ERRORS:
stackoverflow

SEE ALSO:
settransfer, currentscreen

curveto x_1 y_1 x_2 y_2 x_3 y_3 **curveto** –

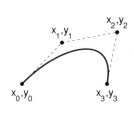

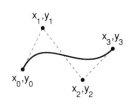

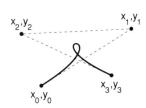

adds a Bézier cubic section to the current path between the current point, referred to here as (x_0, y_0), and the point (x_3, y_3), using (x_1, y_1) and (x_2, y_2) as the Bézier cubic control points. After constructing the curve, **curveto** makes (x_3, y_3) become the new current point. If the current point is undefined (because the current path is empty), **curveto** executes the error **nocurrentpoint**.

The four points define the shape of the curve geometrically. The curve starts at (x_0, y_0), it is tangent to the line from (x_0, y_0) to (x_1, y_1) at that point, and it leaves the point in that direction. The curve ends at (x_3, y_3), it is tangent to the line from (x_2, y_2) to (x_3, y_3) at that point, and it approaches the point from that direction. The lengths of the lines (x_0, y_0) to (x_1, y_1) and (x_2, y_2) to (x_3, y_3) represent in some sense the 'velocity' of the path at the endpoints. The curve is always entirely enclosed by the convex quadrilateral defined by the four points.

The mathematical formulation of a Bézier cubic curve is derived from a pair of parametric cubic equations:

$$x(t) = a_x t^3 + b_x t^2 + c_x t + x_0$$
$$y(t) = a_y t^3 + b_y t^2 + c_y t + y_0$$

The cubic section produced by **curveto** is the path traced by $x(t)$ and $y(t)$ as t ranges from 0 to 1. The Bézier control points corresponding to this curve are:[1]

$$x_1 = x_0 + c_x/3 \qquad\qquad y_1 = y_0 + c_y/3$$
$$x_2 = x_1 + (c_x + b_x)/3 \qquad y_2 = y_1 + (c_y + b_y)/3$$
$$x_3 = x_0 + c_x + b_x + a_x \qquad y_3 = y_0 + c_y + b_y + a_y$$

ERRORS:
limitcheck, nocurrentpoint, stackunderflow, typecheck

SEE ALSO:
lineto, moveto, arc, arcn, arcto

---

[1] For a more thorough treatment of the mathematics of Bézier cubics, see J. D. Foley and A. Van Dam, *Fundamentals of Interactive Computer Graphics*, Addison-Wesley, 1982.

cvi   num **cvi** integer
          string **cvi** integer

(convert to integer) takes an integer, real, or string object from the stack and produces an integer result. If the operand is an integer, **cvi** simply returns it. If the operand is a real, it truncates any fractional part (i.e., rounds it toward 0) and converts it to an integer. If the operand is a string, it interprets the characters of the string as a number according to the POSTSCRIPT syntax rules; if that number is a real, **cvi** converts it to an integer.

cvi executes a **rangecheck** error if a real is too large to convert to an integer. (See the **round**, **truncate**, **floor**, and **ceiling** operators, which remove fractional parts without performing type conversion.)

EXAMPLE:
> (3.3E1) cvi $\Rightarrow$ 33
> −47.8 cvi $\Rightarrow$ −47
> 520.9 cvi $\Rightarrow$ 520

ERRORS:
invalidaccess, rangecheck, stackunderflow, syntaxerror, typecheck, undefinedresult

SEE ALSO:
cvr, ceiling, floor, round, truncate

cvlit   any **cvlit** any

(convert to literal) makes the object on the top of the operand stack have the literal attribute (instead of executable).

ERRORS:
stackunderflow

SEE ALSO:
cvx, xcheck

cvn   string **cvn** name

(convert to name) converts the string operand to a name object that is lexically the same as the string. The name object is executable if the string was.

EXAMPLE:
>   (abc) cvn ⇒ /abc
>   (abc) cvx cvn ⇒ abc

ERRORS:
invalidaccess, rangecheck, stackunderflow, typecheck

SEE ALSO:
cvs, type

cvr   num **cvr** real
     string **cvr** real

(convert to real) takes an integer, real, or string object and produces a real result. If the operand is an integer, **cvr** converts it to a real. If the operand is a real, **cvr** simply returns it. If the operand is a string, it interprets the characters of the string as a number according to the POSTSCRIPT syntax rules; if that number is an integer, **cvr** converts it to a real.

ERRORS:
invalidaccess, rangecheck, stackunderflow, syntaxerror, typecheck, undefinedresult

SEE ALSO:
cvi

cvrs   num radix string **cvrs** substring

(convert to string with radix) produces a text representation of the number *num* in the specified *radix*, stores the text into the supplied *string* (overwriting some initial portion of its value), and returns a string object designating the substring actually used. If *string* is too small to hold the result of the conversion, **cvrs** executes the error **rangecheck**.

If *num* is a real, **cvrs** first converts it to an integer by application of **cvi**. *radix* is expected to be a positive decimal integer in the range 2 to 36. Digits greater than 9 in the resulting string are represented by the letters 'A' through 'Z'.

EXAMPLE:
```
/str 10 string def
100 8 str cvrs ⇒ (144)        % 100₁₀ is 144₈
200 16 str cvrs ⇒ (C8)
```

ERRORS:
invalidacess, rangecheck, stackunderflow, typecheck

SEE ALSO:
cvs

cvs   any string **cvs** substring

(convert to string) produces a text representation of an arbitrary object *any*, stores the text into the supplied *string* (overwriting some initial portion of its value), and returns a string object designating the substring actually used. If the *string* is too small to hold the result of conversion, **cvs** executes the error **rangecheck**.

If *any* is a number, **cvs** produces a string representation of that number. If *any* is a boolean, **cvs** produces either the string 'true' or the string 'false'. If *any* is a string, **cvs** copies its contents into *string*. If *any* is a name or an operator, **cvs** produces the text representation of that name (or the operator's name). If *any* is any other type, **cvs** produces the text '--nostringval--'.

EXAMPLE:
```
/str 20 string def
123 456 add str cvs ⇒ (579)
mark str cvs ⇒ (--nostringval--)
```

ERRORS:
invalidaccess, rangecheck, stackunderflow, typecheck

SEE ALSO:
cvi, cvr, string, type

cvx   any **cvx** any

(convert to executable) makes the object on top of the operand stack have the executable attribute (instead of literal).

ERRORS:
stackunderflow

SEE ALSO:
cvlit, xcheck

def   key value **def** –

associates *key* with *value* in the current dictionary (the one on the top of the dictionary stack; see section 3.5). If *key* is already present in the current dictionary, **def** simply replaces its value. Otherwise, **def** creates a new entry for *key* and stores *value* with it.

EXAMPLE:
```
/ncnt 1 def             % define ncnt to be 1 in current dict
/ncnt ncnt 1 add def    % ncnt now has value 2
```

ERRORS:
dictfull, invalidaccess, limitcheck, stackunderflow, typecheck

SEE ALSO:
store, put

defaultmatrix   matrix **defaultmatrix** matrix

replaces the value of *matrix* with the default transformation matrix for the current output device and pushes this modified matrix back on the operand stack.

ERRORS:
rangecheck, stackunderflow, typecheck

SEE ALSO:
currentmatrix, initmatrix, setmatrix

definefont   key font **definefont** font

registers *font* as a font dictionary associated with *key* (usually a name), as discussed in section 5.3. **definefont** first checks that *font* is a well-formed font dictionary (i.e., contains all required key-value pairs). It inserts an additional entry whose key is **FID** and whose value is an object of type fontID; the dictionary must be large enough to accommodate this additional entry. It makes the dictionary's access read-only. Finally, it associates *key* with *font* in the global font dictionary **FontDirectory**.

Subsequent invocation of **findfont** with *key* will return *font*. Note that since a font dictionary is an ordinary POSTSCRIPT object, a font registered by **definefont** between a **save** and a matching **restore** will be unregistered by the **restore**.

ERRORS:
dictfull, invalidfont, stackunderflow, typecheck

SEE ALSO:
makefont, scalefont, setfont, FontDirectory

dict   int **dict** dict

creates an empty dictionary with a maximum capacity of *int* elements and pushes the created dictionary object on the operand stack. *int* is expected to be a non-negative integer.

ERRORS:
rangecheck, stackunderflow, typecheck, VMerror

SEE ALSO:
begin, end, length, maxlength

dictfull   (error)

occurs when a **def**, **put**, or **store** operator attempts to define a new entry in a dictionary that is already full (i.e., whose **length** and **maxlength** are already equal). A dictionary has a fixed limit on the number of entries (with distinct keys) that it can hold; this limit is established by the operand to the **dict** operator that creates the dictionary.

SEE ALSO:
def, put, store

dictstack   array **dictstack** subarray

stores all elements of the dictionary stack into *array* and returns an object describing the initial *n*-element subarray of *array*, where *n* is the current depth of the dictionary stack. **dictstack** copies the topmost dictionary into element *n*−1 of *array* and the bottommost one into element 0 of *array*. The dictionary stack itself is unchanged. If the length of *array* is less than the depth of the dictionary stack, **dictstack** executes a **rangecheck** error.

ERRORS:
invalidaccess, rangecheck, stackunderflow, typecheck

SEE ALSO:
countdictstack

dictstackoverflow   (error)

The dictionary stack has grown too large. Too many **begin**s (without corresponding **end**s) have pushed too many dictionaries on the dictionary stack. See appendix B for the limit on the size of the dictionary stack.

Before invoking this error, the interpreter creates an array containing all elements of the dictionary stack (stored as if by **dictstack**), pushes this array on the operand stack, and resets the dictionary stack to contain only **systemdict** and **userdict**.

SEE ALSO:
begin

dictstackunderflow   (error)

An attempt has been made to remove (**end**) the bottommost instance of **userdict** from the dictionary stack. This occurs if an **end** is executed for which there was no corresponding **begin**.

SEE ALSO:
end

div   num$_1$ num$_2$ **div** quotient

divides *num$_1$* by *num$_2$*, producing a result that is always a real (even if both operands are integers; use **idiv** if an integer result is desired).

EXAMPLE:
```
3 2 div ⇒ 1.5
4 2 div ⇒ 2.0
```

ERRORS:
stackunderflow, typecheck, undefinedresult

SEE ALSO:
idiv, add, mul, sub, mod

dtransform   dx dy **dtransform** dx′ dy′
dx dy matrix **dtransform** dx′ dy′

With no *matrix* operand, **dtransform** (delta transform) transforms the distance vector (*dx*, *dy*) by the CTM to produce the corresponding distance vector (*dx′*, *dy′*) in device space. If the *matrix* operand is supplied, **dtransform** transforms the distance vector by *matrix* rather than by CTM.

A delta transformation is similar to a normal transformation (see section 4.4), but the translation components (t_x and t_y) of the transformation matrix are not used, thus making the distance vectors position-less in both user space and device space. This is useful for determining how distances map from user space to device space.

ERRORS:
stackunderflow, typecheck

SEE ALSO:
idtransform, transform, itransform

dup   any **dup** any any

duplicates the top element on the operand stack. Note that **dup** copies only the object itself; the value of a composite object is not copied but is shared (see section 3.4).

ERRORS:
stackoverflow, stackunderflow

SEE ALSO:
copy, index

echo   boolean **echo** –

specifies whether characters from the standard input file are to be echoed to the standard output file during interactive mode operation. The applicability of this setting is somewhat environment-dependent. By default, the POSTSCRIPT interpreter echoes the input to the output while opening the special files named '%statementedit' and '%lineedit'. One situation in which turning off echoing is appropriate is password input. See the introduction to the file operators in section 3.8.

ERRORS:
stackunderflow, typecheck

SEE ALSO:
file

end   – **end** –

pops the current dictionary off the dictionary stack, making the dictionary below it the current dictionary. If **end** tries to pop the bottommost instance of **userdict**, it executes the error operator **dictstackunderflow**.

ERRORS:
dictstackunderflow

SEE ALSO:
begin, dictstack, countdictstack

eoclip   – **eoclip** –

intersects the inside of the current clipping path with the inside of the current path to produce a new (smaller) current clipping path. The inside of the current path is determined by the even-odd rule (see section 4.6), while the inside of the current clipping path is determined by whatever rule was used at the time that path was created. Before computing the intersection, the **eoclip** operator implicitly closes any open subpaths of the current path.

Except for the choice of insideness rule, the behavior of **eoclip** is identical to that of **clip**.

ERRORS:
limitcheck

SEE ALSO:
clip, clippath, initclip

eofill   – **eofill** –

paints the inside of the current path with the current color, using the even-odd rule to determine what points are inside. Except for the choice of insideness rule, the behavior of **eofill** is identical to that of **fill**.

ERRORS:
limitcheck

SEE ALSO:
fill

eq any_1 any_2 **eq** bool

pops two objects from the operand stack and pushes the boolean value *true* if they are equal, *false* if not. The definition of equality depends on the types of the objects being compared. Simple objects are equal if their types and values are the same. Strings are equal if their lengths and individual elements are equal. Other composite objects (arrays and dictionaries) are equal only if they share the same value; separate values are considered unequal, even if all the components of those values are the same.

Some type conversions are performed by **eq**. Integers and reals can be compared freely: an integer and a real representing the same mathematical value are considered equal by **eq**. Strings and names can likewise be compared freely: a name defined by some sequence of characters is equal to a string whose elements are the same sequence of characters.

The literal/executable and access attributes of objects are not considered in comparisons between objects.

EXAMPLE:
```
4.0 4 eq ⇒ true          % a real and an integer may be equal
(abc) (abc) eq ⇒ true    % strings with equal elements are equal
(abc) /abc eq ⇒ true     % a string and a name may be equal
[1 2 3] dup eq ⇒ true    % an array is equal to itself
[1 2 3] [1 2 3] eq ⇒ false  % distinct array objects not equal
```

ERRORS:
invalidaccess, stackunderflow

SEE ALSO:
ne, le, lt, ge, gt

erasepage   – **erasepage** –

erases the entire current page by painting it with gray level 1, which is ordinarily white (but may be some other color if an atypical transfer function has been defined). The entire page is erased, regardless of the clip path currently in force. **erasepage** affects only the contents of raster memory; it does not modify the graphics state, nor does it cause a page to be transmitted to the output device.

erasepage is executed automatically by **showpage**. There are few situations in which a POSTSCRIPT page description should execute **erasepage** explicitly, since the operator affects portions of the current page outside the current clip path. It is usually more appropriate to erase just the inside of the current clip path (see **clippath**); then the page description can be embedded within another, composite page without undesirable effects.

ERRORS: (none)

SEE ALSO:
showpage, clippath, fill

errordict   – **errordict** dict

pushes the dictionary object **errordict** on the operand stack (see section 3.6). **errordict** is not actually an operator; it is a name in **systemdict** associated with the dictionary object itself.

ERRORS:
stackoverflow

SEE ALSO:
systemdict, userdict

exch   any$_1$ any$_2$ **exch** any$_2$ any$_1$

exchanges the top two elements on the operand stack.

EXAMPLE:
    1 2 exch $\Rightarrow$ 2 1

ERRORS:
stackunderflow

SEE ALSO:
dup, roll, index, pop

exec   any **exec** –

pushes the operand on the execution stack, thereby executing it immediately. The effect of executing an object depends on the object's type and literal/executable attribute; this is discussed in detail in section 3.6. In particular, executing a literal object will cause it just to be pushed back on the operand stack. Executing a procedure, however, will cause the procedure to be called.

EXAMPLE:
```
(3 2 add) cvx exec ⇒ 5
3 2 /add exec ⇒ 3 2 /add
3 2 /add cvx exec ⇒ 5
```

In the first line, the string '3 2 add' is made executable and then executed. Executing a string causes its characters to be scanned and interpreted according to the POSTSCRIPT syntax rules.

In the second line, the literal objects '3', '2', and 'add' are pushed on the operand stack, then **exec** is applied to the 'add'. Since the 'add' is a literal name, executing it simply causes it to be pushed back on the operand stack; the **exec** in this case has no useful effect.

In the third line, the literal name 'add' on the top of the operand stack is made executable by **cvx**. Applying **exec** to this executable name causes it to be looked up and the **add** operation to be performed.

ERRORS:
stackunderflow

SEE ALSO:
xcheck, cvx, run

execstack   array **execstack** subarray

stores all elements of the execution stack into *array* and returns an object describing the initial *n*-element subarray of *array*, where *n* is the current depth of the execution stack. **execstack** copies the topmost object into element *n*−1 of *array* and the bottommost one into element 0 of *array*. The execution stack itself is unchanged. If the length of *array* is less than the depth of the execution stack, **execstack** executes a **rangecheck** error.

ERRORS:
invalidaccess, rangecheck, stackunderflow, typecheck

SEE ALSO:
countexecstack, exec

execstackoverflow   (error)

The execution stack has grown too large; procedure invocation is nested deeper than the POSTSCRIPT interpreter permits. See appendix B for the limit on the size of the execution stack.

SEE ALSO:
exec

executeonly   array **executeonly** array
file **executeonly** file
string **executeonly** string

reduces the access attribute of an array, file, or string object to execute-only (see the description of attributes in section 3.4). Access can only be reduced by this means, never increased. When an object is execute-only, its value cannot be read or modified explicitly by POSTSCRIPT operators (an **invalidaccess** error will result), but it can still be executed by the POSTSCRIPT interpreter, e.g., by invoking it with **exec**.

executeonly affects the access attribute only of the object that it returns; if there exist other objects that share the same value, their access attributes are unaffected.

ERRORS:
invalidaccess, stackunderflow, typecheck

SEE ALSO:
rcheck, wcheck, xcheck, readonly, noaccess

exit   – exit –

terminates execution of the innermost dynamically enclosing instance of a looping context, without regard to lexical relationship. A looping context is a procedure invoked repeatedly by one of the control operators **for**, **loop**, **repeat**, **forall**, or **pathforall**. **exit** pops the execution stack down to the level of that operator. The interpreter then resumes execution at the next object in normal sequence after that operator.

exit does not affect the operand or dictionary stacks. Any objects pushed on those stacks during execution of the looping context remain after the context is exited.

If **exit** would escape from the context of a **run** or **stopped** operator, it executes the **invalidexit** error (still in the context of the **run** or **stopped**). If there is no enclosing looping context, the interpreter prints an error message and executes the built-in operator **quit** (this never occurs during execution of ordinary user programs, since they are enclosed by a **stopped** context).

ERRORS:
invalidexit

SEE ALSO:
for, forall, loop, repeat, pathforall, stop

exp   base exponent **exp** real

raises *base* to the *exponent* power. The operands may be either integers or reals (if the exponent has a fractional part, the result is meaningful only if the base is non-negative). The result is always a real.

EXAMPLE:
    9 0.5 exp ⇒ 3.0
    −9 −1 exp ⇒ −0.111111

ERRORS:
stackunderflow, typecheck, undefinedresult

SEE ALSO:
sqrt, ln, log, mul

false   – **false** false

pushes a boolean object whose value is *false* on the operand stack. (**false** is not actually an operator; it is a name in **systemdict** associated with the boolean value *false*.)

ERRORS:
stackoverflow

SEE ALSO:
true, and, or, not, xor

file   string₁ string₂ **file** file

creates a file object for the file identified by *string*₁, accessing it as specified by *string*₂. Conventions for both file names and access specifications depend on the operating system environment in which the POSTSCRIPT interpreter is running. However, all POSTSCRIPT interpreters provide several standard files with names such as '%stdin' and '%stdout' (see the introduction to the file operators in section 3.8), as well as the following standard access modes specified by *string*₂:

'r'   input file (read-only). In a POSTSCRIPT environment with permanent file storage, the file identified by *string*₁ must already exist; otherwise, an **undefinedfilename** error is executed.

'w'   output file (write-only). In a POSTSCRIPT environment with permanent file storage, the file identified by *string*₁ is overwritten if it already exists or is created if it doesn't.

Once created, the *file* object remains valid until the file is closed either explicitly (by executing **closefile**) or implicitly (by encountering end-of-file while reading or executing the file). A file is also closed by **restore** if the file object was created more recently than the **save** snapshot being restored. There is a limit on the number of files that can be open simultaneously; see appendix B.

EXAMPLE:
    (%stdin) (r) file ⇒ % standard input file object

ERRORS:
invalidfileaccess, limitcheck, stackunderflow, typecheck, undefinedfilename

SEE ALSO:
closefile, currentfile, read, write, status

fill   − fill −

paints the area enclosed by the current path with the current color. Any previous contents of that area on the current page are obscured, so areas may be erased by filling with color set to white.

Before painting, **fill** implicitly closes any open subpaths of the current path. The inside of the current path is determined by the normal POSTSCRIPT non-zero winding number rule (see section 4.6).

fill implicitly performs a **newpath** after it has finished filling the current path. To preserve the current path across a **fill** operation, use the sequence: **gsave fill grestore**.

ERRORS:
limitcheck

SEE ALSO:
eofill, stroke, clip

findfont   key **findfont** font

obtains a font dictionary identified by the specified *key* and pushes it on the operand stack (see section 5.2). *key* may be a key previously passed to **definefont**, in which case the font dictionary associated with *key* (in **FontDirectory**) is returned.

If *key* is not found, **findfont** takes an action that varies according to the environment in which the POSTSCRIPT interpreter is operating. In some environments, **findfont** may attempt to read a font definition from a file and to execute a **definefont** for that font. In other environments, **findfont** substitutes a default font or executes the error **invalidfont**.

findfont is not actually a POSTSCRIPT operator but a built-in procedure. It may be redefined by a POSTSCRIPT program that requires different strategies for finding fonts.

ERRORS:
invalidfont, stackunderflow, typecheck

SEE ALSO:
scalefont, makefont, setfont, definefont, FontDirectory

flattenpath   – **flattenpath** –

replaces the current path with an equivalent path that preserves all straight line segments but has all **curveto** segments replaced by sequences of **lineto** (straight line) segments that approximate the curves. If the current path does not contain any **curveto** segments, **flattenpath** leaves it unchanged.

This 'flattening' of curves to straight line segments is done automatically when a path is used to control painting (e.g., by **stroke** or **fill**). Only rarely does a program need to flatten a path explicitly (see **pathbbox**). The accuracy of the approximation to the curve is controlled by the current flatness parameter in the graphics state (see **setflat**).

ERRORS:
limitcheck

SEE ALSO:
setflat, curveto, lineto, pathbbox

floor num_1 **floor** num_2

returns the greatest integer value less than or equal to num_1. The type of the result is the same as the type of the operand.

EXAMPLE:
3.2 floor $\Rightarrow$ 3.0
−4.8 floor $\Rightarrow$ −5.0
99 floor $\Rightarrow$ 99

ERRORS:
stackunderflow, typecheck

SEE ALSO:
ceiling, round, truncate, cvi

flush   – flush –

causes any buffered characters for the standard output file to be delivered immediately. In general, a program requiring output to be sent immediately (such as during real-time two-way interactions) should call **flush** after generating that output.

ERRORS:
ioerror

SEE ALSO:
flushfile, print

flushfile   file **flushfile** –

If *file* is an output file, **flushfile** causes any buffered characters for that file to be delivered immediately. In general, a program requiring output to be sent immediately (such as during real-time two-way interactions) should call **flushfile** after generating that output.

If *file* is an input file, **flushfile** reads and discards data from *file* until the end-of-file indication is encountered. This is useful during error recovery, and is used for that purpose by the POSTSCRIPT control program.

ERRORS:
ioerror, stackunderflow, typecheck

SEE ALSO:
flush, read, write

FontDirectory   – **FontDirectory** dict

pushes the global dictionary of fonts on the operand stack. This dictionary associates font names with font dictionaries. Entries are placed in **FontDirectory** by **definefont** and are looked up by **findfont**. This dictionary may be read explicitly by POSTSCRIPT dictionary operators but may not be changed (because it is read-only). **FontDirectory** is not actually an operator; it is a name in **systemdict** associated with the dictionary object itself.

While **FontDirectory** contains all fonts present in POSTSCRIPT's VM, it does not necessarily describe all the fonts available to a POSTSCRIPT program. In some environments, **findfont** may be able to locate a font that is not defined in **FontDirectory**, e.g., by reading it from a file.

ERRORS:
stackoverflow

SEE ALSO:
definefont, findfont

for   initial increment limit proc **for** –

executes *proc* repeatedly, passing it a sequence of values from *initial* by steps of *increment* to *limit*. The **for** operator expects *initial*, *increment* and *limit* to be numbers. It maintains a temporary internal variable, known as the *control variable*, which it first sets to *initial*. Then, before each repetition, it compares the control variable with the termination value *limit*; if *limit* has not been exceeded, it pushes the control variable on the operand stack, executes *proc*, and adds *increment* to the control variable.

The termination condition depends on whether *increment* is positive or negative. If *increment* is positive, **for** terminates when the control variable becomes greater than *limit*. If *increment* is negative, **for** terminates when the control variable becomes less than *limit*. If *initial* itself meets the termination condition, **for** does not execute *proc* at all. If *proc* executes the **exit** operator, **for** terminates prematurely.

Usually, *proc* will use the value on the operand stack for some purpose. However, if *proc* does not remove the value, it will remain there; successive executions of *proc* will cause successive values of the control variable to accumulate on the operand stack.

EXAMPLE:

    0 1 1 4 {add} for $\Rightarrow$ 10
    1 2 6 {} for $\Rightarrow$ 1 3 5
    3 –.5 1 {} for $\Rightarrow$ 3.0 2.5 2.0 1.5 1.0

In the first example, the value of the control variable is added to whatever is on the stack, so 1, 2, 3, and 4 are added in turn to a running sum whose initial value is 0. The second example has an empty procedure, so the successive values of the loop counter are left on the stack. The last example counts backwards from 3 to 1 by halves, leaving the successive values on the stack.

ERRORS:
stackoverflow, stackunderflow, typecheck

SEE ALSO:
repeat, loop, forall, pathforall, exit

forall
    array proc **forall** –
        dict proc **forall** –
     string proc **forall** –

enumerates the elements of the first operand, executing the procedure *proc* for each element. If the first operand is an array or string, **forall** pushes an element on the operand stack and executes *proc* for each element in the array or string, beginning with the element whose index is 0 and continuing sequentially. The objects pushed on the operand stack are the array or string elements themselves; in the case of a string, these elements are integers in the range 0 to 255, *not* one-character strings.

If the first operand is a dictionary, **forall** pushes both a key and a value on the operand stack and executes *proc* for each key-value pair in the dictionary. The order in which **forall** enumerates the entries in the dictionary is arbitrary. New entries put in the dictionary during execution of *proc* may or may not be included in the enumeration.

If the array, dictionary, or string is empty (i.e., has length 0), **forall** does not execute *proc* at all. If *proc* executes the **exit** operator, **forall** terminates prematurely.

Although **forall** does not leave any results on the operand stack when it is finished, the execution of *proc* may leave arbitrary results there. In particular, if *proc* does not remove each enumerated element from the operand stack, the elements will accumulate there.

EXAMPLE:
    0 [13 29 3 –8 21] {add} forall ⇒ 58
    /d 2 dict def
    d /abc 123 put
    d /xyz (test) put
    d {} forall ⇒ /xyz (test) /abc 123

ERRORS:
invalidaccess, stackunderflow, typecheck

SEE ALSO:
for, repeat, loop, pathforall, exit

framedevice   matrix width height proc **framedevice** –

installs a frame buffer as the raster memory for an output device and establishes some of the properties of that device. This operator sets up a full page frame buffer $8 \times width$ pixels wide by *height* pixels high; the width and height should be consistent with the physical properties of the raster output device. **framedevice** derives a clipping path from the *width*, *height*, and *matrix* information and establishes it as the current clip path in the graphics state.

The *matrix* operand is used as the default transformation matrix for the device. It should map default user coordinates into the device coordinate system. **framedevice** establishes this matrix as the current transformation matrix (CTM) in the graphics state.

The *proc* operand is a procedure that will be executed as part of the execution of the **showpage** and **copypage** operators. This procedure's task is to cause the contents of the frame buffer to be transmitted to the physical output device. This generally involves executing one or more special device-dependent operators. Such operators are different for each physical device and are not documented in this manual. For most devices, *proc* is also responsible for implementing the **#copies** convention described under **showpage**.

framedevice is ordinarily invoked by higher-level procedures for setting up specific raster output devices; it is not usually executed directly by user programs (see section 4.9). Not all devices use frame buffers, so the **framedevice** operator may not be defined in some POSTSCRIPT implementations.

ERRORS:
stackunderflow, typecheck

SEE ALSO:
banddevice, nulldevice, showpage

ge   num$_1$ num$_2$ **ge** bool
string$_1$ string$_2$ **ge** bool

pops two objects from the operand stack and pushes the boolean value *true* if the first operand is greater than or equal to the second, *false* otherwise. If both operands are numbers, **ge** compares their mathematical values. If both operands are strings, **ge** compares them element by element (treating the elements as integers in the range 0 to 255) to determine whether the first string is lexically greater than or equal to the second. If the operands are of other types (or one is a string and the other is a number), **ge** executes the **typecheck** error.

EXAMPLE:
    4.2 4 ge ⇒ true
    (abc)(d) ge ⇒ false
    (aba)(ab) ge ⇒ true
    (aba)(aba) ge ⇒ true

ERRORS:
invalidaccess, stackunderflow, typecheck

SEE ALSO:
gt, eq, ne, le, lt

get   array index **get** any
              dict key **get** any
          string index **get** int

gets a single element from the value of an array, dictionary, or string.

If the first operand is an array or string, **get** treats the second operand as an *index* and returns the array or string element identified by the index (counting from zero). *index* must be in the range 0 to *n*−1, where *n* is the length of the array or string; if it is outside this range, **get** will execute a **rangecheck** error.

If the first operand is a dictionary, **get** looks up the second operand as a key in the dictionary and returns the associated value. If the key is not present in the dictionary, **get** executes the **undefined** error.

EXAMPLE:
```
[31 41 59] 0 get ⇒ 31
[0 (a mixed-type array) [] {add 2 div}]
        2 get ⇒ []              % an empty array

/mykey (myvalue) def
currentdict /mykey get ⇒ (myvalue)

(abc) 1 get ⇒ 98               % character code for 'b'
(a) 0 get ⇒ 97
```

ERRORS:
invalidaccess, rangecheck, stackunderflow, typecheck, undefined

SEE ALSO:
put, getinterval

getinterval   array index count **getinterval** subarray
                    string index count **getinterval** substring

creates a new array or string object whose value consists of some subsequence of the original array or string. The subsequence consists of *count* elements starting at the specified *index* in the original array or string. The elements in the subsequence are shared between the original and new objects (see the discussion of simple versus composite objects in section 3.4).

The returned subarray or substring is an ordinary array or string object whose length is *count* and whose elements are indexed starting at 0. Thus, the element at index 0 in *subarray* is the same as the element at index *index* in the original *array*.

getinterval requires *index* to be a valid index in the original array or string and *count* to be a non-negative integer such that *index+count* is not greater than the length of the original array or string.

EXAMPLE:
> [9 8 7 6 5] 1 3 getinterval $\Rightarrow$ [8 7 6]
> (abcde) 1 3 getinterval $\Rightarrow$ (bcd)
> (abcde) 0 0 getinterval $\Rightarrow$ ()   % an empty string

ERRORS:
invalidaccess, rangecheck, stackunderflow, typecheck

SEE ALSO:
get, putinterval

grestore   – grestore –

resets the current graphics state from the one on the top of the graphics state stack and pops the graphics state stack, thereby restoring the graphics state in effect at the time of the matching **gsave**. This operator provides a simple way to undo complicated transformations and context modification without having to reestablish all graphics state parameters individually (see section 4.3).

If there is no matching **gsave** or if the most recent **gsave** preceded the most recent unmatched **save**, **grestore** does not pop the graphics state stack.

ERRORS: (none)

SEE ALSO:
gsave, grestoreall

grestoreall   – grestoreall –

repeatedly pops the graphics state stack until it encounters either the bottommost graphics state or one that was saved by **save** as opposed to **gsave**, leaving that state on top of the graphics state stack. It then resets the current graphics state from that saved one.

ERRORS: (none)

SEE ALSO:
gsave, grestore

gsave   – gsave –

pushes a copy of the current graphics state on the graphics state stack. All elements of the graphics state are saved, including the CTM, current path, clip path, and identity of the raster output device (but not the contents of raster memory). The saved state may later be restored by a matching **grestore** (see section 4.3).

The **save** operator implicitly performs a **gsave**, but restoring a context saved by **save** is slightly different from restoring one saved by **gsave** (see the descriptions of **grestore** and **grestoreall**).

Note that unlike **save**, **gsave** does not return a save object on the operand stack to represent the saved state. **gsave** and **grestore** work in a strictly stack-like fashion (except for the wholesale restoration performed by **restore** and **grestoreall**).

ERRORS:
limitcheck

SEE ALSO:
grestore, grestoreall, restore, save

gt   num$_1$ num$_2$ **gt** bool
            string$_1$ string$_2$ **gt** bool

> pops two objects from the operand stack and pushes the boolean value *true* if the first operand is greater than the second, *false* otherwise. If both operands are numbers, **gt** compares their mathematical values. If both operands are strings, **gt** compares them element by element (treating the elements as integers in the range 0 to 255) to determine whether the first string is lexically greater than the second. If the operands are of other types (or one is a string and the other is a number), **gt** executes the **typecheck** error.
>
> ERRORS:
> **invalidaccess, stackunderflow, typecheck**
>
> SEE ALSO:
> **ge, eq, ne, le, lt**

handleerror   (error)

> is looked up in **errordict** and executed to report error information saved by the default error handlers (see section 3.8). There is also a procedure named **handleerror** in **systemdict**; it merely calls the one in **errordict**.

identmatrix   matrix **identmatrix** matrix

> replaces the value of *matrix* with the value of the identity matrix, i.e., [1.0 0.0 0.0 1.0 0.0 0.0], and pushes this modified matrix back on the operand stack. The identity matrix transforms any coordinate to itself.
>
> ERRORS:
> **rangecheck, stackunderflow, typecheck**
>
> SEE ALSO:
> **matrix, currentmatrix, defaultmatrix, initmatrix**

idiv int_1 int_2 **idiv** quotient

divides int_1 by int_2 and returns the integer part of the quotient, with any fractional part discarded. Both operands of **idiv** must be integers and the result is an integer.

EXAMPLE:
```
3 2 idiv ⇒ 1
4 2 idiv ⇒ 2
–5 2 idiv ⇒ –2
```

ERRORS:
rangecheck, stackunderflow, typecheck, undefinedresult

SEE ALSO:
div, add, mul, sub, mod, cvi

idtransform   dx′ dy′ **idtransform** dx dy
dx′ dy′ matrix **idtransform** dx dy

With no *matrix* operand, **idtransform** (inverse delta transform) transforms the device space distance vector (dx', dy') by the inverse of CTM to produce the corresponding distance vector (dx, dy) in user space. If the *matrix* operand is supplied, **idtransform** transforms the distance vector by the inverse of *matrix* rather than by the inverse of CTM.

A delta transformation is similar to a normal transformation (see section 4.4), but the translation components (t_x and t_y) of the transformation matrix are not used, thus making the distance vectors be positionless in both user space and device space. **idtransform** is the inverse of **dtransform**; it is useful for determining how distances map from device space to user space.

ERRORS:
stackunderflow, typecheck, undefinedresult

SEE ALSO:
dtransform, transform, itransform

if   bool proc **if**   –

removes both operands from the stack, then executes *proc* if *bool* is *true*. The **if** operator pushes no results of its own on the operand stack, but the *proc* may do so (see section 3.6).

EXAMPLE:
    3 4 lt {(3 is less than 4)} if ⇒ (3 is less than 4)

ERRORS:
stackunderflow, typecheck

SEE ALSO:
ifelse

ifelse   bool $proc_1$ $proc_2$ **ifelse**   –

removes all three operands from the stack, then executes $proc_1$ if *bool* is *true* or $proc_2$ if *bool* is *false*. The **ifelse** operator pushes no results of its own on the operand stack, but the procedure it executes may do so (see section 3.6).

EXAMPLE:
    4 3 lt {(TruePart)} {(FalsePart)} ifelse
        ⇒ (FalsePart)   % since 4 is not less than 3

ERRORS:
stackunderflow, typecheck

SEE ALSO:
if

image   width height bits/sample matrix proc **image** –

renders a sampled image onto the current page. The description here only summarizes the **image** operator; see section 4.7 for full details.

The sampled image is a rectangular array of *width* × *height* sample values, each of which consists of *bits/sample* bits of data (1, 2, 4, or 8). The data is received as a sequence of characters, i.e., 8-bit integers in the range 0 to 255. If *bits/sample* is less than 8, sample values are packed left to right within a character (but see the note in section 4.7).

The image is considered to exist in its own coordinate system. The rectangular boundary of the image has its lower left corner at (0, 0) and its upper right corner at (*width, height*). The *matrix* operand specifies a transformation from user space to the image coordinate system.

image executes *proc* repeatedly to obtain the actual image data. *proc* must return (on the operand stack) a string containing any number of additional characters of sample data. (If *proc* returns a string of length zero, **image** will terminate execution prematurely.) The sample values are assumed to be received in a fixed order: (0, 0) through (*width*–1, 0), then (0, 1) through (*width*–1, 1), etc.

Use of the **image** operator after a **setcachedevice** within the context of a **BuildChar** procedure is not permitted (an **undefined** error results); however, use of **imagemask** in that context is permitted (see the **setcachedevice** operator and section 5.7).

EXAMPLE:

```
/picstr 256 string def        % string to hold image data
45 140 translate              % locate lower left corner of image
132 132 scale                 % map image to 132 point square

256 256 8                     % dimensions of source image
[256 0 0 –256 0 256]          % map unit square to source
{currentfile                  % read image data from program file
 picstr readhexstring pop}
image

4c47494b4d4c524c4d50535051554c5152 ...
5959565c5 ... (131072 hex digits of image data)
```

ERRORS:
stackunderflow, typecheck, undefinedresult, undefined

SEE ALSO:
imagemask

imagemask   width height invert matrix proc **imagemask** –

is similar to the **image** operator; however, it treats the source image as a *mask* of 1 bit samples that are used to control where to apply paint (with the current color) and where not to. See the description of the **image** operator and the presentation of sampled images in section 4.7.

imagemask uses the *width*, *height*, *matrix*, and *proc* operands in precisely the same way as **image**. The *invert* operand is a boolean that determines the polarity of the mask. If *invert* is *false*, portions of the image corresponding to source sample values of 0 are painted, while those corresponding to sample values of 1 are left unchanged. If *invert* is *true*, sample values of 1 are painted and sample values of 0 are left unchanged.

imagemask is most useful for printing characters represented as bitmaps. Such bitmaps represent masks through which a color is to be transferred; the bitmaps themselves do not have a color (see section 4.7).

EXAMPLE:

```
45 228 translate             % locate lower left corner of square
132 132 scale                % scale 1 unit to 132 points

0 0 moveto 0 1 lineto        % fill square with gray background
1 1 lineto 1 0 lineto closepath
.9 setgray fill

0 setgray                    % paint mask black
24 23                        % dimensions of source mask
true                         % paint the 1 bits
[24 0 0 –23 0 23]            % map unit square to mask
{<003B00 002700 002480 0E4940 114920
  14B220 3CB650 75FE88 17FF8C 175F14
  1C07E2 3803C4 703182 F8EDFC B2BBC2
  BB6F84 31BFC2 18EA3C 0E3E00 07FC00
  03F800 1E1800 1FF800>}     % mask data
imagemask
```

ERRORS:
stackunderflow, typecheck, undefinedresult

SEE ALSO:
image

index $\text{any}_n \ldots \text{any}_0$ n **index** $\text{any}_n \ldots \text{any}_0 \text{ any}_n$

removes the non-negative integer n from the operand stack, counts down to the nth element from the top of the stack, and pushes a copy of that element on the stack.

EXAMPLE:
>   (a)(b)(c)(d) 0 index $\Rightarrow$ (a)(b)(c)(d)(d)
>   (a)(b)(c)(d) 3 index $\Rightarrow$ (a)(b)(c)(d)(a)

ERRORS:
rangecheck, stackunderflow, typecheck

SEE ALSO:
copy, dup, roll

initclip   – initclip –

replaces the current clip path parameter in the graphics state by the default clip path for the current output device. This path usually corresponds to the boundary of the maximum image area for the current output device (its dimensions are the ones established by the **framedevice** or **banddevice** device setup operator).

There are few situations in which a POSTSCRIPT page description should execute **initclip** explicitly. A page description that executes **initclip** usually produces incorrect results if it is embedded within another, composite page.

ERRORS: (none)

SEE ALSO:
clip, eoclip, clippath, initgraphics

initgraphics   – initgraphics –

resets several values in the current graphics state to their default values:

- current transformation matrix (default for current device)
- current path (empty)
- current point (undefined)
- current clipping path (default for current device)
- current color (black)
- current line width (one user space unit)
- current line cap style (butt end caps)
- current line join style (miter joins)
- current dash description (undashed, i.e., solid lines)
- current miter limit (10)

The **initgraphics** operator leaves the other graphics state parameters unchanged; these include the current output device, font, transfer function, halftone screen, and flatness. This operator affects only the graphics state, not the contents of raster memory or the output device.

initgraphics is equivalent to the POSTSCRIPT sequence:

```
initmatrix newpath initclip
1 setlinewidth 0 setlinecap 0 setlinejoin
[] 0 setdash 0 setgray 10 setmiterlimit
```

There are few situations in which a POSTSCRIPT page description should execute **initgraphics** explicitly. A page description that executes **initgraphics** usually produces incorrect results if it is embedded within another, composite page. A program requiring information about its initial graphics state should read and save that state at the beginning of the program rather than assume that the default state prevailed initially.

ERRORS: (none)

SEE ALSO:
grestoreall

initmatrix   – initmatrix –

sets the current transformation matrix (CTM) to the default matrix for the current output device. This matrix transforms the default user coordinate system to device space (see section 4.4). A device's default matrix is initially established by the **framedevice** or **banddevice** operator.

There are few situations in which a POSTSCRIPT page description should execute **initmatrix** explicitly. A page description that executes **initmatrix** usually produces incorrect results if it is embedded within another, composite page.

ERRORS: (none)

SEE ALSO:
defaultmatrix, currentmatrix, setmatrix

interrupt   (error)

processes an external request to interrupt execution of a POSTSCRIPT program. When the interpreter receives an interrupt request, it executes **interrupt** as if it were an error (i.e., it looks up the name 'interrupt' in **errordict**). Execution of **interrupt** is sandwiched between execution of two objects being interpreted in normal sequence.

The precise nature of an external interrupt request depends on the environment in which the POSTSCRIPT interpreter is running. In typical environments, receipt of a control-C character from a serial communication channel gives rise to the **interrupt** error. This permits a user to explicitly abort a POSTSCRIPT computation. The default definition of **interrupt** executes a **stop**.

invalidaccess   (error)

An attempt has been made to reference an array, dictionary, file, or string object in a way that violates its access attribute (e.g., store into a read-only array). This error also occurs if **pathforall** is executed when the current path includes the result of a **charpath**.

SEE ALSO:
rcheck, wcheck, readonly, executeonly, noaccess

invalidexit   (error)

An **exit** has been executed for which there is no dynamically enclosing looping context (**for**, **loop**, **repeat**, or **pathforall**), or it has attempted to leave the context of a **run** or **stopped** operator.

invalidfileaccess   (error)

The access string specification to the **file** operator is unacceptable (see the **file** operator description).

invalidfont   (error)

Either the operand to **findfont** is not a valid font name or the operand to **makefont** or **setfont** is not a well-formed font dictionary. (The **invalidfont** error may also be executed by other font operators upon discovering a font dictionary to be malformed in some way.)

invalidrestore   (error)

An improper **restore** has been attempted. One or more of the operand, dictionary, or execution stacks contains composite objects whose values were created more recently than the **save** whose context is being restored. Since **restore** would destroy those values but the stacks are unaffected by **restore**, the outcome would be undefined and cannot be allowed.

SEE ALSO:
restore, save

invertmatrix   matrix$_1$ matrix$_2$ **invertmatrix** matrix$_2$

replaces the value of *matrix$_2$* with the result of inverting *matrix$_1$* and pushes the modified *matrix$_2$* back on the operand stack. The result of inverting a matrix is that if *matrix$_1$* transforms a coordinate (x, y) to (x', y') then *matrix$_2$* transforms (x', y') to (x, y) (see section 4.4).

ERRORS:
stackunderflow, typecheck, undefinedresult

SEE ALSO:
itransform, idtransform

ioerror   (error)

An exception (other than end-of-file) has occurred during execution of one of the file operators. The nature of the exception is environment-dependent, but may include such events as parity or checksum errors, broken network connections, etc. Attempting to write to an input file or to a file that has been closed will also cause an **ioerror**. Occurrence of an **ioerror** does not cause the file to become closed unless it was already closed or the error occurs during **closefile**.

itransform   x′ y′ **itransform** x y
x′ y′ matrix **itransform** x y

With no *matrix* operand, **itransform** (inverse transform) transforms the device space coordinate (x', y') by the inverse of CTM to produce the corresponding user space coordinate (x, y). If the *matrix* operand is supplied, **itransform** transforms (x', y') by the inverse of *matrix* rather than by the inverse of CTM.

EXAMPLE:
To achieve consistent line weights among parallel lines appearing on a page, it is necessary for the lines to be positioned uniformly relative to output device pixels; otherwise, some lines may be rendered one pixel thicker than others. It is a simple matter to specify positions in device-independent user space, yet achieve device-dependent positioning, by adjusting user space coordinates according to the following method:

transform round exch round exch itransform

Given x and y values on the operand stack representing a position in user space, this sequence of operations transforms that position to device space, rounds it to the nearest output pixel boundary, and inverse transforms it back to user space.

ERRORS:
stackunderflow, typecheck, undefinedresult

SEE ALSO:
transform, dtransform, idtransform, invertmatrix

known   dict key **known** bool

returns the boolean value *true* if there is an entry in the dictionary *dict* whose key is *key*; otherwise it returns *false*. *dict* does not have to be on the dictionary stack.

EXAMPLE:
```
/mydict 5 dict def
mydict /total 0 put
mydict /total known ⇒ true
mydict /badname known ⇒ false
```

ERRORS:
invalidaccess, stackunderflow, typecheck

SEE ALSO:
where, load, get

kshow   proc string **kshow**   –

prints the characters of *string* in a manner similar to **show**, but allowing user intervention between characters. If the character codes in *string* are $c_0, c_1, \ldots c_n$, **kshow** proceeds as follows. First it shows c_0 at the current point, updating the current point by c_0's width. Then it pushes the character codes c_0 and c_1 on the operand stack (as integers) and executes *proc*. The *proc* may perform any actions it wishes; typically it will modify the current point to affect the subsequent placement of c_1. **kshow** continues by showing c_1, pushing c_1 and c_2 on the stack, executing *proc*, and so on. It finishes by pushing c_{n-1} and c_n on the stack, executing *proc*, and finally showing c_n.

When *proc* is called for the first time, the graphics state (in particular, the user coordinate system) is the same as it was at the time **kshow** was invoked except that the current point has been updated by the width of c_0. Execution of *proc* is permitted to have any side-effects, including changes to the graphics state. Such changes persist from one call of *proc* to the next and may affect graphical output for the remainder of **kshow**'s execution and afterward.

The name **kshow** is derived from 'kern-show'. To *kern* characters is to adjust the spacing between adjacent pairs of characters in order to achieve a visually pleasing result. The **kshow** operator enables user-defined kerning as well as other manipulations, since arbitrary computations can be performed between each pair of characters.

ERRORS:
invalidaccess, invalidfont, nocurrentpoint, stackunderflow, typecheck

SEE ALSO:
show, ashow, awidthshow, widthshow

le   num$_1$ num$_2$ **le** bool
            string$_1$ string$_2$ **le** bool

pops two objects from the operand stack and pushes the boolean value *true* if the first operand is less than or equal to the second, *false* otherwise. If both operands are numbers, **le** compares their mathematical values. If both operands are strings, **le** compares them element by element (treating the elements as integers in the range 0 to 255) to determine whether the first string is lexically less than or equal to the second. If the operands are of other types (or one is a string and the other is a number), **le** executes the **typecheck** error.

ERRORS:
invalidaccess, stackunderflow, typecheck

SEE ALSO:
lt, eq, ne, ge, gt

length   array **length** int
              dict **length** int
            string **length** int

depends on the type of its operand. If the operand is an array or string, **length** returns the number of elements in its value. If the operand is a dictionary, **length** returns the current number of key-value pairs it contains (as opposed to its maximum capacity, which is returned by **maxlength**).

EXAMPLE:
        [1 2 4] length $\Rightarrow$ 3
        [] length $\Rightarrow$ 0   % an array of zero length
        /ar 20 array def ar length $\Rightarrow$ 20

        /mydict 5 dict def
        mydict length $\Rightarrow$ 0
        mydict /firstkey (firstvalue) put
        mydict length $\Rightarrow$ 1

        (abc\n) length $\Rightarrow$ 4   % the '\n' is one character
        () length $\Rightarrow$ 0

ERRORS:
invalidaccess, stackunderflow, typecheck

SEE ALSO:
maxlength, array, dict, string

limitcheck   (error)

A POSTSCRIPT implementation limit has been exceeded (e.g., too many files have been opened simultaneously, or a path has become too complex). Appendix B gives the actual values for all such limits.

lineto   x y **lineto** –

appends a straight line segment to the current path (see section 4.5). The line extends from the current point to the point (x, y) in user space; (x, y) then becomes the current point. If the current point is undefined (because the current path is empty), **lineto** executes the error **nocurrentpoint**.

ERRORS:
limitcheck, nocurrentpoint, stackunderflow, typecheck

SEE ALSO:
rlineto, moveto, arc, curveto, closepath

ln   num **ln** real

returns the natural logarithm (base e) of *num*. The result is a real.

EXAMPLE:
    10 ln $\Rightarrow$ 2.30259
    100 ln $\Rightarrow$ 4.60517

ERRORS:
stackunderflow, typecheck, undefinedresult

SEE ALSO:
log, exp

load　key **load** value

searches for *key* in each dictionary on the dictionary stack, starting with the topmost (current) dictionary. If *key* is found in some dictionary, **load** pushes the associated value on the operand stack. If *key* is not found in any dictionary on the dictionary stack, **load** executes the error **undefined**.

load looks up *key* in precisely the same way as the interpreter looks up executable names that it encounters during execution. However, **load** always pushes the associated value on the operand stack; it never executes that value.

EXAMPLE:
```
/avg {add 2 div} def
/avg load ⇒ {add 2 div}
```

ERRORS:
invalidaccess, stackunderflow, typecheck, undefined

SEE ALSO:
where, get

log　num **log** real

returns the common logarithm (base 10) of *num*. The result is a real.

EXAMPLE:
```
10 log ⇒ 1.0
100 log ⇒ 2.0
```

ERRORS:
stackunderflow, typecheck, undefinedresult

SEE ALSO:
ln, exp

loop   proc **loop** –

repeatedly executes *proc* until *proc* executes the **exit** operator, at which point interpretation resumes at the object next in sequence after the **loop**. Control also leaves *proc* if the **stop** operator is executed.

If *proc* never executes **exit** or **stop**, an infinite loop results, which can be broken only via an external interrupt (see **interrupt**).

ERRORS:
stackunderflow, typecheck

SEE ALSO:
for, repeat, forall, pathforall, exit

lt   num$_1$ num$_2$ **lt** bool
string$_1$ string$_2$ **lt** bool

pops two objects from the operand stack and pushes the boolean value *true* if the first operand is less than the second, *false* otherwise. If both operands are numbers, **lt** compares their mathematical values. If both operands are strings, **lt** compares them element by element (treating the elements as integers in the range 0 to 255) to determine whether the first string is lexically less than the second. If the operands are of other types (or one is a string and the other is a number), **lt** executes the **typecheck** error.

ERRORS:
invalidaccess, stackunderflow, typecheck

SEE ALSO:
le, eq, ne, ge, gt

makefont   font matrix **makefont** font′

applies *matrix* to *font*, producing a new *font′* whose characters are transformed by *matrix* when they are printed. **makefont** first creates a copy of *font*, then it replaces the new font's **FontMatrix** entry with the result of concatenating the existing **FontMatrix** with *matrix*, and finally it returns the result as *font′*.

Printing characters from the transformed font produces the same results as printing from the original font after having transformed user space by the same matrix. **makefont** is essentially a convenience operator that permits the desired transformation to be encapsulated in the font description itself.

The most common transformation is to scale a font by a uniform factor in both x and y. Another operator, **scalefont**, is a special case of the more general **makefont** and should be used for such uniform scaling.

The POSTSCRIPT font machinery keeps track of font dictionaries recently created by **makefont**. Calling **makefont** multiple times with the same *font* and *matrix* will usually return the same *font′* rather than create a new one each time. However, it is usually more efficient for a POSTSCRIPT program to apply **makefont** only once for each font that it needs and to keep track of the resulting font dictionaries on its own.

See chapter 5 for general information about fonts and section 4.4 for a discussion of transformations.

EXAMPLE:
    /Helvetica findfont [10 0 0 12 0 0] makefont setfont

This obtains the standard Helvetica font, which is defined with a one unit line height, and scales it by a factor of 10 in the x dimension and 12 in the y dimension. This produces a 12 unit high font (i.e., a 12 point font in default user space) whose characters are 'condensed' in the x dimension.

ERRORS:
stackunderflow, typecheck

SEE ALSO:
scalefont, setfont, findfont

mark – **mark** mark

pushes a mark (an object whose type is mark, not the **mark** operator itself) on the operand stack. All marks are identical, and the operand stack may contain any number of them at once.

The primary use of marks is to indicate the stack position of the beginning of an indefinitely long list of operands being passed to an operator or procedure. The ']' operator (array construction) is the most common operator that works this way; it treats as operands all elements of the stack down to a mark that was pushed by the '[' operator ('[' is a synonym for **mark**). It is possible to define procedures that work similarly; operators such as **counttomark** and **cleartomark** are useful within such procedures.

ERRORS:
stackoverflow

SEE ALSO:
counttomark, cleartomark, pop

matrix – **matrix** matrix

creates a 6-element POSTSCRIPT array object, fills it in with the values of an identity matrix, i.e., [1.0 0.0 0.0 1.0 0.0 0.0], and pushes this array on the operand stack.

EXAMPLE:
matrix ⇒ [1.0 0.0 0.0 1.0 0.0 0.0]
6 array identmatrix ⇒ [1.0 0.0 0.0 1.0 0.0 0.0]

The two lines in the example yield identical results.

ERRORS:
stackoverflow

SEE ALSO:
currentmatrix, defaultmatrix, initmatrix, setmatrix, array

maxlength   dict **maxlength** int

returns the maximum number of key-value pairs that *dict* can hold, as defined by the operand of the **dict** operator that created *dict*. (See also the **length** operator, which returns the number of entries a dictionary presently contains.)

EXAMPLE:
```
/mydict 5 dict def
mydict length ⇒ 0
mydict maxlength ⇒ 5
```

ERRORS:
invalidaccess, stackunderflow, typecheck

SEE ALSO:
length, dict

mod int_1 int_2 **mod** remainder

returns the remainder that results from dividing int_1 by int_2. The sign of the result is the same as the sign of the dividend int_1. Both operands must be integers; the result is an integer.

EXAMPLE:
```
5 3 mod ⇒ 2
5 2 mod ⇒ 1
–5 3 mod ⇒ –2
```

The last line of the example demonstrates that **mod** is a *remainder* operation rather than a true *modulo* operation.

ERRORS:
stackunderflow, typecheck, undefinedresult

SEE ALSO:
idiv, div

moveto   x y **moveto** –

starts a new subpath of the current path. **moveto** sets the current point in the graphics state to the user space coordinate (x, y) without adding any line segments to the current path.

If the previous path operation in the current path was also a **moveto** (or **rmoveto**), that point is deleted from the current path and the new **moveto** point replaces it.

ERRORS:
limitcheck, stackunderflow, typecheck

SEE ALSO:
rmoveto, lineto, curveto, arc, closepath

mul num_1 num_2 **mul** product

returns the product of num_1 and num_2. If both operands are integers and the result is within integer range, the result is an integer; otherwise, the result is a real.

ERRORS:
stackunderflow, typecheck, undefinedresult

SEE ALSO:
div, idiv, add, sub, mod

ne any_1 any_2 **ne** bool

pops two object from the operand stack and pushes the boolean value *false* if they are equal, *true* if not. What it means for objects to be equal is presented in the description of the **eq** operator.

ERRORS:
invalidaccess, stackunderflow

SEE ALSO:
eq, ge, gt, le, lt

neg   num$_1$ **neg** num$_2$

returns the negative of *num$_1$*. The type of the result is the same as the type of *num$_1$* (unless *num$_1$* is the most negative integer, in which case the result is a real).

EXAMPLE:
    4.5 neg $\Rightarrow$ –4.5
    –3 neg $\Rightarrow$ 3

ERRORS:
stackunderflow, typecheck

SEE ALSO:
abs

newpath   – **newpath** –

initializes the current path to be empty, causing the current point to become undefined.

ERRORS: (none)

SEE ALSO:
closepath, stroke, fill, clip, gsave

noaccess   array **noaccess** array
                dict **noaccess** dict
                file **noaccess** file
                string **noaccess** string

reduces the access attribute of an array, dictionary, file, or string object to none (see the description of attributes in section 3.4). The value of a no-access object cannot be executed or accessed directly by POSTSCRIPT operators. No-access objects are of no use to POSTSCRIPT programs but serve certain internal purposes that are not documented in this manual.

For an array, file, or string, **noaccess** affects the access attribute only of the object that it returns; if there exist other objects that share the same value, their access attributes are unaffected. However, in the case of a dictionary, **noaccess** affects the *value* of the object, so all dictionary objects sharing the same dictionary are affected.

ERRORS:
invalidaccess, stackunderflow, typecheck

SEE ALSO:
rcheck, wcheck, xcheck, readonly, executeonly

nocurrentpoint   (error)

The current path is empty, and thus there is no current point, but an operator requiring a current point has been executed (e.g., **lineto**, **curveto**, **currentpoint**, **show**). The most common cause of this error is neglecting to perform an initial **moveto**.

SEE ALSO:
moveto

not   bool$_1$ **not** bool$_2$
      int$_1$ **not** int$_2$

If the operand is a boolean, **not** returns its logical negation. If the operand is an integer, **not** returns the bitwise complement (one's complement) of its binary representation.

EXAMPLE:
    true not $\Rightarrow$ false   % a complete truth table
    false not $\Rightarrow$ true

    52 not $\Rightarrow$ –53

ERRORS:
stackunderflow, typecheck

SEE ALSO:
and, or, xor, if

null   – **null** null

pushes a literal null object (not the **null** operator itself) on the operand stack.

ERRORS:
stackoverflow

SEE ALSO:
array, type

nulldevice   – nulldevice –

installs the 'null device' as the current output device. The null device corresponds to no physical output device and has no raster memory associated with it. Marks placed on the current page by painting operators (e.g., **show** or **stroke**) are discarded; output operators (**showpage** and **copypage**) do nothing. However, in all other respects the null device behaves like a real raster output device: the graphics operators have their normal side-effects on the graphics state, the character operators invoke the font machinery (including the font cache), and so on.

nulldevice sets the default transformation matrix to be the identity transform [1.0 0.0 0.0 1.0 0.0 0.0]. A POSTSCRIPT program may change this to any other matrix (using **setmatrix**) if it desires to simulate the device coordinate system of some real device. **nulldevice** also establishes the clipping path as a degenerate path consisting of a single point at the origin.

The null device is useful for exercising the POSTSCRIPT graphics and font machinery for such purposes as accumulating characters in the font cache, operating on paths, computing bounding boxes for graphical shapes, and performing coordinate transformations using CTM without generating output. Such manipulations should be bracketed by **gsave** and **grestore** so that the former device can be reinstated and the other side-effects of **nulldevice** undone.

ERRORS: (none)

SEE ALSO:
banddevice, framedevice

or   bool$_1$ bool$_2$ **or** bool$_3$
         int$_1$ int$_2$ **or** int$_3$

If the operands are booleans, **or** returns their logical disjunction. If the operands are integers, **or** returns the bitwise 'inclusive or' of their binary representations.

EXAMPLE:
> true true or $\Rightarrow$ true   % a complete truth table
> true false or $\Rightarrow$ true
> false true or $\Rightarrow$ true
> false false or $\Rightarrow$ false
>
> 17 5 or $\Rightarrow$ 21

ERRORS:
stackunderflow, typecheck

SEE ALSO:
and, not, xor

pathbbox   – **pathbbox** ll$_x$ ll$_y$ ur$_x$ ur$_y$

returns the bounding box of the current path in the current user coordinate system. The results are four real numbers: lower left x, lower left y, upper right x, and upper right y. These coordinates describe a rectangle, oriented with its sides parallel to the x and y axes in user space, that completely encloses all elements of the path. If the current path is empty, **pathbbox** executes the error **nocurrentpoint**.

pathbbox first computes the bounding box of the current path in *device* space. It then transforms these coordinates to user space (by the inverse of CTM) and computes the bounding box of the resulting figure in user space. If the user coordinate system is rotated (other than by multiples of 90 degrees) or skewed, **pathbbox** may return a bounding box that is larger than expected.

If the path includes curve segments, the bounding box encloses the control points of the curves as well as the curves themselves. To obtain a bounding box that fits the path more tightly, one should first 'flatten' the curve segments by executing **flattenpath**.

ERRORS:
nocurrentpoint, stackoverflow

SEE ALSO:
flattenpath, clippath, charpath

pathforall   move line curve close **pathforall** –

removes four operands from the stack, all of which must be procedures. **pathforall** then enumerates the current path in order, executing one of the four procedures for each element in the path. The four basic kinds of elements in a path are **moveto**, **lineto**, **curveto**, and **closepath**. (The relative variants **rmoveto**, **rlineto**, and **rcurveto** are converted to the corresponding absolute forms; **arc**, **arcn**, and **arcto** are converted to sequences of **curveto**.) For each element in the path, **pathforall** pushes the element's coordinates on the operand stack and executes one of the four procedures, as follows:

moveto	push x y; execute *move*
lineto	push x y; execute *line*
curveto	push x_1 y_1 x_2 y_2 x_3 y_3; execute *curve*
closepath	execute *close*

The operands passed to the procedures are coordinates in user space; **pathforall** transforms them from device space to user space using the inverse of the CTM. Ordinarily, these coordinates will be the same as the ones originally entered by **moveto**, **lineto**, etc. However, if the CTM has been changed since the path was constructed, the coordinates reported by **pathforall** will be different from the ones originally entered.

Among other uses, **pathforall** enables a path constructed in one user coordinate system to be read out in another user coordinate system.

If **charpath** was used to construct any portion of the current path, **pathforall** is not allowed; its execution will produce an **invalidaccess** error.

ERRORS:
stackoverflow, stackunderflow, typecheck

SEE ALSO:
moveto, lineto, curveto, closepath

pop   any **pop** −

removes the top element from the operand stack and discards it.

EXAMPLE:
        1 2 3 pop $\Rightarrow$ 1 2
        1 2 3 pop pop $\Rightarrow$ 1

ERRORS:
stackunderflow

SEE ALSO:
clear, dup

print   string **print** −

writes the characters of *string* to the standard output file (see section 3.8). The **print** operator provides the simplest means to send text to a host computer or an interactive user. Note that **print** is a *file* operator that has nothing to do with painting character shapes on the current page (see **show**) or with sending the current page to a raster output device (see **showpage**).

ERRORS:
stackunderflow, typecheck

SEE ALSO:
write, flush, =, ==

prompt   − **prompt** −

is a procedure executed by the POSTSCRIPT interpreter whenever it is
ready for a new statement to be entered by the user during interactive
operation (see section 3.8). The initial definition of **prompt** is
'{(PS>) print flush}'.

SEE ALSO:
echo

pstack   ⊢ any$_1$ ... any$_n$ **pstack** ⊢ any$_1$ ... any$_n$

writes text representations of every object on the stack to the standard
output file, but leaves the stack unchanged. **pstack** applies the '**==**'
operator to each element of the stack, starting with the topmost element. See the '**==**' operator for a description of its effects.

ERRORS:
stackoverflow

SEE ALSO:
stack, =, ==

put   array index any **put** –
            dict key any **put** –
            string index int **put** –

replaces a single element of the value of an array, dictionary, or string.

If the first operand is an array or string, **put** treats the second operand as an *index* and stores the third operand at the position identified by the index (counting from zero). *index* must be in the range 0 to $n-1$, where n is the length of the array or string; if it is outside this range, **put** will execute a **rangecheck** error.

If the first operand is a dictionary, **put** uses the second operand as a key and the third operand as a value, and it stores this key-value pair into *dict*. If *key* is already present as a key in *dict*, **put** simply replaces its value by *any*. Otherwise, **put** creates a new entry for *key* and associates *any* with it; if *dict* is already full, **put** executes the error **dictfull**.

EXAMPLE:
            /ar [5 17 3 8] def
            ar 2 (abcd) put
            ar $\Rightarrow$ [5 17 (abcd) 8]

            /d 5 dict def
            d /abc 123 put
            d {} forall $\Rightarrow$ /abc 123

            /st (abc) def
            st 0 65 put   % 65 is ASCII code for character 'A'
            st $\Rightarrow$ (Abc)

ERRORS:
dictfull, invalidaccess, rangecheck, stackunderflow, typecheck

SEE ALSO:
get, putinterval

putinterval   array$_1$ index array$_2$ **putinterval** –
                    string$_1$ index string$_2$ **putinterval** –

replaces a subsequence of the elements of the first array or string by the entire contents of the second array or string. The subsequence that is replaced begins at the specified *index* in the first array or string; its length is the same as the length of the second array or string.

The objects are actually copied from the second array or string to the first, as if by a sequence of individual **get**s and **put**s. In the case of arrays, if the copied elements are themselves composite objects, the values of those objects become shared between *array$_2$* and *array$_1$* (see the discussion of simple versus composite objects in section 3.4).

putinterval requires *index* to be a valid index in *array$_1$* or *string$_1$* such that *index* plus the length of *array$_2$* or *string$_2$* is not greater than the length of *array$_1$* or *string$_1$*.

EXAMPLE:
```
/ar [5 8 2 7 3] def
ar 1 [(a) (b) (c)] putinterval
ar ⇒ [5 (a) (b) (c) 3]

/st (abc) def
st 1 (de) putinterval
st ⇒ (ade)
```

ERRORS:
invalidaccess, rangecheck, stackunderflow, typecheck

SEE ALSO:
getinterval, put

quit   – **quit** –

terminates operation of the interpreter. The precise action of **quit** depends on the environment in which the POSTSCRIPT interpreter is running; it may give control to an operating system command interpreter, halt or restart the machine, etc.

The definition of the **quit** operator in **systemdict** is ordinarily masked by another definition of **quit** in **userdict**, which is usually searched before **systemdict**. The default definition of **quit** in **userdict** is the same as **stop**, which terminates the current POSTSCRIPT program but not the interpreter as a whole.

In POSTSCRIPT implementations running on computers with an operating system and a file system, **quit** saves a snapshot of the VM in a file before terminating the interpreter. The next time the interpreter is started, it automatically reloads the VM from the file (see section 3.7).

ERRORS: (none)

SEE ALSO:
stop, start

rand   – **rand** int

returns a random integer in the range 0 to $2^{31}-1$, produced by a pseudo-random number generator. The random number generator's state can be reset by **srand** and interrogated by **rrand**.

ERRORS:
stackoverflow

SEE ALSO:
srand, rrand

rangecheck   (error)

A numeric operand's value is outside the range expected by an operator (e.g., an array or string index is out of bounds, a negative number appears where a non-negative number is required, etc.)

rcheck
array **rcheck** bool
dict **rcheck** bool
file **rcheck** bool
string **rcheck** bool

tests whether the operand's access permits its value to be read explicitly by POSTSCRIPT operators. **rcheck** returns *true* if the operand's access is unlimited or read-only, *false* otherwise.

ERRORS:
stackunderflow, typecheck

SEE ALSO:
executeonly, noaccess, readonly, wcheck

rcurveto
dx_1 dy_1 dx_2 dy_2 dx_3 dy_3 **rcurveto** –

(relative curveto) adds a Bézier cubic section to the current path in the same manner as **curveto**; however, the three number pairs are interpreted as displacements relative to the current point (x_0, y_0) rather than as absolute coordinates. That is, **rcurveto** constructs a curve from (x_0, y_0) to (x_0+dx_3, y_0+dy_3), using (x_0+dx_1, y_0+dy_1) and (x_0+dx_2, y_0+dy_2) as Bézier control points. See the description of **curveto** for complete information.

ERRORS:
limitcheck, nocurrentpoint, stackunderflow, typecheck, undefinedresult

SEE ALSO:
curveto, rlineto, rmoveto

read
file **read** *if not end-of-file*: byte true
if end-of-file: false

reads the next character from the input file *file*, pushes it on the stack as an integer, and pushes *true* as an indication of success. If an end-of-file indication is encountered before a character has been read, **read** closes the file and returns *false*. If some other error indication is encountered (e.g., parity or checksum error), **read** executes **ioerror**.

ERRORS:
invalidaccess, ioerror, stackunderflow, typecheck

SEE ALSO:
readhexstring, readline, readstring, bytesavailable

readhexstring   file string **readhexstring** substring bool

reads characters from *file*, expecting to encounter a sequence of hexadecimal digits '0' through '9' and 'A' through 'F' (or 'a' through 'f'). **readhexstring** interprets each successive pair of digits as a two-digit hexadecimal number representing an integer value in the range 0 to 255. It then stores these values into successive elements of *string* (starting at index 0) until either the entire string has been filled or an end-of-file indication is encountered in *file*. Finally, **readhexstring** returns the substring of *string* that was actually filled and a boolean indicating the outcome (*true* normally, *false* if end-of-file was encountered before the string was filled).

readhexstring ignores any characters that are not valid hexadecimal digits, so the data in *file* may be interspersed with spaces, newlines, etc., without changing the interpretation of the data itself.

Hexadecimal is the preferred external representation for arbitrary binary data such as sampled images, since the hexadecimal representation can be stored in files and transmitted over communication channels without concern over preempted control characters, maximum line lengths, and similar restrictions imposed by operating systems and other software.

ERRORS:
invalidaccess, ioerror, rangecheck, stackunderflow, typecheck

SEE ALSO:
read, readline, readstring

readline   file string **readline** substring bool

reads a line of characters (terminated by a newline character) from *file* and stores them into successive elements of *string*. **readline** then returns the substring of *string* that was actually filled and a boolean indicating the outcome (*true* normally, *false* if end-of-file was encountered before a newline character was read).

The terminating newline character is not stored into *string* or included at the end of the returned *substring*. If **readline** completely fills *string* before encountering a newline character, it executes the error **rangecheck**.

ERRORS:
invalidaccess, ioerror, rangecheck, stackunderflow, typecheck

SEE ALSO:
read, readhexstring, readline

readonly   array **readonly** array
              dict **readonly** dict
              file **readonly** file
           string **readonly** string

reduces the access attribute of an array, dictionary, file, or string object to read-only (see the description of attributes in section 3.4). Access can only be reduced by this means, never increased. When an object is read-only, its value cannot be modified by POSTSCRIPT operators (an **invalidaccess** error will result), but it can still be read by operators or executed by the POSTSCRIPT interpreter.

For an array, file, or string, **readonly** affects the access attribute only of the object that it returns; if there exist other objects that share the same value, their access attributes are unaffected. However, in the case of a dictionary, **readonly** affects the *value* of the object, so all dictionary objects sharing the same dictionary are affected.

ERRORS:
invalidaccess, stackunderflow, typecheck

SEE ALSO:
executeonly, noaccess, rcheck, wcheck

readstring   file string **readstring** substring bool

reads characters from *file* and stores them into successive elements of *string* until either the entire string has been filled or an end-of-file indication is encountered in *file*. **readstring** then returns the substring of *string* that was actually filled and a boolean indicating the outcome (*true* normally, *false* if end-of-file was encountered before the string was filled). All character codes are treated the same, namely as integers in the range 0 to 255; there are no special characters (in particular, the newline character is not treated specially).

ERRORS:
invalidaccess, ioerror, rangecheck, stackunderflow, typecheck

SEE ALSO:
read, readhexstring, readline

renderbands   proc **renderbands** −

enumerates the bands of raster data for the current output device, which must have been installed by the **banddevice** operator. **renderbands** may be called only from the output procedure given as an operand to **banddevice**. This operator is not defined in implementations of the POSTSCRIPT interpreter that do not include a **banddevice** operator.

renderbands divides the current page into a sequence of rectangular bands of pixels (the size of a band is implementation-dependent). Then, for each band, **renderbands** interprets the display list representing the current page, paints the band buffer with whatever marks fall into the current band, and executes *proc*. This procedure's task is to cause the contents of the band buffer to be transmitted to the physical output device. This generally involves executing one or more special device-dependent operators. Such operators are different for each physical device and are not documented in this manual.

ERRORS:
typecheck

SEE ALSO:
banddevice

repeat   int proc **repeat** –

executes *proc int* times, where *int* is a non-negative integer. The **repeat** operator removes both operands from the stack before executing *proc* for the first time. If *proc* executes the **exit** operator, **repeat** terminates prematurely. **repeat** leaves no results of its own on the stack, but *proc* may do so.

EXAMPLE:
```
4 {(abc)} repeat ⇒ (abc)(abc)(abc)(abc)
1 2 3 4 3 {pop} repeat ⇒ 1    % pops 3 values (down to the 1)
4 {} repeat ⇒                 % does nothing four times
mark 0 {(won't happen)} repeat ⇒ mark
```

In the last example, a zero repeat count meant that the procedure is not executed at all, hence the mark is still topmost on the stack.

ERRORS:
rangecheck, stackunderflow, typecheck

SEE ALSO:
for, loop, forall, pathforall, exit

resetfile   file **resetfile** –

discards buffered characters belonging to a file object. For an input file, **resetfile** discards any characters that have been received from the source but not yet consumed; for an output file, it discards any characters that have been written to the file but not yet delivered to their destination.

resetfile may have other side-effects that depend on the properties of the underlying file. For example, it may restart communication over a channel that was blocked waiting for buffer space to become available. **resetfile** never waits for characters to be received or transmitted.

ERRORS:
stackunderflow, typecheck

SEE ALSO:
file, closefile, flushfile

restore   save **restore** –

resets the virtual memory (VM) to the state represented by the supplied
save object, i.e., the state at the time the corresponding **save** was executed. See section 3.7 for a description of the VM and of the effects of
save and **restore**.

restore can reset the VM to the state represented by any save object
that is still valid, not necessarily the one produced by the most recent
save. After restoring the VM, **restore** invalidates its *save* operand,
along with any other save objects created more recently than that one.
That is, a VM snapshot can be used only once; to make it possible to
restore the same environment repeatedly, it is necessary to do a new
save each time.

restore does not alter the contents of the operand, dictionary, or execution stack (except to pop its *save* operand). If any of these stacks contain array, dictionary, file, name, save, or string objects that are newer
than the snapshot being restored, **restore** executes the **invalidrestore**
error.

restore does alter the graphics state stack: it performs the equivalent of
a **grestoreall** and then removes the graphics state created by **save** from
the graphics state stack.

ERRORS:
invalidrestore, rangecheck, stackunderflow, typecheck

SEE ALSO:
save, grestoreall, vmstatus

reversepath   – **reversepath** –

replaces the current path with an equivalent one whose segments are
defined in the reverse order. Precisely, **reversepath** reverses the directions and order of segments within each subpath of the current path;
however, it does not alter the order of the subpaths in the path with
respect to each other.

ERRORS: (none)

SEE ALSO:
fill, eofill, clip, eoclip

rlineto   dx dy **rlineto** –

(relative lineto) appends a straight line segment to the current path in the same manner as **lineto**; however, the number pair is interpreted as a displacement relative to the current point (x, y) rather than as an absolute coordinate. That is, **rlineto** constructs a line from (x, y) to $(x+dx, y+dy)$ and makes $(x+dx, y+dy)$ be the new current point.

ERRORS:
limitcheck, nocurrentpoint, stackunderflow, typecheck

SEE ALSO:
lineto, rmoveto, rcurveto

rmoveto   dx dy **rmoveto** –

(relative moveto) starts a new subpath of the current path in the same manner as **moveto**; however, the number pair is interpreted as a displacement relative to the current point (x, y) rather than as an absolute coordinate. That is, **rmoveto** makes $(x+dx, y+dy)$ be the new current point, without connecting it to the previous point. If the current point is undefined (because the current path is empty), **rmoveto** executes the error operator **nocurrentpoint**.

ERRORS:
limitcheck, nocurrentpoint, stackunderflow, typecheck

SEE ALSO:
moveto, rlineto, rcurveto

roll any_{n-1} ... any_0 n j **roll** $any_{(j-1) \bmod n}$ ... any_0 any_{n-1} ... $any_{j \bmod n}$

performs a circular shift of the objects any_{n-1} through any_0 on the operand stack by the amount j. Positive j indicates upward motion on the stack whereas negative j indicates downward motion.

n must be a non-negative integer and j must be an integer. **roll** first removes these operands from the stack; there must be at least n additional elements. **roll** then performs a circular shift of these n elements by j positions.

If j is positive, each shift consists of removing an element from the top of the stack and inserting it between element $n-1$ and element n of the stack, moving all intervening elements one level higher on the stack. If j is negative, each shift consists of removing element $n-1$ of the stack and pushing it on the top of the stack, moving all intervening elements one level lower on the stack.

EXAMPLE:
    (a)(b)(c) 3 −1 roll ⇒ (b)(c)(a)
    (a)(b)(c) 3 1 roll ⇒ (c)(a)(b)
    (a)(b)(c) 3 0 roll ⇒ (a)(b)(c)

ERRORS:
rangecheck, stackoverflow, stackunderflow, typecheck

SEE ALSO:
exch, index, copy, pop

rotate　　　angle **rotate**　–
　　　　　　　angle matrix **rotate**　matrix

With no *matrix* operand, **rotate** builds a temporary matrix R:

$$
\begin{array}{ccc}
\cos\theta & \sin\theta & 0 \\
-\sin\theta & \cos\theta & 0 \\
0 & 0 & 1
\end{array}
$$

where θ is the operand *angle* in degrees, and concatenates this matrix with the current transformation matrix (CTM). Precisely, **rotate** replaces the CTM by $R \times$ CTM. The effect of this is to rotate the user coordinate system axes about their origin by *angle* degrees (positive is counterclockwise) with respect to their former orientation. The position of the user coordinate origin and the sizes of the x and y units are unchanged.

If the *matrix* operand is supplied, **rotate** replaces the value of *matrix* by R and pushes the modified *matrix* back on the operand stack (see section 4.4 for a discussion of how matrices are represented as POSTSCRIPT arrays). In this case, **rotate** does not affect the CTM.

ERRORS:
stackunderflow, typecheck

SEE ALSO:
scale, translate, concat

round　　num$_1$ **round** num$_2$

returns the integer value nearest to *num$_1$*. If *num$_1$* is equally close to its two nearest integers, **round** returns the greater of the two. The type of the result is the same as the type of the operand.

EXAMPLE:
```
3.2 round ⇒ 3.0
6.5 round ⇒ 7.0
−4.8 round ⇒ −5.0
−6.5 round ⇒ −6.0
99 round ⇒ 99
```

ERRORS:
stackunderflow, typecheck

SEE ALSO:
ceiling, floor, truncate, cvi

rrand – **rrand** int

returns an integer representing the current state of the random number generator used by **rand**. This may later be presented as an operand to **srand** to reset the random number generater to the current position in the sequence of numbers produced.

ERRORS:
stackoverflow

SEE ALSO:
rand, srand

run string **run** –

executes the contents of the file identified by *string*; i.e., interprets the characters in that file as a POSTSCRIPT program. When **run** encounters end-of-file or terminates for some other reason (e.g., **stop**), it closes the file.

run is essentially a convenience operator for the sequence

(r) file cvx exec

except for its behavior upon abnormal termination. Additionally, the context of a **run** may not be left by executing **exit**; an attempt to do so produces the error **invalidexit**.

The **run** operator leaves no results on the operand stack, but the program executed by **run** may alter the stacks arbitrarily.

ERRORS:
ioerror, limitcheck, stackunderflow, typecheck, undefinedfilename

SEE ALSO:
exec, file

save   – **save** save

creates a snapshot of the current state of the virtual memory (VM) and returns a *save* object representing that snapshot. Subsequently, this save object may be presented to **restore** in order to reset the VM to this snapshot. See section 3.7 for a description of the VM and of the effects of **save** and **restore**.

save also saves the current graphics state by pushing a copy of it on the graphics state stack in a manner similar to **gsave**. This saved graphics state is restored by **restore** and **grestoreall**.

EXAMPLE:
```
/saveobj save def
% ... (arbitrary computation) ...
saveobj restore              % restore saved VM state
```

ERRORS:
limitcheck, stackoverflow

SEE ALSO:
restore, gsave, grestoreall, vmstatus

scale
s_x s_y **scale** –
s_x s_y matrix **scale** matrix

With no *matrix* operand, **scale** builds a temporary matrix S:

$$\begin{matrix} s_x & 0 & 0 \\ 0 & s_y & 0 \\ 0 & 0 & 1 \end{matrix}$$

and concatenates this matrix with the current transformation matrix (CTM). Precisely, **scale** replaces the CTM by $S \times$ CTM. The effect of this is to make the x and y units in the user coordinate system be the size of s_x and s_y units in the former user coordinate system. The position of the user coordinate origin and the orientation of the axes are unchanged.

If the *matrix* operand is supplied, **scale** replaces the value of *matrix* by S and pushes the modified *matrix* back on the operand stack (see section 4.4 for a discussion of how matrices are represented as POSTSCRIPT arrays). In this case, **scale** does not affect the CTM.

ERRORS:
stackunderflow, typecheck

SEE ALSO:
rotate, translate, concat

scalefont   font scale **scalefont** font′

applies the scale factor *scale* to *font*, producing a new *font′* whose characters are scaled by *scale* (in both *x* and *y*) when they are printed. **scalefont** first creates a copy of *font*, then it replaces the new font's **FontMatrix** entry with the result of scaling the existing **FontMatrix** by *scale*, and finally it returns the result as *font′*.

Printing characters from the transformed font produces the same results as printing from the original font after having scaled user space by the factor *scale* in both *x* and *y* by means of the **scale** operator. **scalefont** is essentially a convenience operator that permits the desired scale factor to be encapsulated in the font description itself. Another operator, **makefont**, performs more general transformations than simple scaling.

The POSTSCRIPT font machinery keeps track of font dictionaries recently created by **scalefont**. Calling **scalefont** multiple times with the same *font* and *scale* will usually return the same *font′* rather than create a new one each time. However, it is usually more efficient for a POSTSCRIPT program to apply **scalefont** only once for each font that it needs and to keep track of the resulting font dictionaries on its own.

See chapter 5 for general information about fonts and section 4.4 for a discussion of transformations.

EXAMPLE:
        /Helvetica findfont 12 scalefont setfont

This obtains the standard Helvetica font, which is defined with a one unit line height, and scales it by a factor of 12 in both *x* and *y* dimensions. This produces a 12 unit high font (i.e., a 12 point font in default user space) whose characters have the same proportions as those in the original font.

ERRORS:
invalidfont, stackunderflow, typecheck, undefined

SEE ALSO:
makefont, setfont, findfont

search   string seek **search**   *if found*: post match pre true
                                         if not found: string false

looks for the first occurrence of the string *seek* within *string* and returns results of this search on the operand stack. The topmost result is a boolean that indicates whether the search succeeded or not.

If **search** finds a subsequence of *string* whose elements are equal to the elements of *seek*, it splits *string* into three segments: *pre*, the portion of *string* preceding the match; *match*, the portion of *string* that matches *seek*; *post*, the remainder of *string*. It then pushes the string objects *post*, *match*, and *pre* on the operand stack, followed by the boolean *true*. All three of these strings are substrings sharing intervals of the value of the original *string*.

If **search** does not find a match, it pushes the original *string* and the boolean *false*.

EXAMPLE:
    (abbc) (ab) search ⇒ (bc) (ab) () true
    (abbc) (bb) search ⇒ (c) (bb) (a) true
    (abbc) (bc) search ⇒ () (bc) (ab) true
    (abbc) (B) search ⇒ (abbc) false

ERRORS:
invalidaccess, stackoverflow, stackunderflow, typecheck

SEE ALSO:
anchorsearch, token

setcachedevice w_x w_y ll_x ll_y ur_x ur_y **setcachedevice** –

passes width and bounding box information to the POSTSCRIPT font machinery. **setcachedevice** may be executed only within the context of the **BuildChar** procedure for a user-defined font (see section 5.7). **BuildChar** must invoke **setcachedevice** (or **setcharwidth**) *before* executing graphics operators to define and paint the character. **setcachedevice** requests the POSTSCRIPT font machinery to transfer the results of those operators both into the font cache (if possible) and onto the current page.

The operands to **setcachedevice** are all numbers interpreted in the *character* coordinate system (see the **FontMatrix** entry in section 5.3). w_x and w_y comprise the basic width vector for this character, i.e., the normal position of the origin of the next character relative to origin of this one (see section 5.5).

ll_x and ll_y are the coordinates of the lower left corner and ur_x and ur_y are the coordinates of the upper right corner of the character bounding box. The character bounding box is the smallest rectangle, oriented with the character coordinate system axes, that completely encloses all marks placed on the page as a result of executing the character's description. (For a character defined as a path, this may be determined by means of the **pathbbox** operator.) This information is required by the font machinery in order to make decisions about clipping and caching. It is essential that the declared bounding box be correct, i.e., sufficiently large to enclose the entire character. If any marks fall outside this bounding box, they will be clipped off and not moved to the current page.

After execution of a **setcachedevice** and until the termination of the **BuildChar** procedure, use of the operators **setgray**, **sethsbcolor**, **setrgbcolor**, **settransfer**, and **image** will result in an error (**undefined**). Use of the **imagemask** operator, however, is permitted.

ERRORS:
stackunderflow, typecheck, undefined

SEE ALSO:
setcharwidth, setcachelimit, cachestatus

setcachelimit   num **setcachelimit** –

establishes the maximum number of bytes that may be occupied by the pixel array of a single cached character. Any character larger than this (according to the character bounding box information passed to **setcachedevice**) is not saved in the font cache; instead, its description is executed every time the character is encountered.

setcachelimit affects the decision whether to place new characters in the font cache; it does not disturb any characters already in the cache. Making the limit larger allows larger characters to be cached but may decrease the total number of different characters that can be held in the cache simultaneously. Changing this parameter is appropriate only in very unusual situations.

ERRORS:
limitcheck, rangecheck, stackunderflow, typecheck

SEE ALSO:
cachestatus

setcharwidth w_x w_y **setcharwidth** –

is similar to **setcachedevice**, but it passes only width information to the POSTSCRIPT font machinery and it declares that the character being defined is not to be placed in the font cache. This is necessary if the character description needs to execute any of the operators **setgray, sethsbcolor, setrgbcolor, settransfer,** or **image,** since the font cache is incapable of retaining the color information from those operators.

setcharwidth is useful, for example, in defining characters that incorporate two or more specific opaque colors (e.g., opaque black and opaque white). This is unusual; most characters have no inherent color but are painted with the current color within the character's outline, leaving the area outside unpainted (transparent).

ERRORS:
stackunderflow, typecheck, undefined

SEE ALSO:
setcachedevice

setdash   array offset **setdash** –

sets the dash pattern parameter in the graphics state, controlling the dash pattern used during subsequent executions of the **stroke** operator. If *array* is empty (i.e., its length is zero), **stroke** produces a normal, unbroken line. If *array* is not empty, **stroke** produces dashed lines whose pattern is given by the elements of *array*, which must all be non-negative numbers and not all zero.

stroke interprets the elements of *array* in sequence as distances along the path, measured in user space. These distances alternately specify the length of a dash and the length of a gap between dashes. **stroke** uses the contents of *array* cyclically; when it reaches the end of the array, it starts over at the beginning.

Dashed lines wrap around curves and corners just as normal strokes do. The ends of each dash are treated with the current line cap; corners within a dash are treated with the current line join. **stroke** does not take any measures to coordinate the dash pattern with features of the path; it simply dispenses dashes along the path as specified by *array*.

The *offset* operand may be thought of as the 'phase' of the dash pattern relative to the start of the path. It is interpreted as a distance into the dash pattern (measured in user space) at which the pattern should be started. Before beginning to stroke a path, **stroke** cycles through the elements of *array*, adding up distances and alternating dashes and gaps as usual, but without generating any output. When it has travelled the *offset* distance into the dash pattern, it starts stroking the path (from its beginning) using the dash pattern from the point that has been reached.

Each subpath of a path is treated independently; i.e., the dash pattern is restarted (and *offset* applied to it) at the beginning of each subpath.

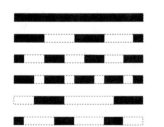

EXAMPLE:

[] 0 setdash	% turn dashing off: solid lines
[3] 0 setdash	% 3-unit on, 3-unit off, ...
[2] 1 setdash	% 1 on, 2 off, 2 on, 2 off, ...
[2 1] 0 setdash	% 2 on, 1 off, 2 on, 1 off, ...
[3 5] 6 setdash	% 2 off, 3 on, 5 off, 3 on, 5 off, ...
[2 3] 11 setdash	% 1 on, 3 off, 2 on, 3 off, 2 on, ...

ERRORS:
limitcheck, stackunderflow, typecheck

SEE ALSO:
currentdash, stroke

setflat   num **setflat** −

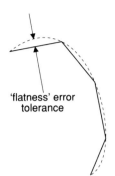

'flatness' error
tolerance

sets the flatness parameter in the current graphics state to *num*, which must be a positive number. This controls the accuracy with which curved path segments are to be rendered on the raster output device by the **stroke**, **fill**, and **clip** operators. Those operators render curves by approximating them with a series of straight line segments. 'Flatness' is an informal term for the error tolerance of this approximation; it is the maximum distance of any point of the approximation from the corresponding point on the true curve, measured in output device pixels.

The choice of flatness value is a tradeoff between accuracy and execution efficiency. Very small values (less than 1 device pixel) produce very accurate curves at high cost, since enormous numbers of tiny line segments must be produced. Larger values produce cruder approximations with substantially less computation. A default value of the flatness parameter is established by the device setup routine for each raster output device; this value is based on characteristics of that device and is the one suitable for most applications.

ERRORS:
stackunderflow, typecheck

SEE ALSO:
currentflat, flattenpath, stroke, fill

setfont   font **setfont** −

establishes the font dictionary to be used by subsequent character operators, such as **show**, **stringwidth**, etc. *font* must be a valid font dictionary previously returned by **findfont**, **scalefont**, or **makefont** (see section 5.2).

EXAMPLE:
```
/Helvetica findfont      % obtain prototype Helvetica font
10 scalefont             % scale it to 10-unit size
setfont                  % establish it as current font
```

ERRORS:
stackunderflow, typecheck

SEE ALSO:
currentfont, scalefont, makefont, findfont

setgray   num **setgray** –

sets the current color parameter in the graphics state to a gray shade corresponding to *num*. *num* must be a number between 0 and 1, with 0 corresponding to black, 1 corresponding to white, and intermediate values corresponding to intermediate shades of gray. This establishes the color used subsequently to paint shapes such as lines, areas, and characters on the current page. See section 4.8 for more information on gray-scale rendition.

The use of **setgray** after a **setcachedevice** operation within the scope of a **BuildChar** procedure is not permitted (an **undefined** error results).

ERRORS:
stackunderflow, typecheck, undefined

SEE ALSO:
currentgray, sethsbcolor, setrgbcolor

sethsbcolor   hue saturation brightness **sethsbcolor** –

sets the current color parameter in the graphics state to a color described by the parameters *hue*, *saturation*, and *brightness*, each of which must be a number in the range 0 to 1. This establishes the color used subsequently to paint shapes such as lines, areas, and characters on the current page. See section 4.8 for an explanation of these color parameters.

The use of **sethsbcolor** after a **setcachedevice** operation within the scope of a **BuildChar** procedure is not permitted (an **undefined** error results).

ERRORS:
stackunderflow, typecheck, undefined

SEE ALSO:
currenthsbcolor, setgray, setrbgcolor

setlinecap int **setlinecap** –

sets the current line cap parameter in the graphics state to *int*, which must be one of the integers 0, 1, or 2. This establishes the shape to be put at the ends of open subpaths painted by the **stroke** operator (see section 4.6). The integers select the following shapes:

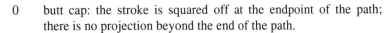

0   butt cap: the stroke is squared off at the endpoint of the path; there is no projection beyond the end of the path.

1   round cap: a semicircular arc with diameter equal to the line width is drawn around the endpoint and filled in.

2   projecting square cap: the stroke continues beyond the endpoint of the path for a distance equal to half the line width and is squared off.

ERRORS:
rangecheck, stackunderflow, typecheck

SEE ALSO:
currentlinecap, setlinejoin, stroke

int **setlinejoin** –

sets the current line join parameter in the graphics state to *int*, which must be one of the integers 0, 1, or 2. This establishes the shape to be put at corners in paths painted by the **stroke** operator (see section 4.6). The integers select the following shapes:

0   miter join: the outer edges of the strokes for the two segments are extended until they meet at an angle, as in a picture frame. (If the segments meet at too sharp an angle, a bevel join is used instead; this is controlled by the miter limit parameter established by **setmiterlimit**.)

1   round join: a circular arc with diameter equal to the line width is drawn around the point where the segments meet and is filled in, producing a rounded corner. (**stroke** actually draws a full circle at this point. If path segments shorter than one-half the line width meet at sharp angles, an unintentional 'wrong side' of this circle may appear.)

2   bevel join: the meeting path segments are finished with butt end caps (see **setlinecap**); then the resulting notch beyond the ends of the segments is filled with a triangle.

Join styles are significant only at points where consecutive segments of a path connect at an angle; segments that meet or intersect fortuitously receive no special treatment. Curved lines are actually rendered as sequences of straight line segments, and the current line join is applied to the 'corners' between those segments. However, for typical values of the flatness parameter (see **setflat**), the corners are so shallow that the difference between join styles is not visible.

ERRORS:
rangecheck, stackunderflow, typecheck

SEE ALSO:
currentlinejoin, setlinecap, stroke, setmiterlimit

setlinewidth   num **setlinewidth** –

sets the current line width parameter in the graphics state to *num*. This controls the thickness of lines rendered by subsequent execution of the **stroke** operator. Precisely, **stroke** paints all points whose perpendicular distance from the current path, in user space, is less than or equal to one-half the absolute value of *num*. The effect actually produced in device space depends on the current transformation matrix (CTM) in effect at the time of the **stroke**. If the CTM specifies scaling by different factors in the x and y dimensions, the thickness of stroked lines in device space will vary according to their orientation.

A line width of zero is acceptable: it is interpreted as the thinnest line that can be rendered at device resolution (i.e., one device pixel wide). Some devices are incapable of reproducing one-pixel lines, and on high-resolution devices such lines are nearly invisible. Since the results of rendering such 'zero-width' lines are device dependent, their use is not recommended.

ERRORS:
stackunderflow, typecheck

SEE ALSO:
currentlinewidth, stroke

setmatrix   matrix **setmatrix** –

replaces the current transformation matrix (CTM) in the graphics state by the value of *matrix*. This establishes an arbitrary transformation from user space to device space, without reference to the former CTM. Except in device setup procedures, use of **setmatrix** should be very rare. POSTSCRIPT programs should ordinarily *modify* the CTM (by use of the **translate**, **scale**, **rotate**, and **concat** operators) rather than replace it altogether.

ERRORS:
rangecheck, stackunderflow, typecheck

SEE ALSO:
currentmatrix, defaultmatrix, initmatrix, rotate, scale, translate, concat

setmiterlimit   num **setmiterlimit** −

sets the current miter limit parameter in the graphics state to *num*, which must be a number greater than or equal to 1. The miter limit controls the **stroke** operator's treatment of corners when miter joins have been specified (see **setlinejoin**). When path segments connect at a sharp angle, a miter join results in a spike that extends well beyond the connection point. The purpose of the miter limit is to cut off such spikes when they become objectionably long.

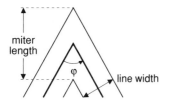

At any given corner, the *miter length* is the distance from the point at which the inner edges of the stroke intersect to the point at which the outside edges of the strokes intersect (i.e., the diagonal length of the miter). This distance increases as the angle between the segments decreases. If the ratio of the miter length to the line width exceeds the miter limit parameter, **stroke** treats the corner with a bevel join instead of a miter join.

The ratio of miter length to line width is directly related to the angle φ between the segments by the formula:

miter length / *line width* = 1 / sin(φ/2)

Examples of miter limit values are: 1.415 cuts off miters (converts them to bevels) at angles less than 90 degrees, 2.0 cuts off miters at angles less than 60 degrees, and 10.0 cuts off miters at angles less than 11 degrees. The default value of the miter limit is 10. Setting the miter limit to 1 cuts off miters at all angles so that bevels are always produced even when miters are specified.

ERRORS:
rangecheck, stackunderflow, typecheck

SEE ALSO:
currentmiterlimit, stroke, setlinejoin

setrgbcolor   red green blue **setrgbcolor** –

sets the current color parameter in the graphics state to a color described by the parameters *red*, *green*, and *blue*, each of which must be a number in the range 0 to 1. This establishes the color used subsequently to paint shapes such as lines, areas, and characters on the current page. See section 4.8 for an explanation of these color parameters.

The use of **setrgbcolor** after a **setcachedevice** operation within the scope of a **BuildChar** procedure is not permitted (an **undefined** error results).

ERRORS:
stackunderflow, typecheck

SEE ALSO:
currentrgbcolor, setgray, sethsbcolor

setscreen   frequency angle proc **setscreen** –

sets the current halftone screen definition in the graphics state. The *frequency* operand is a number that specifies the screen frequency, measured in halftone cells per inch in device space. The *angle* operand specifies the number of degrees by which the halftone screen is to be rotated with respect to the device coordinate system. The *proc* operand is a POSTSCRIPT procedure defining the spot function, which determines the order in which pixels within a halftone cell are whitened to produce any desired shade of gray. See section 4.8 for complete information about halftone screens.

Each device setup procedure establishes a default screen that is known to work well for that device. It is a rare POSTSCRIPT program that needs to specify its own screen definition.

ERRORS:
limitcheck, rangecheck, stackunderflow, typecheck

SEE ALSO:
currentscreen, settransfer

setttransfer   proc **settransfer** –

sets the current transfer function parameter in the graphics state. The *proc* operand must be a POSTSCRIPT procedure that may be called with a number in the range 0 to 1 (inclusive) on the operand stack and will return a number in the same range. This procedure maps *user gray* values (e.g., those specified to **setgray**) to *device gray* values (fraction of all pixels that are to be whitened). See section 4.8 for a complete explanation.

The use of **settransfer** after a **setcachedevice** operation within the scope of a **BuildChar** procedure is not permitted (an **undefined** error results).

ERRORS:
stackunderflow, typecheck

SEE ALSO:
currenttransfer, setscreen

show   string **show** –

prints the characters identified by the elements of *string* on the current page starting at the current point, using the font face, size, and orientation specified by the most recent **setfont**. The spacing from each character of the string to the next is determined by the character's width, which is an (x, y) displacement that is part of the character's definition. When it is finished, **show** adjusts the current point in the graphics state by the sum of the widths of all the characters printed. **show** requires that the current point initially be defined (e.g., by a **moveto**); otherwise it executes the error **nocurrentpoint**.

See chapter 5 for complete information about the definition, manipulation, and rendition of fonts.

ERRORS:
invalidaccess, invalidfont, nocurrentpoint, stackunderflow, typecheck

SEE ALSO:
ashow, awidthshow, widthshow, kshow, charpath, moveto, setfont

showpage   – **showpage** –

transmits the current page to the current output device, causing any marks painted on the page actually to appear. **showpage** then performs the equivalent of **erasepage** and **initgraphics** in preparation for the next page. (A related operator, **copypage**, does not perform these resetting actions.)

For a device that produces physical output (e.g., printed paper), **showpage** looks up the name **#copies** in the context of the current dictionary stack. The associated value, which must be a non-negative integer, determines the number of copies of the output to be produced. The default value of **#copies** is 1, defined in **userdict**; this may be overridden either by redefining **#copies** in **userdict** or by defining **#copies** in some dictionary higher on the dictionary stack.

The precise manner in which the current page is transmitted to the output device is device-dependent; it is specified by the *proc* operand of the **framedevice** or **banddevice** operator originally used to install the device in the current graphics state.

EXAMPLE:
```
/#copies 5 def
showpage
```

This prints 5 copies of the current page and then erases the current page.

ERRORS: (none)

SEE ALSO:
copypage, erasepage

sin   angle **sin** real

returns the sine of *angle*, which is interpreted as an angle in degrees. The result is a real.

ERRORS:
stackunderflow, typecheck

SEE ALSO:
cos, atan

sqrt num **sqrt** real

> returns the square root of *num*, which must be a non-negative number. The result is a real.
>
> ERRORS:
> **rangecheck, stackunderflow, typecheck**
>
> SEE ALSO:
> **exp**

srand int **srand** –

> initializes the random number generator with the seed *int*, which may be any integer value. Executing **srand** with a particular value causes subsequent invocations of **rand** to generate a reproducible sequence of results.
>
> ERRORS:
> **stackunderflow, typecheck**
>
> SEE ALSO:
> **rand, rrand**

stack ⊢ any$_1$ ... any$_n$ **stack** ⊢ any$_1$ ... any$_n$

> writes text representations of every object on the stack to the standard output file, but leaves the stack unchanged. **stack** applies the '**=**' operator to each element of the stack, starting with the topmost element. See the '**=**' operator for a description of its effects.
>
> ERRORS:
> **stackoverflow**
>
> SEE ALSO:
> **pstack, =, ==, count**

stackoverflow (error)

> The operand stack has grown too large. Too many objects have been pushed on the stack and not popped off. See appendix B for the limit on the size of the operand stack.
>
> Before invoking this error, the interpreter creates an array containing all elements of the operand stack (stored as if by **astore**), resets the operand stack to empty, and pushes the array on the operand stack.

stackunderflow   (error)

An attempt has been made to remove an object from the operand stack when it is empty. This usually occurs because some operator did not have all of its required operands on the stack.

StandardEncoding   − **StandardEncoding** array

pushes the standard encoding vector on the operand stack. This is a 256-element array, indexed by character codes, whose values are the character names for those codes. See section 5.4 for an explanation of encoding vectors. **StandardEncoding** is not actually an operator; it is a name in **systemdict** associated with the array object itself.

StandardEncoding is the encoding vector used by most standard text fonts but not by special fonts such as Symbol. A new text font having no unusual encoding requirements should specify its **Encoding** entry to be the value of **StandardEncoding** rather than define its own private array. The contents of the standard encoding vector are tabulated in appendix A.

ERRORS:
stackoverflow

start   − **start** −

is executed by the POSTSCRIPT interpreter when it starts up. After setting up the VM (restoring it from a file if appropriate), the interpreter executes the name **start** in the context of the default dictionary stack (**userdict** and **systemdict**). The procedure associated with the name **start** is expected to provide whatever top-level control is required, e.g., for receiving page descriptions, interacting with a user, recovering from errors, etc. The precise definition of **start** depends on the environment in which the POSTSCRIPT interpreter is operating; it is not of any interest to ordinary POSTSCRIPT programs.

SEE ALSO:
quit

status   file **status** bool

returns *true* if *file* is still valid (i.e., is associated with an open file), *false* otherwise.

ERRORS:
stackunderflow, typecheck

SEE ALSO:
file, closefile

stop   – **stop** –

terminates execution of the innermost dynamically enclosing instance of a **stopped** context, without regard to lexical relationship. A **stopped** context is a procedure (or other executable object) invoked by the **stopped** operator. **stop** pops the execution stack down to the level of the **stopped** operator. The interpreter then pushes the boolean *true* on the operand stack and resumes execution at the next object in normal sequence after the **stopped**. (It thus appears that **stopped** returned the value *true*, whereas it normally returns *false*.)

stop does not affect the operand or dictionary stacks. Any objects pushed on those stacks during the execution of the **stopped** context remain after the context is terminated.

If **stop** is executed when there is no enclosing **stopped** context, the interpreter prints an error message and executes the built-in operator **quit** (this never occurs during execution of ordinary user programs).

ERRORS: (none)

SEE ALSO:
stopped, exit

stopped   any **stopped** bool

> executes *any*, which is typically but not necessarily a procedure, executable file, or executable string object. If *any* runs to completion normally, **stopped** returns *false* on the operand stack. If *any* terminates prematurely as a result of executing **stop**, **stopped** returns *true* on the operand stack. Regardless of the outcome, the interpreter resumes execution at the next object in normal sequence after **stopped**.
>
> This mechanism provides an effective way for a POSTSCRIPT program to 'catch' errors or other premature terminations, retain control, and perhaps perform its own error recovery. See the discussions about errors in sections 3.6 and 3.8.
>
> EXAMPLE:
> > { ... } stopped {handleerror} if
>
> If execution of the procedure '{...}' causes an error, an error message is printed (by **handleerror**). In any event, normal execution continues at the token following the **if**.
>
> ERRORS:
> **stackunderflow**
>
> SEE ALSO:
> **stop**

store   key value **store** –

> searches for *key* in each dictionary on the dictionary stack, starting with the topmost (current) dictionary. If *key* is found in some dictionary, **store** replaces its value by the *value* operand. If *key* is not found in any dictionary on the dictionary stack, **store** creates a new entry with *key* and *value* in the current dictionary (the one on the top of the dictionary stack).
>
> EXAMPLE:
> > /abc 123 store
> > /abc where {} {currentdict} ifelse /abc 123 put
>
> The two lines of the example have the same effect.
>
> ERRORS:
> **dictfull, invalidaccess, limitcheck, stackunderflow**
>
> SEE ALSO:
> **def, put, where**

string   int **string** string

creates a string of length *int*, each of whose elements is initialized with the integer 0, and pushes this string on the operand stack. The *int* operand must be a non-negative integer not greater than the maximum allowable string length (see appendix B).

ERRORS:
limitcheck, rangecheck, stackunderflow, typecheck, VMerror

SEE ALSO:
length, array, dict, type

stringwidth   string **stringwidth** w_x w_y

calculates the change in the current point that would occur if *string* were given as the operand to **show** with the current font. w_x and w_y are computed by adding together the widths of all the individual characters in *string* and converting the result to user space. Thus, they form a distance vector in *x* and *y* describing the width of the entire string in user space. See section 5.5 for a discussion about character widths.

In order to obtain the character widths, **stringwidth** may actually execute the descriptions of one or more of the characters in the current font and may cause the results to be placed in the font cache. However, **stringwidth** prevents the graphics operators that are executed from actually painting anything into the current page.

ERRORS:
invalidaccess, invalidfont, stackunderflow, typecheck

SEE ALSO:
show, setfont

stroke   – stroke –

paints a line following the current path and using the current color. This line is centered on the path, has sides parallel to the path segments, and has a width (thickness) given by the current line width parameter in the graphics state (see **setlinewidth**). **stroke** paints the joints between connected path segments with the current line join (see **setlinejoin**) and the ends of open subpaths with the current line cap (see **setlinecap**). The line is either solid or broken according to the dash pattern established by **setdash**.

The parameters in the graphics state controlling line rendition (line width, line join, and so forth) are consulted at the time **stroke** is executed; their values during the time the path is being constructed are irrelevant.

If a subpath is degenerate (consists of a single point), **stroke** paints it only if round line caps have been specified, producing a filled circle centered at that point. If butt or projecting square line caps have been specified, **stroke** produces no output, since the orientation of the caps would be indeterminate.

stroke implicitly performs a **newpath** after it has finished painting the current path. To preserve the current path across a **stroke** operation, use the sequence: **gsave stroke grestore**.

ERRORS:
limitcheck

SEE ALSO:
setlinewidth, setlinejoin, setmiterlimit, setlinecap, setdash

strokepath   – strokepath –

replaces the current path with one enclosing the shape that would result if the **stroke** operator were applied to the current path. The path resulting from **strokepath** is suitable as the implicit operand to **fill**, **clip**, or **pathbbox**. In general, this path is not suitable for **stroke**, as it may contain interior segments or disconnected subpaths produced by **strokepath**'s stroke to outline conversion process.

ERRORS:
limitcheck

SEE ALSO:
fill, clip, stroke, pathbbox, charpath

sub   num$_1$ num$_2$ **sub** difference

returns the result of subtracting *num$_2$* from *num$_1$*. If both operands are integers and the result is within integer range, the result is an integer; otherwise, the result is a real.

ERRORS:
stackunderflow, typecheck, undefinedresult

SEE ALSO:
add, div, mul, idiv, mod

syntaxerror   (error)

The scanner has encountered program text that does not conform to the POSTSCRIPT syntax rules (see section 3.3). This can occur either during interpretation of an executable file or string object or during explicit invocation of the **token** operator.

Since the POSTSCRIPT syntax is simple, the set of possible causes for a **syntaxerror** is very small:

- an opening string or procedure bracket, '(', '<', or '{', is not matched by a corresponding closing bracket before the end of the file or string being interpreted;

- a closing string or procedure bracket, ')', '>', or '}', appears for which there is no previous matching opening bracket;

- a character other than a hexadecimal digit or white space character appears within a hexadecimal string literal bracketed by '<...>'.

Erroneous tokens such as malformed numbers do not produce a **syntaxerror**; such tokens are instead treated as name objects (often producing an **undefined** error when executed). Tokens that exceed implementation limits, such as names that are too long or numbers whose values are too large, produce a **limitcheck** (see appendix B).

systemdict   – **systemdict** dict

> pushes the dictionary object **systemdict** on the operand stack (see section 3.4). **systemdict** is not actually an operator; it is a name in **systemdict** associated with the dictionary object itself.
>
> ERRORS:
> **stackoverflow**
>
> SEE ALSO:
> **errordict, userdict**

timeout   (error)

> A time limit has been exceeded; i.e., a POSTSCRIPT program has executed for too long or has waited an excessive amount of time for some external event to occur.
>
> The POSTSCRIPT language does not define any standard causes for **timeout** errors. However, a POSTSCRIPT interpreter running in a particular environment provides a set of timeout facilities appropriate for that environment. The timeout facilities available in one POSTSCRIPT implementation are described in appendix D.

token   file **token** *if found*: any true
                                     if not found: false
          string **token** *if found*: post any true
                                     if not found: false

reads characters from *file* or *string*, interpreting them according to the POSTSCRIPT syntax rules (see section 3.3), until it has scanned and constructed an entire object.

In the *file* case, **token** normally pushes the scanned object followed by *true*. However, if **token** reaches end-of-file before encountering any characters besides white space, it closes *file* and returns *false*.

In the *string* case, **token** normally pushes *post* (the substring of *string* beyond the portion consumed by **token**), the scanned object, and *true*. However, if **token** reaches the end of *string* before encountering any characters besides white space, it simply returns *false*.

In either case, the *any* result is an ordinary POSTSCRIPT object. It may be simple (an integer, real, or name) or composite (a string bracketed by '(...)' or an executable array bracketed by '{...}'). The object returned by **token** is the same as the object that would be encountered by the interpreter if the *file* or *string* were executed directly. The only differences are that **token** scans just a single object and it always pushes that object on the operand stack rather than executing it.

token consumes all characters of the token and sometimes consumes the terminating character as well. If the token is a name or a number followed by a white space character, **token** consumes the white space character (only the first one if there are several). If the token is terminated by a special character that is part of the token (i.e., ')', '>', ']', or '}'), **token** consumes that character but no following ones. If the token is terminated by a special character that is part of the next token (i.e., '/', '(', '<', '[', or '{'), **token** does not consume that character but leaves it in the input sequence.

EXAMPLE:
     (15(St1) {1 2 add}) token ⇒ ((St1) {1 2 add}) 15 true
     ((St1) {1 2 add}) token ⇒ ({1 2 add}) (St1) true
     ({1 2 add}) token ⇒ () {1 2 add} true
     () token ⇒ false

ERRORS:
invalidaccess, ioerror, rangecheck, stackoverflow, stackunderflow, syntaxerror, typecheck, undefinedresult

SEE ALSO:
search, anchorsearch, read

transform
x y **transform** x′ y′
x y matrix **transform** x′ y′

With no *matrix* operand, **transform** transforms the user space coordinate (x, y) by CTM to produce the corresponding device space coordinate $(x′, y′)$. If the *matrix* operand is supplied, **transform** transforms (x, y) by *matrix* rather than by CTM.

ERRORS:
stackunderflow, typecheck

SEE ALSO:
itransform, dtransform, idtransform

translate
t_x t_y **translate** –
t_x t_y matrix **translate** matrix

With no *matrix* operand, **translate** builds a temporary matrix T:

$$\begin{matrix} 1 & 0 & 0 \\ 0 & 1 & 0 \\ t_x & t_y & 1 \end{matrix}$$

and concatenates this matrix with the current transformation matrix (CTM). Precisely, **translate** replaces the CTM by $T \times$ CTM. The effect of this is to move the origin of the user coordinate system by t_x units in the x direction and t_y units in the y direction relative to the former user coordinate system. The sizes of the x and y units and the orientation of the axes are unchanged.

If the *matrix* operand is supplied, **translate** replaces the value of *matrix* by T and pushes the modified matrix back on the operand stack (see section 4.4 for a discussion of how matrices are represented as POSTSCRIPT arrays). In this case, **translate** does not affect the CTM.

ERRORS:
rangecheck, stackunderflow, typecheck

SEE ALSO:
rotate, scale, concat, setmatrix

true   – **true** true

pushes a boolean object whose value is *true* on the operand stack. (**true** is not actually an operator; it is a name in **systemdict** associated with the boolean value *true*.)

ERRORS:
stackoverflow

SEE ALSO:
false, and, or, not, xor

truncate num_1 **truncate** num_2

truncates *num* toward zero by removing its fractional part. The type of the result is the same as the type of the operand.

EXAMPLE:
>3.2 truncate $\Rightarrow$ 3.0
>−4.8 truncate $\Rightarrow$ −4.0
>99 truncate $\Rightarrow$ 99

ERRORS:
stackunderflow, typecheck

SEE ALSO:
ceiling, floor, round, cvi

type   any **type** name

returns a POSTSCRIPT name object that identifies the type of the object *any*. The result is one of the following names:

arraytype	nametype
booleantype	nulltype
dicttype	operatortype
filetype	realtype
fonttype	savetype
integertype	stringtype
marktype	

(The name 'fonttype' identifies an object of type *fontID*; it has nothing to do with a font dictionary, which is identified by 'dicttype' just the same as any other dictionary.)

The returned name has the executable attribute. This makes it convenient to perform type-dependent processing of an object simply by executing the name returned by **type** in the context of a dictionary that defines all the type names to have procedure values (this is how '==' works).

ERRORS:
stackunderflow

typecheck   (error)

Some operand's type is different from what an operator expects. This is probably the most frequent error encountered. It is often the result of faulty stack manipulation, such as operands supplied in the wrong order or procedures leaving results on the stack when they aren't supposed to.

undefined   (error)

A name used as a dictionary key in some context cannot be found. This occurs if a name is looked up explicitly in a specified dictionary (**get**) or in the current dictionary stack (**load**) and is not found. It also occurs if an executable name is encountered by the interpreter and is not found in any dictionary on the dictionary stack.

A few POSTSCRIPT operators are disabled in certain contexts (e.g., **setgray** after a **setcachedevice** in a **BuildChar** procedure); attempting to execute such a disabled operator results in an **undefined** error.

SEE ALSO:
known, where, load, exec, get

undefinedfilename   (error)

A file identified by a name string operand of **file** or **run** cannot be found or cannot be opened. The **undefinedfilename** error also occurs if the special file '%statementedit' or '%lineedit' is opened when the standard input file has reached end-of-file.

SEE ALSO:
file, run

undefinedresult   (error)

A numeric computation would produce a meaningless result or one that cannot be represented as a POSTSCRIPT number. Possible causes include numeric overflow or underflow, division by zero, or inverse transformation of a non-invertible matrix. See appendix B for the limits of the values representable as integers and reals.

unmatchedmark   (error)

A mark object is sought on the operand stack by the ']', **cleartomark**, or **counttomark** operator, but none is present.

SEE ALSO:
counttomark, cleartomark,]

unregistered   (error)

An operator object has been executed for which the interpreter has no built-in action. This represents an internal malfunction in the POSTSCRIPT interpreter and should never occur.

userdict   – **userdict** dict

pushes the dictionary object **userdict** on the operand stack (see section 3.4). **userdict** is not actually an operator; it is a name in **systemdict** associated with the dictionary object itself.

ERRORS:
stackoverflow

SEE ALSO:
systemdict, errordict

usertime   – **usertime** int

returns the value of a clock that increments by 1 for every millisecond of execution by the POSTSCRIPT interpreter. The value has no defined meaning in terms of calendar time or time-of-day; its only use is interval timing. The accuracy and stability of the clock depends on the environment in which the POSTSCRIPT interpreter is running.

ERRORS:
stackoverflow

version   – **version** string

returns a string that identifies the version of the POSTSCRIPT language and interpreter being used. This identification includes no information about the hardware or operating system environment in which the POSTSCRIPT interpreter is running. The POSTSCRIPT version described in this manual is identified by the string '23.0'.

ERRORS:
stackoverflow

VMerror   (error)

An error has occurred in the virtual memory (VM) machinery. The most likely problems are:

- An attempt to create a new composite object (string, array, or dictionary) would exhaust VM resources. Either the program's requirements exceed available capacity or (more likely) the program has failed to use the **save/restore** facility appropriately (see section 3.7).

- The interpreter has attempted to perform an operation that should be impossible due to access restrictions (e.g., store into **systemdict**, which is read-only). This represents an internal error in the interpreter.

vmstatus   – **vmstatus** level used maximum

> returns three integers describing the state of the POSTSCRIPT virtual memory (VM). *level* is the current depth of **save** nesting, i.e., the number of **save**s that haven't been matched by a **restore**. *used* and *maximum* measure VM resources in units of 8-bit bytes; *used* is the number of bytes currently in use and *maximum* is the maximum available capacity. (However, in certain environments, the interpreter may be able to increase *maximum* dynamically by obtaining more storage from the operating system).
>
> ERRORS:
> **stackoverflow**
>
> SEE ALSO:
> **save, restore**

wcheck   array **wcheck** bool
              dict **wcheck** bool
              file **wcheck** bool
              string **wcheck** bool

> tests whether the operand's access permits its value to be written explicitly by POSTSCRIPT operators. **wcheck** returns *true* if the operand's access is unlimited, false otherwise.
>
> ERRORS:
> **stackunderflow, typecheck**
>
> SEE ALSO:
> **rcheck, readonly, executeonly, noaccess**

where   key **where** *if found*: dict true
                           if not found: false

> determines which dictionary on the dictionary stack (if any) contains an entry whose key is *key*. **where** searches for *key* in each dictionary on the dictionary stack, starting with the topmost (current) dictionary. If *key* is found in some dictionary, **where** returns that dictionary object and the boolean *true*. If *key* is not found in any dictionary on the dictionary stack, **where** simply returns *false*.
>
> ERRORS:
> **invalidaccess, stackoverflow, stackunderflow**
>
> SEE ALSO:
> **known, load, get**

widthshow c_x c_y char string **widthshow** –

prints the characters of *string* in a manner similar to **show**. But while doing so, **widthshow** adjusts the width of each occurrence of the character *char* by adding c_x to its *x* width and c_y to its *y* width, thus modifying the spacing between it and the next character. *char* is an integer in the range 0 to 255 used as a character code. This operator enables fitting a string of text to a specific width by adjusting the width of all occurrences of some specific character (such as the space character). For example, this is useful for setting justified text.

EXAMPLE:

Normal spacing
Wide word spacing

```
/Helvetica findfont 12 scalefont setfont
45 458 moveto (Normal spacing) show
45 444 moveto 6 0 8#040 (Wide word spacing) widthshow
```

ERRORS:
nocurrentpoint, stackunderflow, typecheck

SEE ALSO:
show, ashow, awidthshow, kshow, stringwidth

write   file int **write** –

appends a single character to the output file *file*. The *int* operand should be an integer in the range 0 to 255 representing a character code (values outside this range are reduced modulo 256). If *file* is not a valid output file or some error is encountered, **write** executes **ioerror**.

ERRORS:
invalidaccess, ioerror, stackunderflow, typecheck

SEE ALSO:
read, writehexstring, writestring, file

writehexstring   file string **writehexstring** –

writes all the characters of *string* to *file* as hexadecimal digits. For each element of *string* (an integer in the range 0 to 255), **writehexstring** appends a two-digit hexadecimal number composed of the characters '0' through '9' and 'a' through 'f'.

EXAMPLE:
```
(%stdout)(w) file (abz) writehexstring
```

writes the six characters '61627a' to the standard output file.

ERRORS:
invalidaccess, ioerror, stackunderflow, typecheck

SEE ALSO:
readhexstring, write, writestring, file

writestring   file string **writestring** –

writes the characters of *string* to the output file *file*. **writestring** does not append a newline character or otherwise interpret the value of *string*.

ERRORS:
invalidaccess, ioerror, stackunderflow, typecheck

SEE ALSO:
readstring, write, writehexstring, file

xcheck   any **xcheck** bool

tests whether the operand has the executable or literal attribute, returning *true* if it is executable or *false* if it is literal. (This has nothing to do with the object's access attribute, e.g., execute-only; see section 3.4.)

ERRORS:
stackunderflow

SEE ALSO:
cvx, cvlit

xor $bool_1\ bool_2$ **xor** $bool_3$
           $int_1\ int_2$ **xor** int_3

If the operands are booleans, **xor** pushes their logical 'exclusive or'. If the operands are integers, **xor** pushes the bitwise 'exclusive or' of their binary representations.

EXAMPLE:

    true true xor $\Rightarrow$ false   % a complete truth table
    true false xor $\Rightarrow$ true
    false true xor $\Rightarrow$ true
    false false xor $\Rightarrow$ false

    7 3 xor $\Rightarrow$ 4
    12 3 xor $\Rightarrow$ 15

ERRORS:
stackunderflow, typecheck

SEE ALSO:
or, and, not

APPENDIX **A**

STANDARD FONTS

The Adobe Type Library includes a wide variety of fonts that may be used by POSTSCRIPT programs. Among them are 13 standard fonts that are resident in the Apple LaserWriter, the Linotype Linotronic 300 typesetter, and other POSTSCRIPT printers.

This appendix describes the standard font set. The set consists of four faces each of Times and Helvetica, derived from the Mergenthaler Type Library under license from Allied Corporation. Also included are a Symbol font containing mathematical and special characters and a fixed-pitch Courier font. For each standard font, this appendix provides some sample text and a detailed description of the available character set. It then documents the standard encoding used for the text fonts and the separate encoding used for the Symbol font. (For more information on encoding, see section 5.4.)

A considerable amount of information concerning fonts is available to POSTSCRIPT programs, including character widths, side bearings, and bounding boxes. A program can obtain information about a font by executing POSTSCRIPT operators such as **stringwidth** (see section 5.5) or by accessing the font dictionary directly (section 5.3).

243

11 point text on 13 point linespacing

Times-Roman (with Italic, Bold, and BoldItalic)

The graphic signs called letters are so completely blended with the stream of written thought that their presence therein is as unperceived as *the ticking of a clock in the measurement of time.* To try to learn and ***repeat their excellence*** is to put oneself under training in a simple and severe school of design. **–William Addison Dwiggins**

Times-Italic

Architecture began like all scripts. First there was the alphabet. A stone was laid and that was a letter, and each letter was a hieroglyph, and on each hieroglyph there rested a group of ideas. –Victor Hugo

Times-Bold

Decisive, too, for the quality of a letter is that its various parts, though of limited expressiveness in themselves should combine into a harmonious unity charged with imagination and feeling. –Albert Windisch

Times-BoldItalic

It can be considered a special merit of our time that creative forces are again concerned with the problem of type design – a problem which has been faced by the best artists of every age. –Walter Tiemann

8 point The graphic signs called letters are so completely blended with the stream of written thought that their presence ther

9 point The graphic signs called letters are so completely blended with the stream of written thought that their p

10 point The graphic signs called letters are so completely blended with the stream of written thought

11 point The graphic signs called letters are so completely blended with the stream of written

12 point The graphic signs called letters are so completely blended with the stream of w

14 point The graphic signs called letters are so completely blended with th

18 point The graphic signs called letters are so completely b

24 point The graphic signs called letters are so c

18 point

abcdefghijklmnopqrstuvwxyz åçëîñòšú
ABCDEFGHIJKLMNOPQRSTUVWXYZ
ÅÇËÎÑÒŠÚ — ıłøßŁØæœfiflÆŒ(_@&†‡§¶)
1234567890--¤$¢¥£ƒ<·/*/+|=\^#>%~‰
«?!»•‹„""‚'.;:‚"'›{`´^~‾˘¨˙°˝˛ˇ}...[¡¿ªº]

18 point

abcdefghijklmnopqrstuvwxyz åçëîñòšú
ABCDEFGHIJKLMNOPQRSTUVWXYZ
ÅÇËÎÑÒŠÚ — ıłøßŁØæœfiflÆŒ(_@&†‡§¶)
1234567890--¤$¢¥£ƒ<·//+|=\^#>%~‰*
«?!»•‹„""‚'.;:‚"'›{`´^~‾˘¨˙°˝˛ˇ}...[¡¿ªº]

18 point

abcdefghijklmnopqrstuvwxyz åçëîñòšú
ABCDEFGHIJKLMNOPQRSTUVWXYZ
ÅÇËÎÑÒŠÚ — ıłøßŁØæœfiflÆŒ(_@&†‡§¶)
1234567890--¤$¢¥£ƒ<·/*/+|=\^#>%~‰
«?!»•‹„""‚'.;:‚"'›{`´^~‾˘¨˙°˝˛ˇ}...[¡¿ªº]

18 point

abcdefghijklmnopqrstuvwxyz åçëîñòšú
ABCDEFGHIJKLMNOPQRSTUVWXYZ
ÅÇËÎÑÒŠÚ — ıłøßŁØæœfiflÆŒ(_@&†‡§¶)
1234567890--¤$¢¥£ƒ<·/*/+|=\^#>%~‰
«?!»•‹„""‚'.;:‚"'›{`´^~‾˘¨˙°˝˛ˇ}...[¡¿ªº]

245

11 point text on 13 point linespacing

Helvetica (with Oblique, Bold, and BoldOblique)

I am Type! I bring into the light of day the precious stores of knowledge and wisdom long hidden in the grave of ignorance. I coin for you *the enchanting tale the philosopher's moralizing*, and the poet's phantasies. Through me, **Socrates and Plato** become your faithful friends who ever surround you.
– **Frederic Goudy**

Helvetica-Oblique

The typographer who can serve his art modestly and with a sensitive understanding of the special demands made by each type face sill be the one to achieve the finest results.
– Paul Renner

Helvetica-Bold

Of all the arts, architecture is nearest akin to typography. Both are equally related to their function. In both, that which wholly fulfills its purpose is beautiful.
– Helmut Presser

Helvetica-BoldOblique

No other art is more justified than typography in looking ahead to future centuries;for the creations of typography benefit coming generations as much as present ones.
– Giambattista Bodoni

8 point The graphic signs called letters are so completely blended with the stream of written thought that their pr

9 point The graphic signs called letters are so completely blended with the stream of written thought t

10 point The graphic signs called letters are so completely blended with the stream of written

11 point The graphic signs called letters are so completely blended with the stream o

12 point The graphic signs called letters are so completely blended with the str

14 point The graphic signs called letters are so completely blended w

18 point The graphic signs called letters are so complet

24 point The graphic signs called letters ar

18 point

abcdefghijklmnopqrstuvwxyz åçëîñòšú
ABCDEFGHIJKLMNOPQRSTUVWXYZ
ÅÇËÎÑÒŠÚ — ıłø ßŁØæœfiflÆŒ(_@&†‡§¶)
1234567890-–—¤$¢¥£ƒ<·/*/+|=\^#>%~‰
«?!»•‹„""‚'.;:‚"›{ ´˜¯˘˙¨˚˝¸ˇˆ}…[¡¿ªº]

18 point

abcdefghijklmnopqrstuvwxyz åçëîñòšú
ABCDEFGHIJKLMNOPQRSTUVWXYZ
ÅÇËÎÑÒŠÚ — ıłø ßŁØæœfiflÆŒ(_@&†‡§¶)
1234567890-–—¤$¢¥£ƒ<·//+|=\^#>%~‰*
«?!»•‹„""‚'.;:‚"›{ ´˜¯˘˙¨˚˝¸ˇˆ}…[¡¿ªº]

18 point

abcdefghijklmnopqrstuvwxyz åçëîñòšú
ABCDEFGHIJKLMNOPQRSTUVWXYZ
ÅÇËÎÑÒŠÚ — ıłøßŁØæœfiflÆŒ(_@&†‡§¶)
1234567890-–—¤$¢¥£ƒ<·/*/+|=\^#>%~‰
«?!»•‹„""‚'.;:‚"›{ ´˜¯˘˙¨˚˝¸ˇˆ}…[¡¿ªº]

18 point

abcdefghijklmnopqrstuvwxyz åçëîñòšú
ABCDEFGHIJKLMNOPQRSTUVWXYZ
ÅÇËÎÑÒŠÚ — ıłøßŁØæœfiflÆŒ(_@&†‡§¶)
1234567890-–—¤$¢¥£ƒ<·/*/+|=\^#>%~‰
«?!»•‹„""‚'.;:‚"›{ ´˜¯˘˙¨˚˝¸ˇˆ}…[¡¿ªº]

10 point text on 11 point linespacing

Courier
(with Oblique,
Bold, and
BoldOblique)

Each single letter is a small, well-balanced figure in itself. There are bad types, too; however, in a good type-face *each letter rests complete in itself*. To us, who are **used to reading**, a letter has become an abstract idea, a mere means of understanding.
– *Romano Guardini*

Courier-Oblique

The contemporary typographer regards his work from the design point of view and concentrates on the true essence of his task, to create graphic design.
– Emerich Kner

Courier-Bold

Machines exist; let us then exploit them to create beauty – a modern beauty, while we are about it. For we live in the twentieth century.
– Aldous Huxley

Courier-BoldOblique

Neither may the clarity of the single letter be given up for the sake of rhythm, nor may formal beauty be sacrificed to mere clarity or misconceived utility.
– Jan Tschichold

8 point   The graphic signs called letters are so completely blended with the stream

9 point   The graphic signs called letters are so completely blended with the

10 point   The graphic signs called letters are so completely blended

11 point   The graphic signs called letters are so completely

12 point   The graphic signs called letters are so completely

14 point   The graphic signs called letters are so

18 point   The graphic signs called letters

24 point   The graphic signs called

248

18 point
abcdefghijklmnopqrstuvwxyz åçëîñòšú
ABCDEFGHIJKLMNOPQRSTUVWXYZ
ÅÇËÎÑÒŠÚ — ıłøßŁØ(_@&†‡§¶)…[¡¿ªº]
1234567890--¤$¢¥£ƒ<·/*/+|=\^#>%~
«?!»•<„"",''.;:,"'>{`´^~¯˘·¨°¸"˛˘}

18 point
abcdefghijklmnopqrstuvwxyz åçëîñòšú
ABCDEFGHIJKLMNOPQRSTUVWXYZ
ÅÇËÎÑÒŠÚ — ıłøßŁØ(_@&†‡§¶)…[¡¿ªº]
1234567890--¤$¢¥£ƒ<·//+|=\^#>%~*
«?!»•<„"",''.;:,"'>{`´^~¯˘·¨°¸"˛˘}

18 point
abcdefghijklmnopqrstuvwxyz åçëîñòšú
ABCDEFGHIJKLMNOPQRSTUVWXYZ
ÅÇËÎÑÒŠÚ — ıłøßŁØ(_@&†‡§¶)…[¡¿ªº]
1234567890--¤$¢¥£ƒ<·/*/+|=\^#>%~
«?!»•<„"",''.;:,"'>{`´^~¯˘·¨°¸"˛˘}

18 point
abcdefghijklmnopqrstuvwxyz åçëîñòšú
ABCDEFGHIJKLMNOPQRSTUVWXYZ
ÅÇËÎÑÒŠÚ — ıłøßŁØ(_@&†‡§¶)…[¡¿ªº]
1234567890--¤$¢¥£ƒ<·/*/+|=\^#>%~
«?!»•<„"",''.;:,"'>{`´^~¯˘·¨°¸"˛˘}

Sample Symbol uses

$$a \oplus (b \otimes c) = (a \oplus b) \otimes (a \oplus c)$$

$$\gamma p \supset \Gamma * P$$

$$\neg (p \vee q) = \neg p \wedge \neg q$$
$$\neg (p \wedge q) = \neg p \vee \neg q$$

$$\varepsilon = \min_{x > 0} (x \mid (1 + x) \neq 1)$$

$$w (\xi' - \xi'') = \sum_{i=1}^{m} |C_i \cap \{ \xi' \}| \cdot |C_i \cap \{ \xi'' \}| \text{ if } \xi', \xi'' \in L \text{ and } \xi' \neq \xi''$$

$$\bigcup_{i=1}^{n} Z_i (t) \subseteq M$$
$$Z_i (t) \cap Z_j (t) = \emptyset \quad (i \neq j)$$

proposition	true if and only if
$(\forall u) s (p)$	$S \cap T'_p = \emptyset$
$(\exists u) s (p)$	$S \cap T_p \neq \emptyset$
$(\forall u) s (\sim p)$	$S \cap T_p = \emptyset$
$(\exists u) s (\sim p)$	$S \cap T'_p \neq \emptyset$
$\sim((\forall u) s (p))$	$S \cap T'_p \neq \emptyset$
$\sim((\exists u) s (p))$	$S \cap T_p = \emptyset$

$$kp^{k/2}t^{-1}I_k (at) \Leftrightarrow \left| \frac{s + \sqrt{s^2 - 4\lambda\mu}}{2\lambda} \right|^{-k}$$

12 point

αβχδεφγηικλμνοπθρστυωξψζφϖϑς ∫ ⌠ { ⎡ } [⎤] (⎛)

ΑΒΧΔΕΦΓΗΙΚΛΜΝΟΠΘΡΣΤΥΩΞΨΖΥ | { } | | | |

= ≠ ≡ ≈ ≅ < > ≤ ≥ ∧ ∨ ∴ − + ± × ÷ ¬ ∝ ⌡ ∪ ⌊ ∪

∀ ∃ ∍ ∩ ∪ ⊃ ⊂ ⊇ ⊆ ⊄ ∈ ∉ ∅ ⊗ ⊕ ∞

↔ ← ↑ → ↓ ⇔ ⇐ ⇑ ⇒ ⇓ ° ′ ″ ⌡ ℵ ℑ ℜ ℘

… 〈 ◊ ® © ™ ® © ™ Σ ∏ 〉 ∠ ⊥ ∇ ♣ ♦ ♥ ♠

16 point

αβχδεφγηικλμνοπθρστυωξψζφϖϑς ∫ ⌠ { ⎡ } [⎤] (⎛)

ΑΒΧΔΕΦΓΗΙΚΛΜΝΟΠΘΡΣΤΥΩΞΨΖΥ | { } | | | |

= ≠ ≡ ≈ ≅ < > ≤ ≥ ∧ ∨ ∴ − + ± × ÷ ¬ ∝ ⌡ ∪ ⌊ ∪

∀ ∃ ∍ ∩ ∪ ⊃ ⊂ ⊇ ⊆ ⊄ ∈ ∉ ∅ ⊗ ⊕ ∞

↔ ← ↑ → ↓ ⇔ ⇐ ⇑ ⇒ ⇓ ° ′ ″ ⌡ ℵ ℑ ℜ ℘

… 〈 ◊ ® © ™ ® © ™ Σ ∏ 〉 ∠ ⊥ ∇ ♣ ♦ ♥ ♠

251

octal	0	1	2	3	4	5	6	7
\00x								
\01x								
\02x								
\03x								
\04x		!	"	#	$	%	&	'
\05x	(	)	*	+	,	-	.	/
\06x	0	1	2	3	4	5	6	7
\07x	8	9	:	;	<	=	>	?
\10x	@	A	B	C	D	E	F	G
\11x	H	I	J	K	L	M	N	O
\12x	P	Q	R	S	T	U	V	W
\13x	X	Y	Z	[	\	]	^	_
\14x	`	a	b	c	d	e	f	g
\15x	h	i	j	k	l	m	n	o
\16x	p	q	r	s	t	u	v	w
\17x	x	y	z	{	|	}	~	
\20x								
\21x								
\22x								
\23x								
\24x		¡	¢	£	⁄	¥	ƒ	§
\25x	¤	'	"	«	‹	›	fi	fl
\26x		–	†	‡	·		¶	•
\27x	‚	„	"	»	…	‰		¿
\30x		`	´	^	~	¯	˘	˙
\31x	¨		°	¸		˝	˛	ˇ
\32x	—							
\33x								
\34x		Æ		ª				
\35x	Ł	Ø	Œ	º				
\36x		æ				1		
\37x	ł	ø	œ	ß				

■ ASCII control character

□ not assigned

octal	0	1	2	3	4	5	6	7
\00x								
\01x								
\02x								
\03x								
\04x		!	∀	#	∃	%	&	∋
\05x	(	)	*	+	,	−	.	/
\06x	0	1	2	3	4	5	6	7
\07x	8	9	:	;	<	=	>	?
\10x	≅	Α	Β	Χ	Δ	Ε	Φ	Γ
\11x	Η	Ι	ϑ	Κ	Λ	Μ	Ν	Ο
\12x	Π	Θ	Ρ	Σ	Τ	Υ	ς	Ω
\13x	Ξ	Ψ	Ζ	[	∴	]	⊥	_
\14x		α	β	χ	δ	ε	φ	γ
\15x	η	ι	φ	κ	λ	μ	ν	ο
\16x	π	θ	ρ	σ	τ	υ	ϖ	ω
\17x	ξ	ψ	ζ	{	|	}	~	
\20x								
\21x								
\22x								
\23x								
\24x		ϒ	′	≤	⁄	∞	ƒ	♣
\25x	♦	♥	♠	↔	←	↑	→	↓
\26x	°	±	″	≥	×	∝	∂	•
\27x	÷	≠	≡	≈	…	|	—	↵
\30x	ℵ	ℑ	ℜ	℘	⊗	⊕	∅	∩
\31x	∪	⊃	⊇	⊄	⊂	⊆	∈	∉
\32x	∠	∇	®	©	™	∏	√	·
\33x	¬	∧	∨	⇔	⇐	⇑	⇒	⇓
\34x	◊	⟨	®	©	™	∑	⎛	|
\35x	⎝	⎡	|	⎣	⎧	⎨	⎩	|
\36x		⟩	∫	⌠	|	⌡	⎞	|
\37x	⎠	⎤	|	⎦	⎫	⎬	⎭	

The following tables list the character names and character codes in Adobe's standard text fonts and in the Symbol font. For each character, the character itself is shown along with its POSTSCRIPT character name and octal character code. Unencoded characters are also shown; their character code is noted with '–'.

Standard Text Characters

char	name	octal	char	name	octal	char	name	octal
	space	040	\	backslash	134	†	dagger	262
!	exclam	041	]	bracketright	135	‡	daggerdbl	263
"	quotedbl	042	^	asciicircum	136	·	periodcentered	264
#	numbersign	043	_	underscore	137	¶	paragraph	266
$	dollar	044	'	quoteleft	140	•	bullet	267
%	percent	045	a-z	a-z	141-172	,	quotesinglbase	270
&	ampersand	046	{	braceleft	173	„	quotedblbase	271
'	quoteright	047	|	bar	174	"	quotedblright	272
(	parenleft	050	}	braceright	175	»	guillemotright	273
)	parenright	051	~	asciitilde	176	…	ellipsis	274
*	asterisk	052	¡	exclamdown	241	‰	perthousand	275
+	plus	053	¢	cent	242	¿	questiondown	277
,	comma	054	£	sterling	243	`	grave	301
-	hyphen	055	/	fraction	244	´	acute	302
.	period	056	¥	yen	245	^	circumflex	303
/	slash	057	ƒ	florin	246	˜	tilde	304
0-9	zero-nine	060-071	§	section	247	¯	macron	305
:	colon	072	¤	currency	250	˘	breve	306
;	semicolon	073	'	quotesingle	251	·	dotaccent	307
<	less	074	"	quotedblleft	252	¨	dieresis	310
=	equal	075	«	guillemotleft	253	°	ring	312
>	greater	076	‹	guilsinglleft	254	¸	cedilla	313
?	question	077	›	guilsinglright	255	˝	hungarumlaut	315
@	at	100	fi	fi	256	˛	ogonek	316
A-Z	A-Z	101-132	fl	fl	257	ˇ	caron	317
[	bracketleft	133	–	endash	261	—	emdash	320

Unencoded Text Characters

char	name	octal	char	name	octal	char	name	octal
Æ	AE	341	Á	Aacute	–	á	aacute	–
ª	ordfeminine	343	Â	Acircumflex	–	â	acircumflex	–
Ł	Lslash	350	Ä	Adieresis	–	ä	adieresis	–
Ø	Oslash	351	À	Agrave	–	à	agrave	–
Œ	OE	352	Å	Aring	–	å	aring	–
º	ordmasculine	353	Ã	Atilde	–	ã	atilde	–
æ	ae	361	Ç	Ccedilla	–	ç	ccedilla	–
ı	dotlessi	365	É	Eacute	–	é	eacute	–
ł	lslash	370	Ê	Ecircumflex	–	ê	ecircumflex	–
ø	oslash	371	Ë	Edieresis	–	ë	edieresis	–
œ	oe	372	È	Egrave	–	è	egrave	–
ß	germandbls	373	Í	Iacute	–	í	iacute	–
			Î	Icircumflex	–	î	icircumflex	–
			Ï	Idieresis	–	ï	idieresis	–
			Ì	Igrave	–	ì	igrave	–
			Ñ	Ntilde	–	ñ	ntilde	–
			Ó	Oacute	–	ó	oacute	–
			Ô	Ocircumflex	–	ô	ocircumflex	–
			Ö	Odieresis	–	ö	odieresis	–
			Ò	Ograve	–	ò	ograve	–
			Õ	Otilde	–	õ	otilde	–
			Š	Scaron	–	š	scaron	–
			Ú	Uacute	–	ú	uacute	–
			Û	Ucircumflex	–	û	ucircumflex	–
			Ü	Udieresis	–	ü	udieresis	–
			Ù	Ugrave	–	ù	ugrave	–
			Ÿ	Ydieresis	–	ÿ	ydieresis	–
			Ž	Zcaron	–	ž	zcaron	–

Symbol Set

char	name	octal	char	name	octal	char	name	octal
	space	40	Λ	Lambda	114	o	omicron	157
!	exclam	41	M	Mu	115	π	pi	160
∀	universal	42	N	Nu	116	θ	theta	161
#	numbersign	43	O	Omicron	117	ρ	rho	162
∃	existential	44	Π	Pi	120	σ	sigma	163
%	percent	45	Θ	Theta	121	τ	tau	164
&	ampersand	46	P	Rho	122	υ	upsilon	165
∋	suchthat	47	Σ	Sigma	123	ϖ	omega1	166
(	parenleft	50	T	Tau	124	ω	omega	167
)	parenright	51	Y	Upsilon	125	ξ	xi	170
*	asteriskmath	52	ς	sigma1	126	ψ	psi	171
+	plus	53	Ω	Omega	127	ζ	zeta	172
,	comma	54	Ξ	Xi	130	{	braceleft	173
−	minus	55	Ψ	Psi	131	|	bar	174
.	period	56	Z	Zeta	132	}	braceright	175
/	slash	57	[	bracketleft	133	~	similar	176
0-9	zero-nine	60-71	∴	therefore	134	ϒ	Upsilon1	241
:	colon	72	]	bracketright	135	′	minute	242
;	semicolon	73	⊥	perpendicular	136	≤	lessequal	243
<	less	74	_	underscore	137	⁄	fraction	244
=	equal	75		radicalex	140	∞	infinity	245
>	greater	76	α	alpha	141	ƒ	florin	246
?	question	77	β	beta	142	♣	club	247
≅	congruent	100	χ	chi	143	♦	diamond	250
A	Alpha	101	δ	delta	144	♥	heart	251
B	Beta	102	ε	epsilon	145	♠	spade	252
X	Chi	103	φ	phi	146	↔	arrowboth	253
Δ	Delta	104	γ	gamma	147	←	arrowleft	254
E	Epsilon	105	η	eta	150	↑	arrowup	255
Φ	Phi	106	ι	iota	151	→	arrowright	256
Γ	Gamma	107	φ	phi1	152	↓	arrowdown	257
H	Eta	110	κ	kappa	153	°	degree	260
I	Iota	111	λ	lambda	154	±	plusminus	261
ϑ	theta1	112	μ	mu	155	″	second	262
K	Kappa	113	ν	nu	156	≥	greaterequal	263

char	name	octal		char	name	octal		char	name	octal
×	multiply	264		¬	logicalnot	330		}	bracerightmid	375
∝	proportional	265		∧	logicaland	331		⌋	bracerightbt	376
∂	partialdiff	266		∨	logicalor	332				
•	bullet	267		⇔	arrowdblboth	333				
÷	divide	270		⇐	arrowdblleft	334				
≠	notequal	271		⇑	arrowdblup	335				
≡	equivalence	272		⇒	arrowdblright	336				
≈	approxequal	273		⇓	arrowdbldown	337				
…	ellipsis	274		◊	lozenge	340				
|	arrowvertex	275		〈	angleleft	341				
—	arrowhorizex	276		®	registersans	342				
⌐	carriagereturn	277		©	copyrightsans	343				
ℵ	aleph	300		™	trademarksans	344				
ℑ	Ifraktur	301		∑	summation	345				
ℜ	Rfraktur	302		(	parenlefttp	346				
℘	weierstrass	303		|	parenleftex	347				
⊗	circlemultiply	304		(	parenleftbt	350				
⊕	circleplus	305		⌈	bracketlefttp	351				
∅	emptyset	306		|	bracketleftex	352				
∩	intersection	307		⌊	bracketleftbt	353				
∪	union	310		{	bracelefttp	354				
⊃	propersuperset	311		{	braceleftmid	355				
⊇	reflexsuperset	312		{	braceleftbt	356				
⊄	notsubset	313		|	braceex	357				
⊂	propersubset	314		〉	angleright	361				
⊆	reflexsubset	315		∫	integral	362				
∈	element	316		⌠	integraltp	363				
∉	notelement	317		|	integralex	364				
∠	angle	320		⌡	integralbt	365				
∇	gradient	321		)	parenrighttp	366				
®	registerserif	322		|	parenrightex	367				
©	copyrightserif	323		)	parenrightbt	370				
™	trademarkserif	324		⌉	bracketrighttp	371				
∏	product	325		|	bracketrightex	372				
√	radical	326		⌋	bracketrightbt	373				
·	dotmath	327		}	bracerighttp	374				

APPENDIX B

IMPLEMENTATION LIMITS

The POSTSCRIPT language itself imposes no restrictions on the sizes or quantities of things described in the language, such as numbers, arrays, stacks, paths, etc. However, a POSTSCRIPT interpreter running on a particular computer in a particular operating environment does have such limits. The interpreter cannot execute POSTSCRIPT programs that exceed these limits; if it attempts to perform some operation that would exceed one of the limits, it executes the error **limitcheck** (or **VMerror** if it exhausts virtual memory resources).

All the limits are sufficiently large that a POSTSCRIPT page description should never come close to exceeding any of them, since the POSTSCRIPT interpreter has been designed to handle very complex page descriptions. On the other hand, a program that is not a page description might encounter some of these limits, since the interpreter has not been designed with unlimited general programming in mind. There is no formal distinction in POSTSCRIPT between a page description and a general program. However, a POSTSCRIPT interpreter residing in a printer is deliberately optimized for its intended use: to produce raster output according to a fully-specified graphical description generated by some external application program.

Encountering a **limitcheck** during execution of a page description is almost always an indication of an error in the POSTSCRIPT program, such as unbounded recursion on one of the stacks. Encountering a **VMerror** is usually an indication that the program is not using the **save/restore** facility appropriately.

The following table gives the limits for a particular implementation of the POSTSCRIPT interpreter, namely the one in the Apple LaserWriter. These limits are typical of other POSTSCRIPT implementations, but some variations should be expected.

Quantity	Limit	Explanation
integer	2147483647	largest integer value; this value is $2^{31}-1$ and its representation is 16#7FFFFFFF. (However, in most contexts, an integer that would exceed this limit is converted to a real automatically.)
	−2147483648	smallest integer value; this is -2^{31} and its representation is 16#80000000.
real	$\pm10^{38}$	largest and smallest real values (approximately).
	$\pm10^{-38}$	nonzero real values closest to zero (approximately); values closer than these are converted to zero automatically.
	8	significant decimal digits of precision (approximately).
array	65535	maximum length of an array.
dictionary	65535	maximum capacity of a dictionary (key-value pairs).
string	65535	maximum length of a string.
name	128	maximum number of characters in a name.
file	6	maximum number of open files, including the standard input and output files. (A POSTSCRIPT implementation operating in an environment with permanent file storage would have a substantially larger limit.)
userdict	200	capacity of **userdict**. Note that **userdict** starts out with several things defined in it already.
operand stack	500	maximum depth of the operand stack (i.e., the maximum number of elements that may be pushed on and not yet popped off).
dict stack	20	maximum depth of the dictionary stack.

exec stack	250	maximum depth of the execution stack. Each procedure, file, or string whose execution has been suspended occupies one element of this stack. Additionally, control operators such as **for**, **repeat**, and **stopped** push a few additional elements on the stack to control their execution.
interpreter level	10	maximum number of recursive invocations of the POSTSCRIPT interpreter. Graphics operators that call POSTSCRIPT procedures, such as **pathforall**, **show**, **image**, etc., invoke the interpreter recursively.
save level	15	maximum number of active **save**s, i.e., ones that haven't been matched by a **restore**.
gsave level	31	maximum number of active **gsave**s. Note that each **save** also performs a **gsave** implicitly.
path	1500	maximum number of points specified in *all* active path descriptions, including the current path, clip path, and paths saved by **save** and **gsave**.
dash	11	maximum number of elements in a dash pattern; i.e., the maximum length of the array operand of **setdash**.
VM	240000	maximum size of the virtual memory in bytes. (This applies when using the **letter** or **legal** page type. Using the **note** page type raises the VM limit to 345000 bytes. See appendix D.) The current and maximum size of the VM are reported by the **vmstatus** operator.

It is impossible to predict accurately how much VM a program will consume; but it is possible to make a rough estimate. Recall from section 3.7 that VM is occupied primarily by the values of composite objects. Simple objects do not consume VM, nor do composite objects that share the values of other objects.

An array (or procedure) value occupies 8 bytes per element. Array values are created and VM consumed when a program executes the **array** and ']' operators and when the POSTSCRIPT scanner encounters procedures delimited by '{...}'.

A string value occupies 1 byte per element. String values are created and VM consumed when a program executes the **string** operator and when the POSTSCRIPT scanner encounters string literals delimited by '(...)' and '<...>'.

A dictionary value occupies approximately 20 bytes per key-value pair; consumption is based on the dictionary's maximum capacity, regardless of how full it currently is. Dictionary values are created only by the **dict** operator.

Each distinct name occupies approximately 40 bytes plus the length of the name in characters, consumed at the time the name is first encountered by the POSTSCRIPT scanner. Repeated occurrences of a particular name require no additional storage.

The **save/restore** machinery consumes VM in proportion to the magnitude of the changes that must be undone by **restore** (but independent of the total size of VM). **restore** reclaims all VM resources consumed since the corresponding **save**.

Loading an Adobe-supplied POSTSCRIPT font definition typically consumes 20000 to 30000 bytes of VM, depending on the size of the character set and the complexity of the characters. (VM consumption for a font remains essentially constant, regardless of the number of ways in which its characters are scaled, rotated, or otherwise transformed.) Thus, there is a practical limit on the number of different fonts (other than built-in fonts) that may be referenced in a single page description. A spooler program that manages font down-loading for a POSTSCRIPT printer may find it helpful to execute **vmstatus** and to enumerate **FontDirectory** in order to obtain information about VM consumed by fonts.

Once again, remember that the information given here applies only to the Apple LaserWriter and not necessarily to other implementations of the POSTSCRIPT interpreter.

STRUCTURING CONVENTIONS

Introduction

As discussed in section 3.3, the POSTSCRIPT language standard does not specify the overall structure of a POSTSCRIPT program. Any sequence of tokens conforming to the syntax and semantics of the POSTSCRIPT language is a valid program that may be presented to a POSTSCRIPT interpreter for execution.

For a POSTSCRIPT program that is a page description (i.e., a description of a printable document), it is often advantageous to impose an overall program structure. Two conventions for structuring programs are mentioned in the body of this manual.

First, a page description may be organized as a prologue and a script, as discussed in section 2.5. The prologue contains application-dependent definitions; the script describes the particular desired results in terms of those definitions. The prologue is written by a programmer, stored in a place accessible to an application program, and incorporated as a standard preface to each page description created by the application. The script is usually generated automatically by an application program.

Second, the script of a multiple-page document may be organized as a sequence of independent single-page descriptions that depend only on the prologue and not on each other. Each page's execution is bracketed by **save** and **restore**, isolating it from side-effects of other pages (and also ensuring that VM resources are reclaimed). This is discussed in section 3.7.

If a POSTSCRIPT program conforms to both of these conventions, other programs may operate on its text in various useful ways: reorder the pages of the script, extract subsets of the pages for printing or for inclusion in other documents, and so on. One can imagine applications that treat POSTSCRIPT programs simply as files of text data: they accept one or more POSTSCRIPT programs as input, transform them in some way, and produce a POSTSCRIPT program as output.

Beyond these simple conventions, programs that manage previously generated POSTSCRIPT page descriptions, such as 'printer spooler' utilities, may require additional information about those page descriptions. For example, if a page description references special fonts, a spooler may need to transmit those fonts' definitions to the POSTSCRIPT printer ahead of the page description itself.

To facilitate these and other operations, this appendix defines a standard set of *structuring conventions* for POSTSCRIPT programs. A POSTSCRIPT program that obeys the structuring conventions is called *conforming*; a POSTSCRIPT program that does not obey the structuring conventions is called *nonconforming*. The structuring conventions have no effect on the execution of a program by a POSTSCRIPT interpreter; however, many applications that operate on POSTSCRIPT page descriptions (including some printer spoolers) accept only conforming programs as input.

Compliance with these conventions is not an all-or-nothing proposition. Applications that generate POSTSCRIPT page descriptions need not supply all of the information described below. Simple applications (particularly ones running on very small computers) may only be able to specify basic information; larger applications are able to implement the complete specification. A POSTSCRIPT page description is called *minimally conforming* if it obeys the conventions flagged below with '†'. A minimally conforming page description must supply information about program structure and font requirements but may omit any other information.

Comment convention

An essential requirement of the structuring conventions is that one should be able to obtain the structural information from a page description without having to interpret or execute the POSTSCRIPT program itself. That is, the structure must be distinguishable by static analysis of the text of the page description, and it must be straightforward to extract and interpret the structural information.

The structuring conventions make use of POSTSCRIPT *comments* to represent this information. The syntax for comments is described in section 3.3: a comment consists of a '%' followed by any text at all and terminated by a newline character. Comments are totally ignored by the POSTSCRIPT interpreter. However, comments conforming to the file structuring conventions can convey structural information to other programs that operate on page descriptions.

A conforming program includes structural information in the form of complete lines that start with '%!' or '%%' and end at the next newline. Such comments should contain structural information as detailed below. Comments that do not start with '%!' or '%%' or that do not start at the beginning of a line are not interpreted as structural information; they may contain arbitrary text, which is ignored.

The very first line of every POSTSCRIPT program (whether it is conforming or nonconforming) should be a comment that begins with the characters '%!'. This enables a file containing a POSTSCRIPT program to be easily identified as such.[1] It is important that every POSTSCRIPT program start with a '%!' comment, even if it is nonconforming; otherwise, it may not be given the appropriate handling in some operating system environments.

If the POSTSCRIPT program is conforming, the remainder of the first line (after the '%!') should be the version identifier for the structuring conventions that the file obeys. The version described

---

[1]For example, the UNIX operating system has a scheme whereby the first 16 bits of a file's contents are a 'magic number' that identifies the file's type to programs that operate on files of several different types. The '%!' serves as a 16-bit 'magic number' that identifies POSTSCRIPT files. This enables such a file to be treated as a POSTSCRIPT program meant to be executed as opposed to a text file meant to be printed as text.

in this appendix is version 'PS-Adobe-1.0'. A POSTSCRIPT program is taken to be minimally conforming to the file structuring conventions if the version identifier begins with the characters 'PS-Adobe-' (i.e., the first 11 characters of the program are '%!PS-Adobe-'). A program is taken to be fully conforming to the current version of the file structuring conventions if the version identifier consists of 'PS-Adobe-1.0'.

Following the version identifier comment line in a conforming or minimally conforming POSTSCRIPT program is the text of the program itself, interspersed with comment lines containing structural information and other information about the page description. Each comment begins with '%%', followed by a keyword. In comments that require values, the keyword is followed by ':' and one or more values whose interpretation depends on the keyword. (Comments that begin with '%!' are ignored if they appear other than on the first line of the program.)

These comments fall into three classes: *header comments*, *body comments*, and *trailer comments*. Header comments precede any non-comment POSTSCRIPT program text and provide information about the program as a whole. Body comments are interspersed with the program text and serve mainly to delimit the various parts of the page description (the prologue and the individual pages of the script). Trailer comments follow all the non-comment POSTSCRIPT program text and provide additional information about the program as a whole.

Comments must appear exactly in the form shown in the descriptions below: no space characters between the '%%' and the keyword or between the keyword and the ':', one space between the ':' and the first value, one space between values, and newline immediately after the last value. The case of letters in keywords is significant.

Header comments

The header comments begin immediately after the version identifier comment and end at the first occurrence of a line that does not start with '%%' or '%!'. (They may also end at an explicit 'EndComments' comment.)

The order in which header comments appear is not significant unless there is more than one comment with the same keyword. The first occurrence of a comment with a particular keyword is the one whose value prevails; any later comments with the same keyword are ignored. This enables utility programs to override header comments in an existing page description simply by inserting new header comments at the beginning; there is no need to delete the existing comments.

Certain of these header comments can be deferred to the end of the program (i.e., to the trailer comments section). This is for the benefit of application programs that generate page descriptions on-the-fly; such applications might not have the necessary information about fonts, page count, etc., at the beginning of generating a page description, but only at the end. If a particular header comment is to be deferred, a comment with the same keyword and the value '(atend)' must appear in the header comments section.

%%DocumentFonts: $font_1$ $font_2$ ...[†]

where $font_1$, $font_2$, etc. are the POSTSCRIPT font names of fonts used by the document. This comment can be deferred to the end of the program by specifying the value '(atend)' as described above. The font information is useful to utility programs that may need to down-load special fonts to a POSTSCRIPT printer before sending the document.

%%Title: title

The title of the document. The *title* value consists of arbitrary text terminated by newline. This is intended for use in identifying or locating page descriptions; the *title* might be derived from an application-level document name or from a file name.

%%Creator: text

The person or program (or both) that created this POSTSCRIPT document. This may be different from the person printing the document (see the 'For' comment below). The *text* value consists of arbitrary text terminated by newline.

%%CreationDate: text

The date and time at which this POSTSCRIPT document was created. The *text* value consists of arbitrary text terminated by newline; it should be interpretable as a date and time by humans.

%%For: text

> The intended recipient of the printed output produced by executing this document (usually the person who requests printing). The *text* value consists of arbitrary text terminated by newline. If no 'For' comment is present, the intended recipient is assumed to be the same as the value of 'Creator'.

%%Pages: pages

> The number of pages present in this document, i.e., the number of distinct pages that will be produced (by **showpage** or **copypage**) when the document is executed as a POSTSCRIPT program. *pages* should be a non-negative decimal integer. If execution of the document produces *no* pages (for example, the program is meant to be an included illustration), the number should be 0. The specification '(atend)' is permitted.

%%BoundingBox: ll_x ll_y ur_x ur_y

> The bounding box that encloses all the marks painted as a result of executing this program. All four values must be integers; (ll_x, ll_y) and (ur_x, ur_y) are the coordinates of the lower left and upper right corners of the bounding box in the default user coordinate system. This information is of use to composition programs that incorporate this document into a larger one as an included illustration.[2] The specification '(atend)' is permitted.

%%EndComments

> This comment explicitly ends the header comments section of a POSTSCRIPT program (as does any line that does not start with '%%' or '%!').

Body comments

Body comments serve primarily to mark the boundaries between the various parts of a POSTSCRIPT page description (the prologue and the individual pages of the script). An application that operates on the structure of a POSTSCRIPT page description (to extract page subsets, reverse the order of pages, etc.) must pay attention to these boundaries. In particular, whatever it does to

[2]The bounding box information is not especially useful for a multiple-page document. In that case, the values given should enclose the marks painted on all the pages combined; or the 'BoundingBox' comment should be omitted altogether.

individual pages, it must preserve the prologue at the beginning and the trailer (described below) at the end.

%%EndProlog[†]

> marks the end of the prologue section and the beginning of the script section of the document.

%%Page: label ordinal[†]

> marks the beginning of the description of an individual page, thereby terminating the previous page (if any). The *label* and *ordinal* parameters identify the page according to either or both of two schemes. The *label* is a text string not containing white space characters; it identifies the page according to the document's internal numbering scheme (e.g., 'vii', '10-34', etc.) The *ordinal* is a positive integer that specifies the page's position in the document's page sequence (from 1 through *n* for an *n*-page document). If the number in either scheme is not known, a '?' may be substituted. This information is useful to utility programs that extract selected pages from a document; it permits pages to be identified by specifications of the form 'pages vii and ix' or 'the last 10 pages'.

%%PageFonts: $font_1$ $font_2$ ...

> specifies the fonts required by the current page. If this comment is present, it must immediately follow a 'Page' comment. The fonts in a 'PageFonts' comment must be a subset of the fonts in the 'DocumentFonts' header comment. The purpose of 'PageFonts' is to provide a finer degree of detail for utility programs to use, e.g., when extracting page subsets or managing font down-loading for extremely complex documents. Pages without a 'PageFonts' comment are assumed to need all of the fonts listed in 'DocumentFonts'.

%%Trailer[†]

> marks the end of the last page of the document and the beginning of the trailer section (see below). Any non-comment POSTSCRIPT program text that follows this comment is considered to be part of the document as a whole rather than part of the last page; such text might include global cleanup (e.g., by **restore**) of state established by the prologue.

Trailer comments

Following the 'Trailer' body comment and any additional non-comment POSTSCRIPT program text may appear one or more trailer comments. The trailer comments section is composed of one or more of the header comments 'DocumentFonts', 'Pages', and 'BoundingBox'. These contain information that is deferred from the header comments section by the value specification '(atend)', as described earlier.

As with header comments, the order of trailer comments is not significant unless there is more than one comment with the same keyword. In this situation, the *last* trailer comment with a particular keyword is the one that prevails. Note, however, that a trailer comment applies *only* if there exists a header comment that has the same keyword and whose value is '(atend)'.

Example

The following is a skeletal example of a POSTSCRIPT program that conforms to the structuring conventions. The actual POSTSCRIPT program text is not shown, only the structuring comments.

```
%!PS-Adobe-1.0
%%Creator: Anthony Abstract
%%Title: Tropic of Calculus
%%CreationDate: Fri Aug  9 11:33:03 1974
%%Pages: (atend)
%%DocumentFonts: (atend)
%%BoundingBox: 0 0 612 792
%%EndComments
... document prologue goes here ...
%%EndProlog
%%Page: 0 1
... this might be the title page ...
%%Page: 1 2
... the first text page of the document ...
%%Page: 2 3
... the last page of the document ...
%%Trailer
... document trailer (if any) goes here ...
%%DocumentFonts: Times-Roman Times-Italic Times-Bold
%%Pages: 3
```

APPLE LASERWRITER

D.1 INTRODUCTION

The Apple LaserWriter is a low-cost laser printer that contains a POSTSCRIPT interpreter. It executes page descriptions written in the POSTSCRIPT language and produces printed pages at a rate of up to 8 pages per minute. The raster printing technology is xerographic, black-and-white, at 300 pixels per inch. The machine is intended either as a dedicated printer accessed by RS-232 serial communication or as a shared printer accessed through the AppleTalk local-area network.

The LaserWriter supports the entire POSTSCRIPT language that is specified in the main part of this manual. Page descriptions written in the POSTSCRIPT language can be printed on a LaserWriter or on other POSTSCRIPT printers.

Additionally, the LaserWriter has its own features, capabilities, and operating modes that are not necessarily present in other POSTSCRIPT printers. These facilities may be accessed by executing special POSTSCRIPT operators that exist only in the LaserWriter's POSTSCRIPT interpreter. The special operators are intended for use by human users or by host software carrying out user requests; ordinarily, page descriptions should not refer to them, since doing so would impair portability of those descriptions.

This appendix to the *POSTSCRIPT Language Reference Manual* contains detailed information about programming and operating the LaserWriter. This material is primarily of interest to programmers of host software accessing the LaserWriter and to users who may wish to configure a LaserWriter in non-standard ways.

Though the information in this appendix is not part of the standard POSTSCRIPT language, we have included it in the *Reference Manual* to give you an idea of how a real POSTSCRIPT printer operates. The descriptions here apply specifically to the LaserWriter, running version 23.0 of the POSTSCRIPT interpreter. However, it is reasonable to expect that many of these facilities will also be present in other POSTSCRIPT printers and that they will be accessed in similar ways.

This appendix does not repeat basic operating information given in Apple's *LaserWriter* manual, a copy of which accompanies each printer. For information about loading paper, changing toner cartridges, troubleshooting, etc., you should refer to the *LaserWriter* manual. It describes how to set up and operate a LaserWriter in a single standard configuration, namely as a network printer connected to AppleTalk and accessed by application programs running on other AppleTalk hosts.

D.2 BASIC OPERATION

This section gives an overview of the operation and use of the LaserWriter. Subsequent sections deal with the complete details of communication, operating modes, and parameter setting.

Much of the behavior of the LaserWriter is subject to change by the user. In the following descriptions, we assume that all user-adjustable options are set to their standard values, thereby producing the LaserWriter's 'normal' behavior.

Server

The principal function of the LaserWriter is to execute POSTSCRIPT programs sent to it from another computer. In normal operation, the LaserWriter cycles endlessly through the following sequence of steps. First, it sets up a clean initial execution environment (virtual memory) for a user's POSTSCRIPT program, which we will refer to as a 'job'. Then it executes the job by interpreting the standard input file, which is either an AppleTalk connection or a serial channel. When it encounters end-of-file or an error occurs, the LaserWriter cleans up after the user's job and restores the virtual memory to its initial state in preparation for the next job.

Thus, the LaserWriter's main role is as a *server* for execution of POSTSCRIPT programs sent to it by applications running on other computers. Ordinarily, each program is executed solely for its side-effect, namely the generation of printed pages. However, under suitable conditions, a program may change some permanent parameters in the LaserWriter itself, or may perform some computation whose results are sent back over the communication channel rather than causing hardcopy to be produced.

The LaserWriter has two other modes of operation: *interactive*, in which it operates as if it were a personal computer controlled directly by a human user, and *emulation*, in which it emulates the behavior of some other printer. These special modes are detailed in later sections.

Switches and lights

The LaserWriter has two switches and four lights visible on the outside of the machine. Aside from the power switch, there is a four-position switch that, in combination with some parameters previously established, controls the mode of operation and the communication discipline.

The switch positions are labelled '1200', '9600', 'Special', and 'AppleTalk'. These positions are assigned the following meanings, the details of which are described in later sections:

1200	PostScript batch mode operation; serial (RS-232/422) communication via either of the two connectors at 1200 baud, with parity ignored.
9600	PostScript batch mode operation; serial communication using parameters established previously. The default parameters are 9600 baud, parity ignored. Since these parameters can be set under software control, the '9600' switch position may select a baud rate different from 9600.
Special	Diablo 630 emulation mode; serial communication using parameters established previously. The default parameters are 9600 baud, parity ignored.
AppleTalk	PostScript batch mode operation; AppleTalk communication.

Changing the switch setting has immediate effect; if a job is in progress, it is aborted by execution of a PostScript **interrupt**.

The lights are intended to provide a simple visual indication of what the LaserWriter is doing. There are three colored lights on the front panel (green, yellow, and red) labelled with suggestive icons; additionally, there is a light on the rear of the machine labelled 'Test'. The lights are used in combination to indicate various states of operation:

idle	If the green light is on continuously, the machine is completely idle and awaiting the next user job to be executed.
warming up	If green is flashing and the other lights are off continuously, the printer is warming up (this should take no longer than two minutes).
busy	If green is alternating with a single quick flash of the yellow light, the server is busy executing a user job (or, immediately after power-on, computing the test page to be printed).
waiting	If green is alternating with two quick flashes of the yellow light, the server is in the midst of executing a user job but is suspended waiting to receive more data over the communication channel (AppleTalk or serial I/O).
no paper	If the yellow light is on continuously, either the paper tray is empty (or absent) or the printer is in manual feed mode waiting for a sheet of paper to be inserted.
jam	If the red light is on, a sheet of paper has failed to feed from the paper tray or has jammed in the printer. The jam may be cleared by releasing the top of the printer and removing the paper; it is not necessary to turn power off while doing this.

printer failure	If the green, yellow, and red lights are all off, the printer mechanism or electronics have suffered a failure requiring manual intervention and possibly a service call. A common cause of this indication is failure to insert a toner cartridge.
digital logic failure	If the 'Test' light on the rear of the machine is on (either flashing or continuously), a failure has occurred in the digital electronics and the machine is inoperable. If the light is flashing, an error message is being repeatedly transmitted over the 25-pin serial connector at 1200 baud. This indication may occur in combination with any of the other three lights.

Modes of operation

There are three basic modes of server operation: *batch*, *interactive*, and *emulation*. The four-position switch selects among these modes in combination with various communication options.[1]

In batch mode, a job consists of the execution of a single file containing a POSTSCRIPT program. When end-of-file is reached or the POSTSCRIPT program terminates, the job is finished. The only data transmitted from the LaserWriter to the host is that written explicitly to the standard output file (by the POSTSCRIPT **print** operator or by error handlers); the server provides no echoing, editing, or other user amenities. Batch mode is the normal way of operating the LaserWriter as a printing device for another computer.

In interactive mode, a job consists of an arbitrarily long dialogue in which the user issues a POSTSCRIPT statement and the server executes the statement and prompts for the next one. The state of the POSTSCRIPT's virtual memory persists until the user explicitly requests to end the job. While the user is entering a statement, the server echoes characters and provides some limited means for making corrections. Interactive mode is the means by which a user may interact with the LaserWriter from a terminal connected directly to it. This is useful for experimenting with POSTSCRIPT and for using the LaserWriter as a general-purpose computer. More information about interactive mode operation is presented in section D.5.

[1]Actually, the switch selects only between batch and emulation modes. Interactive mode is invoked by a procedure given in section D.5.

In emulation mode, the server emulates the operation of some other printer. In this mode, the LaserWriter does not interpret the incoming characters as a POSTSCRIPT program, but instead treats them as text and control codes understood by the printer being emulated. The LaserWriter has a built-in emulator for the Diablo 630 printer. Complete information about Diablo 630 emulation mode may be found in section D.5.

D.3 COMMUNICATION

The LaserWriter's connection with the outside world is via either AppleTalk or a point-to-point serial link (RS-232 or RS-422). The setting of the four-position switch determines the choice of communication discipline, as described previously.

In the following paragraphs, the connection is referred to as the *communication channel* (or just *channel*). The computer at the other end of the channel is referred to as the *host*. The host uses the channel to send the LaserWriter POSTSCRIPT programs to execute or data on which to operate. (Alternatively, the device at the other end of the channel may be a terminal operated directly by a human user.)

This channel is bidirectional. As well as reading programs and data from the channel, the LaserWriter may send output to the channel, either by explicit request of the program being executed (e.g., the POSTSCRIPT **print** operator) or by some spontaneous event such as an error. In this context, you should remember that **print** results in sending characters to the host computer or terminal, and has nothing to do with causing printed pages to emerge from the LaserWriter.

AppleTalk

Before connecting a LaserWriter to an AppleTalk network, you should first turn the machine off and then set the server mode switch to 'AppleTalk'. Never operate a LaserWriter connected to AppleTalk with the switch set to any but the 'AppleTalk' position. Failure to heed this precaution may leave the machine in an inoperable state or even bring down the entire network.

Connecting a LaserWriter requires that you use an AppleTalk connection box with a 9-pin plug, the same as is used with a Macintosh. A connection box with a 25-pin plug will not work, even though the LaserWriter does have a 25-pin socket.

While the LaserWriter is attached to AppleTalk, it listens for a connection request from another AppleTalk host. The server then executes a job using that connection as its standard input file. Any error messages or other output produced by **print** are sent back to the host over the same connection. Data is carried transparently in both directions; that is, there are no character codes reserved for AppleTalk communication functions.

The AppleTalk protocols define an end-of-file indication. When the POSTSCRIPT interpreter reaches end-of-file, the LaserWriter sends a matching end-of-file indication back to the host, terminates the current job, and starts a new one. Several jobs may be sent in sequence over a single AppleTalk connection. The host is permitted to close the connection any time after sending its end-of-file indication.

While the LaserWriter is busy with one connection, it refuses any additional connection requests. This causes the requesting hosts to queue up and wait for the server to become free. At that time, the server accepts the request from the host that has waited the longest.

AppleTalk communication with the LaserWriter is accomplished by means of the Printer Access Protocol, which makes use of the Apple Transaction Protocol, Datagram Delivery Protocol, and Name Binding Protocol. These protocols are specified in the *Inside LaserWriter* and *Inside AppleTalk* documentation packages published by Apple.

A LaserWriter is identified by a three-part name constructed according to the Name Binding Protocol. The first or *object* part is the printer's individual name, which is initially 'LaserWriter' but may be set to any other value by means of the **setprintername** operator described in section D.6. The second or *type* part is always 'LaserWriter', and the third or *zone* part is unspecified.

It is possible to connect more than one LaserWriter to the same AppleTalk network. If an additional machine has the same name as an existing one, it will automatically choose a new name, such as 'LaserWriter1' or 'LaserWriter2', in order to resolve the conflict.

Serial I/O

The LaserWriter has two serial channels, one wired to a 9-pin (RS-422) connector and the other to a 25-pin (RS-232) connector, either of which can be used for conventional asynchronous serial communication. (The 9-pin connector is also used for connecting to AppleTalk, but serial and AppleTalk communication are incompatible and will never occur at the same time.)

The signal pin assignments for the 9-pin (RS-422) connector are:

1, 3	Signal Ground
4	Transmit Data +
5	Transmit Data −
8	Receive Data +
9	Receive Data −

This is compatible with the Macintosh. It is possible to connect a LaserWriter directly to a Macintosh using an Apple Modem cable and to communicate with it using MacTerminal.

The assignments for the 25-pin (RS-232) connector are:

2	Transmit Data
3	Receive Data
4	Request To Send (optional)
7	Signal Ground
20	Data Terminal Ready (optional)

The 'optional' signals need to be connected only if the host computer requires them. The remaining pins in the 25-pin connector are not used. Technically, the LaserWriter has a DTE type of RS-232 interface. This means it can be connected directly to a terminal port of a host computer, with no signal reversals required. Connecting a LaserWriter to a terminal requires interposing a 'null modem', which at a minimum involves reversing the Transmit Data and Receive Data signals.

When the LaserWriter is in any of the serial I/O modes, it uses one of the two channels to send and receive serial data encoded in ASCII. Certain character codes serve special purposes, such as control-D to mark end-of-file. The server performs a job by reading and executing a POSTSCRIPT program from the serial channel. When it reads the end-of-file character and the program terminates, the server sends an end-of-file character, ends the job, and starts a new one.

At the beginning of a job, both channels are enabled with independent baud rate and parity. The first channel to receive a character is the one chosen for execution of the next job. (The other channel is not disabled; if characters start to arrive on it, they are saved in a buffer and that channel is selected when the current job is finished.)

The details of serial communication are determined by three parameters: channel, baud rate, and parity. These parameters may be changed by invoking the **statusdict** operators **setsccbatch** and **setsccinteractive**, described in section D.6. Serial communication is asynchronous, start-stop, with 8 data bits per character (of which the high-order bit may or may not be used for parity), one start bit, and two stop bits.

The 9- and 25-pin connectors are designated in POSTSCRIPT by the integers 9 and 25. The baud rate is given as an integer, such as 1200 or 9600. The maximum baud rate supported by the LaserWriter is 9600. The parity is specified by an integer in the range 0 to 3, as follows:

0   Ignore: the high-order bit of each 8-bit character received is ignored; the high-order bit of each character transmitted is zero.

1   Odd: the high-order bit of each 8-bit character received is checked for odd parity (a POSTSCRIPT **ioerror** occurs if it is incorrect); each character transmitted has odd parity.

2   Even: like odd, but for even parity.

3   None: all 8 bits of each character are treated as data and no checking is performed.

As described in section D.2, switch setting '1200' establishes communication with standard parameters (1200 baud, parity ignored). Switch settings '9600' and 'Special' use parameters established previously; if no such parameters have been established, the defaults for the latter two switch positions are 9600 baud, parity ignored. If you are attempting to make contact with a LaserWriter for the first time and you don't know how the parameters might have been set by a previous user, you should start with the '1200' setting. A particular user or installation will likely want to establish different standard parameters. The facilities for adjusting these and other parameters are described in section D.6.

The LaserWriter uses a simple serial communication protocol. There are several character codes reserved for communication functions and not passed through to the POSTSCRIPT interpreter. The ASCII character codes are given in decimal.

Character	Code	Function
Control-C	3	interrupt: causes execution of the POSTSCRIPT **interrupt** error (see the description of **interrupt** in chapter 6)
Control-D	4	end-of-file
Control-S	19	stop output (XOFF flow control)
Control-Q	17	start output (XON flow control)
Control-T	20	status query: causes the server to produce a one-line message that describes what it is doing (see below)
Return	13	end-of-line: translated to the POSTSCRIPT *newline* character
Line-feed	10	end-of-line: this is the POSTSCRIPT *newline* character (see section 3.3). If a return and a line-feed are received in sequence, only one newline character is passed to the POSTSCRIPT interpreter. When a newline character is written to the standard output file, it is translated to the two-character sequence return, line-feed.

As may be inferred, the LaserWriter makes use of the XON/XOFF flow control protocol and expects the host to do likewise.[2] That is, when the LaserWriter sends an XOFF character to the host, the host must immediately stop sending characters to the LaserWriter. When the LaserWriter sends XON to the host, the

[2]Another common flow control protocol that makes use of the Data Terminal Ready (DTR) signal is *not* supported by the LaserWriter.

host may resume sending characters to the LaserWriter. (The LaserWriter also heeds XOFF and XON characters received from the host.) Failure to conform to XON/XOFF flow control may result in unexpected occurrences of **ioerror**, caused by overflow of the LaserWriter's input buffer.

There is no way to 'quote' the reserved characters (to pass them through to the POSTSCRIPT interpreter), nor is there any way to transmit characters in the 'high ASCII' range (128 to 255) when using parity settings 0, 1, and 2, which cause the high-order bit of each character to be ignored or used for parity. Thus, the serial link is not a fully transparent channel. However, this causes no difficulty in normal use since the standard POSTSCRIPT character set consists entirely of printable characters (see section 3.3). The language itself provides means for encoding arbitrary characters in strings (the '\nnn' escape sequence). True binary data, such as images and encrypted programs, are transmitted in hexadecimal.

As mentioned earlier, when the server encounters an end-of-file character and the job terminates, it sends an end-of-file character back to the host. This character marks the end of the data (if any) written to the standard output file during execution of the job. This enables the application program running on the host computer to synchronize with the server (if desired) and to correlate a given batch of output with the job that generated it.

Communication dynamics

It is important to keep in mind that data transmitted by the LaserWriter, whether generated by the POSTSCRIPT program being executed or by some spontaneous event such as an error, is logically asynchronous with respect to the data received. This means that the host computer must be prepared to consume data received from the LaserWriter while waiting to send more data to the LaserWriter. If this is not done, the LaserWriter and the host may each end up waiting for the other to consume some data, and a deadlock will result.

Characters written to the standard output file by POSTSCRIPT operators such as **print** typically are not sent immediately but are buffered until a **flush** is executed. (A **flush** is performed automatically at end-of-job and, in interactive mode, at each prompt for user type-in.) If a POSTSCRIPT program writes data that is needed immediately by the host (e.g., in response to an environmental query), it is important that it execute a **flush** after writing the data; otherwise, a deadlock may occur.

Status queries and spontaneous messages

The LaserWriter provides a status query facility that enables the host or user to determine what the LaserWriter is doing. The LaserWriter responds to a status query asynchronously with respect to normal job execution; that is, it sends a response immediately, regardless of what has gone on before or how much input data has been buffered. This facility is intended primarily to enable 'spoolers' (printer control programs) to keep track of the activities of LaserWriters under their control.

The status query mechanism works differently depending on whether AppleTalk or serial communication is in use, but the syntax and semantics of the response are the same in either case.

In the case of AppleTalk, a request to open a connection to a busy LaserWriter yields a rejection packet whose data consists of a status message. There is also a separate status request packet that yields the same information. The path over which the status response packet travels is logically separate from the connection through which the server is receiving its current job.

In the case of serial communication, receipt of a control-T character from either channel elicits a one-line status message over the same channel. This channel need not be the one through which the server is receiving its current job. The message is bracketed by the text sequences '%%[' and ']%%' to enable host software to extract the message from ordinary data generated by the job being executed.

The status message has a standardized syntax that is intended to be machine-readable. It consists of one or more 'key: value' pairs, separated by semicolons. For example:

%%[job: Fred's Memo; status: busy; source: serial 9]%%

The possible keys, values, and meanings of the various fields are as follows:

---

job   the name of the job, as stored in the **jobname** entry in **statusdict** (described in section D.6). This field is omitted if the current job has not defined **jobname**.

status   what the LaserWriter is currently doing: 'idle' (no job in progress), 'busy' (executing user's POSTSCRIPT program), 'waiting' (I/O wait in mid-job), 'printing' (paper in motion), 'PrinterError: *reason*' (no paper, jam, etc.), 'initializing' (during startup), 'printing test page'.

source   'serial 9', 'serial 25', or 'AppleTalk'—the source of the job that the server is currently executing. This field is omitted if the server is idle.

All messages generated spontaneously by the server (as opposed to those produced by execution of **print** by the user's POSTSCRIPT program) conform to the same syntax as status messages.[3] These are:

%%[Error: error; OffendingCommand: operator]%%

An error has been detected by the POSTSCRIPT interpreter and the standard error handler (**handleerror**) has been invoked. *error* is the name of the error operator originally invoked; *operator* is the operator (or other POSTSCRIPT object) being executed at the time of the error. See section 3.8 and chapter 6 for more information about error handling.

%%[PrinterError: reason]%%

A problem has been reported by printer mechanism; the nature of the problem is detailed by *reason* (no paper, no paper tray, jam, cover open, etc.) A printer error can occur only when the machine is actually trying to print a page, i.e., during execution of a **showpage** or **copypage**. After generating this message, the server usually waits for the condition to be corrected and then continues automatically. (The server's behavior upon encountering a printer error is controlled by the **printererror** procedure defined in **statusdict**; see section D.6.)

[3]Note, however, that these messages are sent as ordinary data through the communication channel, in sequence with any other characters written to the standard output file. Consequently, they are always bracketed with '%%[' and ']%%' whether the channel is serial or AppleTalk.

%%[Flushing: rest of job (to end-of-file) will be ignored]%%

Due to a previous error or other abort condition (e.g., **stop** or control-C interrupt), the remainder of the current job is being discarded. The server reads and discards characters from the standard input file until it receives an end-of-file indication.

%%[exitserver: permanent state may be changed]%%

The POSTSCRIPT program has successfully exited from the server's normal **save/restore** context and may now make permanent changes to system parameters or to the VM (see section D.6).

D.4 DETAILS OF SERVER OPERATION

Much of the behavior of the LaserWriter is subject to change by the user. There is a collection of operators and other parameters in a special POSTSCRIPT dictionary named **statusdict**. These are mentioned in the paragraphs below, but complete documentation is deferred to section D.6.

Power-on test page

LaserWriter

When the LaserWriter is turned on, it attempts to print a test page containing various simple text and graphics. The test page is not printed if the **dostartpage** parameter in **statusdict** has been set to *false* or if the printer takes more than three minutes to warm up. The normal startup time is about 50 seconds if the test page is printed and about 25 seconds if it is not.

Certain information about the current communication parameters is encoded in the two graph examples in the middle of the page. The number of tick marks along the bottom of the line graph corresponds to the current switch setting, as follows:

1200	no ticks
9600	1 tick
Special	2 ticks
AppleTalk	3 ticks

The communication parameters selected by the current switch setting (if not AppleTalk) are shown in the bar graph. The height of the two bars indicates the baud rates for the 9 and 25-pin connectors. The color of the bars indicates the parity settings:

Ignore	dark gray
Odd	medium gray (same as apple)
Even	light gray
None	white

At the top of the page is the printer's AppleTalk name (returned by **printername**). At the bottom is the total number of pages that have been printed by this LaserWriter. At the lower left corner of the line graph illustration is the LaserWriter version number; '1.0' corresponds to version 23.0 of the POSTSCRIPT interpreter.

The border is intended to appear exactly one-half inch from the edges of a standard letter-size page (8.5 × 11 inches); also, the left border of the apple illustration and the bottom border of the bar graph illustration intersect at the exact center of the paper. The printer alignment can be adjusted if necessary by invoking the **setmargins** operator in **statusdict**.

Page types

The imageable region of the page is subject to both hardware limits (physical page size and margins required by the printing engine) and software constraints (amount of memory available for the full page frame buffer). Space is traded off between the frame buffer and the POSTSCRIPT virtual memory (VM). The LaserWriter includes built-in device setup procedures for establishing any of three standard 'page types':

---

letter   an imageable region of 8.0 by 10.92 inches, centered on an 8.5 by 11 inch page (that is, with 0.25 inch margins on left and right and 0.04 inch margins on top and bottom). This is the standard page type for all but legal-size paper.

note   an imageable region of 7.69 by 10.16 inches, centered on an 8.5 by 11 inch page. This page type is of interest to jobs that require unusually large amounts of VM for execution; the smaller frame buffer enables the VM to be approximately 100000 bytes larger than normal.

legal   an imageable region of 6.72 by 13.0 inches, centered on an 8.5 by 14 inch page. This is the standard page type for legal-size paper.

For all page types, the point (0, 0) in default user coordinate space is the lower left corner of the entire page, not of the imageable region; that is, the origin lies some distance outside the lower left corner of the imageable region. The coordinate system is arranged this way so that switching page types does not affect the position of graphical objects on the paper but just changes the sizes of the margins.[4]

At the beginning of each job, the software detects whether a letter or legal size paper tray is installed and sets the default page type automatically. If a legal size paper tray is present, page type **legal** is used; otherwise either **letter** or **note** is used according to the **pagetype** parameter previously established (the default is **letter**). A POSTSCRIPT program can override the default page type by executing one of the procedures **letter**, **note**, or **legal** explicitly.

Manual feed

It is possible to feed individual sheets of paper or other material (envelopes, transparency stock, etc.) into the LaserWriter manually. If a program defines **manualfeed** to be *true* in **statusdict**, the printer does not take paper from the paper tray during subsequent **showpage** operations. Instead, for each page printed, the yellow light comes on and the printer waits for a sheet of paper to be inserted into the slot in the right-hand side of the machine (opposite the paper exit slot). If no paper is inserted within **manualfeedtimeout** seconds, a **timeout** error occurs and the job is aborted.

Timeouts

There is a timeout facility for limiting the amount of time the server will remain in various states. There are three timeouts of interest: the *job* timeout, the *manual feed* timeout, and the *wait* timeout. At the beginning of a job, these timeouts are set to default values (initially 0, 60, and 30 seconds respectively). A POSTSCRIPT program can change the timeouts for the current job if it wants to. The operators for controlling timeouts are located in **statusdict** and are described in section D.6.

---

[4]Other page dimensions can be achieved by explicit invocation of the **framedevice** operator, described in chapter 6. This requires some care; it should be attempted only after thorough study of the definitions of the built-in procedures **letter**, **legal**, and **note**.

The manual feed timeout was described above. The job timeout, if nonzero, limits the total amount of time the job will execute; this is to protect the LaserWriter from being tied up by a POSTSCRIPT program that runs for an unexpectedly long time (or forever). The program itself can rejuvenate the timer any number of times during the job if that is desirable.

The wait timeout, if nonzero, limits the time the server will wait to receive additional input for a job that is in progress; this is to protect the LaserWriter from being tied up indefinitely by a host that crashes or is disconnected in the midst of sending a file to the server.

If a nonzero job or wait timeout has been set and it expires, the POSTSCRIPT interpreter executes the **timeout** error from **errordict**. With the standard definition of **timeout**, this causes a job running in batch or emulation mode to terminate. The timeout facility is not ordinarily enabled when the LaserWriter is in interactive mode.

Idle-time font scan conversion

While the server is waiting for a job to begin (i.e., before the first character of a new job has arrived from the source specified by the switch), it utilizes the available time to scan convert a standard selection of characters in commonly-used fonts and point sizes and to load the results into the font cache (see section 5.6). If a subsequent page description happens to use those characters, it will execute faster than it otherwise would.

The characters normally scan converted during idle time are listed below. The sizes marked with an asterisk are pre-scanned and permanently resident in ROM.

- Courier 10* point, full ASCII set (intended for program listings and other 'line printer' applications)
- Times-Roman and Helvetica 10, 12*, and 14 point, alphanumerics and common punctuation
- Times-Bold and Helvetica-Bold 10, 12, and 14 point, lower-case letters only

The standard selection of fonts to be scan converted during idle time may be overridden (except for the ones stored in ROM) by use of the **setidlefonts** operator in **statusdict**. Each font to be scan converted is specified by a sequence of five integers:

font $s_x \times 10$ $s_y \times 10$ *rot*/5 *nchars*

where *font* is a font number taken from the table below, s_x and s_y are the scale factors for *x* and *y*, *rot* is the rotation in degrees, and *nchars* is the number of characters to be converted. The font numbers are:

0	Courier	7	Times-BoldItalic
1	Courier-Bold	8	Helvetica
2	Courier-Oblique	9	Helvetica-Bold
3	Courier-BoldOblique	10	Helvetica-Oblique
4	Times-Roman	11	Helvetica-BoldOblique
5	Times-Bold	12	Symbol
6	Times-Italic		

The characters converted are the first *nchars* characters of the following set, which contains 94 in all:

```
abcdefghijklmnopqrstuvwxyz
ABCDEFGHIJKLMNOPQRSTUVWXYZ
0123456789.,;?:-()'"!+[]$%&*/_=@#'{}<>^~|\
```

For example, the following sequence of numbers (used as operands to **setidlefonts**) would specify conversion of all lower- and upper-case alphabetic characters of Helvetica-Bold in a 12-point size, narrowed by the ratio 10/12, and rotated by 90 degrees:

```
9 100 120 18 52
```

The complete set of fonts to be scan converted is specified as a sequence of integers, interpreted in groups of five as just described. If the sequence is empty, the standard fonts are converted. See the description of **setidlefonts** in section D.6 for more information.

D.5 OTHER OPERATING MODES

As discussed previously, the LaserWriter normally operates in batch mode: it consumes and executes a sequence of POSTSCRIPT programs, which are ordinarily page descriptions intended to produce printed output. However, there are two other operating modes that are sometimes useful: interactive and emulation.

Interactive mode

A human user can interact directly with the LaserWriter's POSTSCRIPT interpreter from a terminal and use the LaserWriter as if it were a personal computer. To facilitate this, the LaserWriter has an interactive mode of operation that provides some simple user amenities.

A terminal with a standard RS-232 interface can be connected directly to the LaserWriter, usually via its 25-pin connector. When making this connection, one must generally use a 'null modem' or 'modem eliminator' that reverses the Transmit Data and Receive Data signals. In place of a terminal, one can use a personal computer running terminal emulation software. For example, a Macintosh running MacTerminal can be connected to the LaserWriter's 9-pin connector using an Apple Modem cable or to its 25-pin connector using an Apple ImageWriter cable.

There are two ways to put the LaserWriter into interactive mode. The first is to select one of the batch mode switch positions ('1200' or '9600'), make sure the attached terminal is set to the correct baud rate and parity, and invoke the POSTSCRIPT procedure named **executive**. That is, type 'executive' followed by return or line-feed. (Since the server is in batch mode, the characters you type are not echoed back to you.) Once you do this, a POSTSCRIPT herald and prompt should appear:

```
PostScript(tm) version 23.0
Copyright (c) 1984 Adobe Systems Incorporated.
PS>
```

Each time the LaserWriter prints the 'PS>' prompt, it is waiting for you to enter a complete POSTSCRIPT statement followed by return or line-feed.[5] It then executes that statement and prints another 'PS>' prompt.

While you are typing, the LaserWriter echoes the characters you type (i.e., sends them back to your terminal, so you can see them). You can use the following special characters to make corrections while entering a statement:

Backspace (control-H)	backs up and erases one character
Delete (rubout)	same as backspace
Control-U	erases the current line
Control-R	re-displays the current line
Control-C	aborts the entire statement and starts over

Interactive mode continues until you type control-D (the serial end-of-file character), execute the POSTSCRIPT **quit** operator, or change the switch setting. Execution of **stop** (due to an error or control-C interrupt) does not terminate the job but simply aborts the statement currently being executed and prompts for a new one.

By changing a system parameter, you can redefine the meaning of the 'Special' switch position so that selecting it invokes interactive instead of emulation mode. For information about this, see the description of **eescratch** parameter 58 in section D.6.

Diablo 630 emulation

Because the LaserWriter is a general-purpose computer, it can be programmed with the capability to *emulate* other printers. That is, it can be connected in place of some other printer and produce output that correctly reproduces the results of that other printer.

The LaserWriter has a built-in emulator for the Diablo 630 daisy wheel printer, which is a product of Diablo Systems, Inc., and which is widely supported by personal computer application programs. This capability is intended mainly for use in printing

---

[5]The way it does this is to execute the **file** operator on the identifying string '%statementedit'. This is a standard POSTSCRIPT file facility, described in section 3.8.

simple text files that are not in POSTSCRIPT form and for processing output from software packages that do not directly support POSTSCRIPT.

If the system parameters have not been changed from their standard values, all that is necessary to invoke the Diablo 630 emulator is to set the server mode switch to the 'Special' position and connect one of the LaserWriter's serial ports to the host's RS-232 interface. The host should then send the text to be printed at 9600 baud (with any parity).

Most of the information about serial communication in section D.3 also applies in the case of Diablo 630 emulation. However, the special meanings of control characters such as control-C, control-D, etc., are disabled; instead, all characters are treated according to the Diablo 630 protocol.

The LaserWriter still sends XON and XOFF characters to control the flow of data from the host. Not all printer drivers in microcomputer operating systems support the XON/XOFF protocol; it may be necessary to issue special commands or to obtain a separate software package to support this protocol. The procedure for dealing with this problem varies from one computer and operating system to another; you must consult your own computer's documentation for the necessary information.

All the parameter settings that can be changed with Diablo 630 commands are initialized as they are in the Diablo 630. For information about these commands, refer to the Diablo 630 documentation.

There are other parameters that in the Diablo 630 require setting hardware switches or changing print wheels; in the LaserWriter these are system parameters that may be adjusted as described in section D.6. The complete set of system parameters pertaining to Diablo 630 emulation is given in the following table. To change them, refer to section D.6.

Parameter	Initial setting
pitch	10
font	Courier
font for bold	Courier-Bold
auto-linefeed	off

The Diablo 630 emulator supports all the standard LaserWriter typefaces. The default font is Courier, which is the fixed-pitch font most commonly used in daisy wheel printers and is the one most likely to give correct results for typical microcomputer application programs. Note that the regular and bold fonts are specified separately. Thus, one could use Courier for regular printing and Courier-Oblique for bold; then the 'bold' text would print as italic instead.

The LaserWriter emulates the Diablo 630 as closely as possible; however, there are some differences of which you should be aware:

The LaserWriter does not have any way to detect that the end of a document has been reached other than by noticing that characters have stopped arriving. All Diablo 630 printer settings (margins, tabs, spacing, etc.) remain in effect for about 30 seconds after the last character is received. Then the LaserWriter automatically performs a Diablo 630 'reset' operation to restore all settings to standard values; i.e., to put margins and spacing back to normal and to clear tab settings and any special word processing modes.

The LaserWriter actually prints a page when it either reaches the bottom of the page or receives a form-feed (control-L) character. If the last page of a document is not full and does not have a form-feed at the end, it will not be printed immediately. Instead, it will be printed when the LaserWriter resets approximately 30 seconds later, or as part of the next document. You should take care to ensure that each document has a final form-feed character so that documents printed in close succession do not get run together.

Some word processors produce 'bold' by double-striking characters. Such characters will not appear bold in output from the LaserWriter. Only the bold produced by issuing the proper Diablo 630 command sequence (escape-O) will result in bold characters.

Times-Roman and Helvetica are narrow fonts that may look squeezed if no adjustment of page width is made by the word processor. Very few word processing programs are capable of producing correctly formatted output using proportionally spaced fonts such as these.

The emulator uses exact positioning on the paper. Output from a word processor that has attempted to compensate for slippage on vertical movement may appear slightly uneven.

The following Diablo 630 commands and features are not supported by the LaserWriter:

- print suppression
- HY-Plot
- extended character set
- ability to download information for print wheels, including program mode
- ability to override printwheel spacing (for proportional spacing), although the offset for proportional spacing can be changed
- page lengths other than 11 inches
- paper feeder control
- hammer energy control
- remote diagnostic
- backward printing control (note, however, that 'reverse printing' is supported)

If you are an IBM-PC user, you may wish to issue the following commands to set up serial port 1 for communication with the LaserWriter. These commands set the baud rate to 9600 and map printer output to the serial port:

```
MODE COM1:9600,n,8,1
MODE LPT1:=COM1:
```

This by itself is not sufficient to support XON/XOFF flow control. Some applications may handle this protocol themselves; otherwise a different printer driver should be installed to avoid communication problems while printing large documents.

D.6 SYSTEM PARAMETERS

The LaserWriter has a fairly extensive collection of parameters that control its behavior. Some of these parameters are stored in non-volatile memory (EEROM), so they persist even when the machine is turned off. Other parameters are volatile and generally remain in effect only through the execution of a single job. This section documents both types of parameters.

All the system parameters are accessed through a special dictionary named **statusdict**, which is separate from **systemdict** and **userdict** (where all the standard POSTSCRIPT operators and procedures are defined). To change system parameters requires that you send the LaserWriter a POSTSCRIPT program that accesses **statusdict** explicitly.[6]

The easiest way to gain access to **statusdict** is to execute **statusdict begin**, which pushes **statusdict** on the dictionary stack. Subsequently (until the matching **end**), the operators defined in **statusdict** may be invoked directly simply by executing their names. Some system parameters are stored in **statusdict** as ordinary data values (integers, booleans, strings, etc.) that may be read by executing their names and changed by using the **def** operator.

The detailed explanations of the **statusdict** operators follow the format described in the introduction to chapter 6. Since the number of operators is relatively small, there is no summary section; instead, the operator descriptions are organized functionally rather than alphabetically.

Changing persistent parameters

Ordinarily, the server brackets each job with **save** and **restore** so that changes made to the virtual memory (VM) by the job do not persist into the next job. To make permanent changes (e.g., to install additional font definitions), it is necessary to escape from this context and execute a job that is not bracketed by **save** and **restore**. This is also necessary in order to execute any of the **statusdict** operators that change the persistent (non-volatile) parameters.

The ability to make permanent changes is controlled by a password. Some LaserWriters are used in a shared environment in which it is undesirable for individual users to change a server's persistent state. In such cases, only a system administrator should be permitted to make such changes. But in the case of a LaserWriter dedicated to a single user or a small group of cooperative users, the users should be permitted to make changes freely.

The system administrator password is a POSTSCRIPT integer. The

---

[6]The name **statusdict** is a vestige of an early design. **statusdict** is the repository for machine- and configuration-dependent operators and values in most implementations of the POSTSCRIPT interpreter. The set of operators and values defined in **statusdict** varies from one POSTSCRIPT implementation to another.

default value is zero, but it may be changed to any other value by executing the **setpassword** operator.

To escape from the normal server **save/restore** context, issue the POSTSCRIPT statement:

> serverdict begin *password* exitserver

where *password* is the system administrator password.[7] If the password is incorrect, **exitserver** executes the error **PasswordIncorrect** (which immediately invokes **stop**, bypassing **errordict**). If the password is correct, however, **exitserver** responds with the message

> %%[exitserver: permanent state may be changed]%%

as a positive acknowledgment to the **exitserver** request. It then performs an implicit **restore**, clears the operand and dictionary stacks, etc., as if it were preparing to execute the next job, but it does not perform another **save**.[8]

The POSTSCRIPT program executed between a successful **exitserver** and the next end-of-file is permitted to invoke the **statusdict** operators that change persistent parameters. Additionally, all changes made by that program to the state of the POSTSCRIPT VM, such as creating new objects, storing values into dictionaries, etc., persist until power-off; the modified VM appears as the initial state of all subsequent jobs.

During execution of this program, the VM is not protected from harmful changes that could cause the server to malfunction. (This is to permit the server itself to be patched, should that become necessary.) Also, VM resources consumed by that program remain in use indefinitely; there is no way to reclaim them other than by turning the LaserWriter off and on.

---

[7]**serverdict** is another special dictionary, distinct from **statusdict**, that contains definitions having to do with controlling the server. The **exitserver** procedure is the only definition in **serverdict** that is of interest to users.

[8]Actually, the server does start a new job, but without sending the usual end-of-file indication on the communication channel. Consequently, the POSTSCRIPT program must *not* issue an **end** to match the **serverdict begin**.

Persistent parameters

The **statusdict** operators for accessing persistent parameters are described below. The volatile parameters are dealt with in a later subsection.

In order to invoke any of the operators that change persistent parameters, it is first necessary to escape from the normal server **save/restore** context as described above; otherwise an **invalidaccess** error will occur. The operators for which this is required are marked with a '†'.

pagecount   – **pagecount** int

returns the number of pages that have been printed by this LaserWriter. (There is no way to reset this value.)

ERRORS:
stackoverflow

pagestackorder   – **pagestackorder** bool

returns *true* if the second page printed faces the back of the first page when it is stacked in the output tray; *false* if the second page faces away from the first. For the current LaserWriter product this is always *false*, meaning that pages are collated in reverse order.

ERRORS:
stackoverflow

setprintername[†]   string **setprintername** –

establishes *string* to be this printer's name. This string is printed on the test page at power-on time; it also defines the name used to identify this LaserWriter on AppleTalk. The *string* should be 31 or fewer characters long, should consist entirely of printing characters, and should not contain the characters ':' or '@'.[9]

ERRORS:
invalidaccess, rangecheck, stackunderflow, typecheck

[9]Those characters are reserved for constructing complete three-part names of the form '*name:type@zone*' used by the AppleTalk Name Binding Protocol. It is ordinarily inappropriate for the printer's name to specify any but the first part of an NBP name.

printername   string **printername** substring

stores the printer's name into the supplied *string* (overwriting some initial portion of its value) and returns a string object designating the substring actually used.

STANDARD VALUE: (LaserWriter)

ERRORS:
invalidaccess, rangecheck, stackunderflow, typecheck

setsccbatch[†]   channel baud parity **setsccbatch** −

sets communication parameters as specified by three integers designating *channel* (9 or 25), *baud* rate, and *parity* (see section D.3). These determine how serial communication is to be performed on that channel when the server mode switch is in the '9600' position (which ordinarily selects batch mode operation). Note that these parameters may be set independently for each of the two channels.

The new baud rate and parity do not take effect until the end of the current job. Setting a channel's baud rate to zero disables the channel; but disabling both channels is not permitted.[10]

EXAMPLE:
     25 9600 2 setsccbatch

This sets the 25-pin channel to 9600 baud with even parity.

ERRORS:
invalidaccess, rangecheck, stackunderflow, typecheck

sccbatch   channel **sccbatch** baud parity

returns the baud rate and parity for the specified *channel* (9 or 25). These are the parameters used when the server mode switch is in the '9600' position.

STANDARD VALUE: 9600 0

ERRORS:
rangecheck, stackoverflow, stackunderflow, typecheck

[10]The 'scc' in **setsccbatch** stands for Serial Communication Controller, which is the device that operates the LaserWriter's two communication channels.

setsccinteractive[†]   channel baud parity **setsccinteractive** –

is similar to **setsccbatch**, but it sets serial communication parameters to be used when the switch is in the 'Special' position (which selects either interactive or emulation mode operation).

ERRORS:
invalidaccess, rangecheck, stackunderflow, typecheck

sccinteractive   channel **sccinteractive** baud parity

returns the baud rate and parity for the specified *channel* (9 or 25). These are the parameters used when the server mode switch is in the 'Special' position.

STANDARD VALUE: 9600 0

ERRORS:
rangecheck, stackoverflow, stackunderflow, typecheck

setdostartpage[†]   bool **setdostartpage** –

specifies whether or not the LaserWriter is to print a test page upon subsequent power-on.

ERRORS:
invalidaccess, stackunderflow, typecheck

dostartpage   – **dostartpage** bool

returns the boolean that specifies whether a test page is printed at power-on.

STANDARD VALUE: true

ERRORS:
stackoverflow

setmargins[†] top left **setmargins** –

adjusts the printer's margins, thereby changing the alignment of the imageable area on the physical page. The *top* and *left* operands are integers that specify distances in device space (the unit size is one device pixel or 1/300 inch). A positive *top* widens the top margin and a negative *top* narrows it relative to the standard margin width. (The top of the page is the edge that emerges first from the printer.) Similarly, a positive *left* widens the left margin and a negative *left* narrows it.

setmargins is intended only for use at installation time to correct any physical alignment errors that may exist; it has nothing to do with setting the dimensions of the imageable area (see **letter**, **note**, and **legal** in section D.4). There are limits to the range of adjustment that is possible. The left margin parameter is quantized in units of 16 pixels, so horizontal centering is possible only to the nearest 8 pixels. Also, the printer hardware imposes margins that cause the image to be clipped if it is moved too close to the edge of the paper; unfortunately, the hardware-imposed margins are not symmetrical about the center of the paper.

ERRORS:
invalidaccess, rangecheck, stackunderflow, typecheck

margins   – **margins** top left

returns the two margin adjustment parameters set by **setmargins**.

STANDARD VALUE: 0 0

ERRORS:
stackoverflow

setpagetype[†] int **setpagetype** –

specifies the default page type to be used subsequently when any except the legal-size paper tray is installed (see section D.4). The value 0 selects page type **letter** and 1 selects **note**.

ERRORS:
invalidaccess, rangecheck, stackunderflow, typecheck

pagetype   – **pagetype** int

returns the default page type parameter.

STANDARD VALUE: 0

ERRORS:
stackoverflow

setdefaulttimeouts[†]   job manualfeed wait **setdefaulttimeouts** –

establishes the default values for the three timeouts (see section D.4). At the beginning of each job, these values are used to initialize the job, manual feed, and wait timeouts. (A POSTSCRIPT program may change a timeout for the remainder of the current job by executing the **setjobtimeout** operator or changing the **manualfeedtimeout** or **waittimeout** value in **statusdict**.) Each parameter must be a non-negative integer denoting a time interval in seconds; the value 0 indicates that the corresponding timeout should never occur.

ERRORS:
invalidaccess, rangecheck, stackunderflow, typecheck

defaulttimeouts   – **defaulttimeouts** job manualfeed wait

returns the default job, manual feed, and wait timeout values.

STANDARD VALUE: 0 60 30

ERRORS:
stackoverflow

setpassword   old new **setpassword** bool

sets the system administrator password, controlling the ability to escape from the server **save/restore** context and make persistent changes to system parameters or to the VM (see the introduction to this section). **setpassword** requires two integer operands: the *old* password and the *new* password. If *old* is the correct old password, **setpassword** changes the password to *new* and returns *true*; otherwise it returns *false*.

STANDARD VALUE: 0

ERRORS:
stackunderflow, typecheck

checkpassword   int **checkpassword** bool

> returns *true* if *int* is equal to the current system administrator password; otherwise it returns *false* (after delaying for one second).
>
> STANDARD VALUE: 0
>
> ERRORS:
> **stackunderflow, typecheck**

setidlefonts[†]   mark font s_x s_y rot nchars ... **setidlefonts** −

> expects the operand stack to contain up to 150 integers in the range 0 to 255, delimited by a *mark* immediately below them. **setidlefonts** removes the *mark* and the integers and remembers them permanently. The integers are interpreted in groups of 5 to specify characters to be scan converted while the LaserWriter is idle, as described in section D.4. An empty list of integers (i.e., just a *mark* on the top of the operand stack) specifies that the standard set of characters is to be scan converted.
>
> ERRORS:
> **invalidaccess, rangecheck, typecheck, unmatchedmark**

idlefonts   − **idlefonts** mark font s_x s_y rot nchars ...

> pushes a *mark* followed by the integers controlling idle time scan conversion (see **setidlefonts**).
>
> STANDARD VALUE: mark
>
> ERRORS:
> **stackoverflow**

seteescratch[†]   index value **seteescratch** −

> writes *value* at position *index* in an array in the EEROM reserved for scratch use. The *index* must be an integer in the range 0 to 63; the *value* must be an integer in the range 0 to 255. The EEROM scratch array is intended for storing persistent parameters not envisioned in the original design of the LaserWriter. Several entries in the array have already been assigned; they are described below.
>
> ERRORS:
> **invalidaccess, rangecheck, stackunderflow, typecheck**

eescratch   index **eescratch** value

returns the value at position *index* in the EEROM scratch array (see **seteescratch**).

STANDARD VALUE: 0

ERRORS:
rangecheck, stackunderflow, typecheck

Additional persistent parameters

Several capabilities have been added to the LaserWriter since the standard set of persistent parameters (just described) was established. Notable among these are the Diablo 630 emulator and the sharing of the 'Special' switch position between interactive and emulation modes. Entries in the EEROM scratch array (accessed by **seteescratch** and **eescratch**) have been assigned to control these capabilities. In the next major revision of the LaserWriter's POSTSCRIPT interpreter, these parameters will be assigned names of their own.

Parameter	Index	Semantics
Special mode	58	selects the function of the 'Special' switch setting: the value 0 means Diablo 630 emulation mode, 1 means POSTSCRIPT interactive mode, and other values are reserved for future capabilities.
Auto-linefeed	59	the value 1 enables the Diablo 630 auto-linefeed feature; any other value disables it.
Pitch	60	selects the Diablo 630 'pitch' (number of characters per inch). Reasonable values are 10, 12, and 15; the default value 0 selects 10 characters per inch.
Bold font	61	selects the 'bold' font used for Diablo 630 emulation. This is a font number taken from the table on page 288, except that if the number is 0 (selecting Courier) then 1 (selecting Courier-Bold) is used instead. (To actually select Courier as the 'bold' font, use some unreasonable font number such as 255.)
Normal font	62	selects the 'normal' font used for Diablo 630 emulation. This is a font number taken from the table on page 288. The default value 0 selects Courier.
–	63	has an internal use which is not documented.

For example, to change the meaning of the 'Special' switch position from Diablo 630 emulation to POSTSCRIPT interactive mode, execute the POSTSCRIPT program:

```
serverdict begin 0 exitserver
statusdict begin
58 1 seteescratch
```

The EEROM in which the persistent parameters are stored can be written only a limited number of times before wearing out. Each location in the EEROM is capable of being written approximately 10,000 times. For this reason, the EEROM is used only for parameters that are expected to change infrequently.

At power-on time, the LaserWriter's POSTSCRIPT interpreter checks the contents of the EEROM for consistency; it reports the result by defining an entry named **eerom** in **statusdict**. Normally, it defines **eerom** to be *true*. If it detects an inconsistency, it defines **eerom** to be a 512-character POSTSCRIPT string into which it reads the entire contents of the EEROM; then it sets the page count to zero and resets all system parameters to their default values. If it finds that the EEROM has failed altogether (perhaps because it has worn out), the interpreter shifts to a simulation of the EEROM parameters in RAM. All the operations for setting and reading parameters continue to work, but the values no longer survive power-off.

Volatile parameters

statusdict contains two operators (**setjobtimeout** and **jobtimeout**) with immediate effects that do not persist from one job to the next. The remaining **statusdict** entries are not operators but are ordinary data values such as booleans, integers, and strings. They may be read and written in the usual way by POSTSCRIPT dictionary operators such as **get** and **put**. There are no restrictions on changing these parameters; the effects of changes persist only until the end of the current job.

There are several additional **statusdict** entries that are not documented. They have to do with the operation of the server and are not intended for execution by user programs.

setjobtimeout   int **setjobtimeout** –

sets the timeout for the current job to the value *int*, a non-negative integer specifying a time interval in seconds. If the current job continues for *int* seconds without either completing or executing **setjobtimeout** again, the POSTSCRIPT interpreter executes a **timeout** error. The value 0 disables the job timeout altogether.

At the beginning of a job, the server initially sets the job timeout to the default job timeout returned by **defaulttimeouts**. (However, in interactive mode, the initial job timeout is always 0.)

ERRORS:
rangecheck, stackunderflow, typecheck

jobtimeout   – **jobtimeout** int

returns the number of seconds remaining before the job timeout will occur. A returned value of 0 means the job will never time out.

STANDARD VALUE: 0

ERRORS:
stackoverflow

manualfeedtimeout   – **manualfeedtimeout** int

is the manual feed timeout currently in effect, i.e., the number of seconds the LaserWriter will wait for a page to be inserted into the manual feed slot. This timeout applies only when the LaserWriter is in manual feed mode, i.e., when **manualfeed** is *true* (see the description of **manualfeed**).

At the beginning of a job, the server initializes **manualfeedtimeout** to the default manual feed timeout returned by **defaulttimeouts**; but a POSTSCRIPT program may change it to any non-negative integer value (by using **def**, **put**, or **store**).

STANDARD VALUE: 60

waittimeout   – **waittimeout**   integer

is the wait timeout currently in effect, i.e., the number of seconds the LaserWriter will wait to receive additional characters from the host before it will give up and abort the current job by executing a **timeout**. At the beginning of a job, the server initializes **waittimeout** to the default wait timeout returned by **defaulttimeouts**; but a POSTSCRIPT program may change it to any non-negative integer value. (However, in interactive mode, the wait timeout is always 0.)

STANDARD VALUE: 30

manualfeed   – **manualfeed**   bool

is a boolean that controls whether paper is to be fed manually (*true*) or from the paper tray (*false*).

STANDARD VALUE: false

prefeed   – **prefeed** bool

is a boolean that enables pre-feeding of paper from the paper tray. Normally, the printer mechanism does not start up and begin to feed paper until **showpage** is executed. Depending on what was printed on the previous page, setting **prefeed** *true* can decrease the time required to print each page by several seconds.

If **prefeed** is *true*, **showpage** begins feeding the *next* sheet of paper after it has completed printing the current page. The paper stops just before reaching the point at which the page image is transferred to it, awaiting execution of the next **showpage**. Meanwhile, the POSTSCRIPT interpreter executes the description of the next page, ending with a **showpage**. If the paper has reached the imaging position by that time, no additional time is lost waiting for paper to be fed.

To maximize printing throughput, a POSTSCRIPT program should set **prefeed** to *true* at the beginning of a job and to *false* immediately *before* executing the last **showpage** of the job. (If **prefeed** is still *true* when the job ends, the LaserWriter may produce an extra blank page.)

This feature should be used with care. Between the time a page is pre-fed and the time the next **showpage** is executed, the printer mechanism runs continuously and the laser is on. Leaving the machine running in this way for long periods of time can result in premature wear.

STANDARD VALUE: false

jobname   – **jobname** string

is a string that specifies the name of the current job. If a POSTSCRIPT program defines **jobname**, status responses generated during the remainder of the current job will include a 'job' field that reports the text of this string (see section D.3). The string should not contain the characters ';' or ']', since that would disrupt the syntax of status messages.

STANDARD VALUE: null

printererror   status tries **printererror** –

> is a procedure called during execution of **showpage** or **copypage** if the printer mechanism reports an error, such as no paper, jam, cover open, etc. The *status* is an integer that encodes details of the error condition; it is device-dependent and is not documented here. *tries* is the number of times **printererror** has previously been called during the same **showpage** or **copypage**. If **printererror** returns, the printing operation is retried; if it aborts (by executing **stop**), the printing operation is abandoned.
>
> The standard **printererror** procedure interprets *status* and generates a 'PrinterError' status message (described in section D.3). It then returns, thus allowing printer errors to be retried indefinitely.

product   – **product** string

> is a string object which is the name of the laser printer product (LaserWriter). The rare program that needs to know what type of printer it is running on should check this string. Also, this string defines the *type* portion of the printer's AppleTalk name.
>
> STANDARD VALUE: (LaserWriter)

revision   – **revision** int

> is an integer designating the current revision level of the machine-dependent portion of the POSTSCRIPT interpreter.
>
> STANDARD VALUE: 0

D.7 KNOWN PROBLEMS

> The POSTSCRIPT interpreter in the LaserWriter is an extremely complex piece of software. Not surprisingly, it contains a few bugs that have been discovered since manufacture of LaserWriters began.
>
> The following problems are known to exist in the initial release of the LaserWriter software (LaserWriter version 1.0, POSTSCRIPT version 23.0). These bugs will be present in the product until the next complete ROM revision. Most of the problems are relatively obscure. Fortunately, it is possible either

to avoid or to work around the problems that affect the LaserWriter's function. You should not worry about the ones that affect only its performance.

Input/output problems

During serial input, if the input buffer becomes full and the LaserWriter sends XOFF to stop transmission from the host, it occasionally fails to send XON to restart transmission. Assuming the wait timeout is enabled (as it ordinarily is), this causes the job to time out and abort, causing the standard input file to be flushed and an XON to be sent. The existence of this bug makes it inadvisable to operate the LaserWriter with the wait timeout disabled, since communication with the host could become hung up indefinitely. This bug occurs only under unusual circumstances that are difficult to describe; it is timing- and data-dependent and is most likely to interfere with Diablo 630 emulation.

If the LaserWriter starts to receive a new job over a serial channel before it has finished executing the previous one, it may erroneously read past the end-of-file character marking the end of the first job, usually causing an error to occur in the second job. This problem occurs only if the first job's last character is a regular character rather than a white space or special character. To avoid this problem, either ensure that all jobs end with a newline character or wait for a job to end (by waiting for the answering end-of-file character) before starting to send the next job.

Disabling one of the serial channels by setting its baud rate to zero (see **setsccbatch**) may cause communication difficulties with the other channel. We recommend that this feature not be used.

The **readline** operator does not recognize return as a newline character, only line-feed. This does not matter for serial communication, since return characters and return, line-feed pairs are converted to newlines. However, for AppleTalk communication, no such translation is done. POSTSCRIPT programs that expect to read data from the program file using **readline** should use line-feed as their newline character.

Under certain circumstances, the POSTSCRIPT scanner incorrectly interprets occurrences of the '\ddd' octal character constant notation within string literals (see section 3.3). This occurs only if the octal constant is less than three digits long and the next character is a letter. To avoid this problem, always use three-digit octal character constants, e.g., '\035' rather than '\35'.

Font and cache problems

If characters are positioned by adjusting the translation component of **currentmatrix** rather than by adjusting **currentpoint** as is ordinarily done, character positioning may be as much as one pixel off, leading to ragged base lines.

The font cache may work at less than full efficiency due to the presence of certain characters that are inappropriately locked in the cache. The performance effects of this bug are slight.

Redefining any of the built-in fonts or fonts derived from them causes the font cache to malfunction under certain complex and hard-to-describe circumstances. The effect is that some characters are displayed in the wrong font or point size or both. To avoid this bug, do not define a new font (using **definefont**) with the same name as any of the built-in fonts.

Two sizes of the same font whose size ratio is 300:72 (e.g., 50 point and 12 point versions of a font) may be confused with each other. This problem is extremely difficult to provoke; but if it occurs, change one of the sizes slightly to avoid the offending ratio.

It is possible to copy an existing font dictionary and then add a **Metrics** entry to the copy in order to create a new with different spacings for the characters (see section 5.7). Unfortunately, this does not always work correctly because the font cache fails to distinguish between characters belonging to the new and old fonts. To work around this bug, it is necessary also to change some *other* significant entry in the new dictionary. The simplest way to do this is to change the **FontBBox** entry to be a *new* array which is a copy of the **FontBBox** array from the original font.

More than two levels of recursion in calls to **BuildChar** procedures may cause the LaserWriter to crash. A user-defined font's **BuildChar** procedure may execute a **show** using a built-in font. But it is unsafe for that user-defined font to be invoked from the **BuildChar** procedure of yet another user-defined font.

Graphics problems

The path created by **strokepath** (or by **charpath** for a stroked font such as Courier) may not be suitable for subsequent clipping or filling if round line caps or line joins are used. Portions of the round line caps or joins may incorrectly be found to be 'outside' the path thus created.

Images built in strips by multiple executions of the **image** operator may contain seams between the strips under certain circumstances. It is better to render an entire image by one execution of **image**.

If the procedure operand of **image** or **imagemask** fails to return a string as it is supposed to, the LaserWriter may cease to be able to render images until the machine is next turned off and on.

If a **gsave** is done and a new transfer function is established by **settransfer**, the subsequent **grestore** may not properly restore the old transfer function. This bug occurs randomly with low probability. (The bug does not affect the restoration of the default transfer function, which is done at the beginning of each job and during any explicit invocation of **letter**, **legal**, or **note**.)

Miscellaneous problems

If manual feed is invoked (by setting **manualfeed** to *true* in **statusdict**) too quickly after printing a previous page using normal feed (from the paper tray), the printer mechanism ignores the request to use manual feed. To avoid this problem, when switching from normal to manual feed be sure at least 5 seconds elapse before issuing the next **showpage**. If necessary, insert a delay explicitly by executing the statement:

```
usertime 5000 add
{dup usertime lt {pop exit} if} loop
```

Exhausting POSTSCRIPT's VM sometimes causes the LaserWriter to crash and restart rather than simply abort the current job with a **VMerror** as it should. Also, if a job uses the **note** page type and then fills the VM close to overflowing, a subsequent attempt by the same job to set any page type causes the LaserWriter to crash and restart.

The Diablo 630 emulator may fail to produce any output if it is sent two or more successive single-page documents that do not end with form-feed characters.

The automatic recovery from total failure of the EEROM device, described on page 303, does not work properly. If the EEROM fails, the LaserWriter will not start up after power-on.

Index

263, 294
reversepath 110, **203**
revision 307
RGB
    See Red-green-blue
rlineto 68, 110, **204**
rmoveto 68, 110, **204**
roll 46, 104, **205**
rotate 62, 63, 66, 75, 109, **206**
round 46, 105, **206**
rrand 47, 105, **207**
RS-232 271, 276, 278, 289, 291
RS-422 276, 278
run 53, 108, **207**

Sample data representation 73
Sampled image 72, 170, 171, 199
save 33, 44, 45, 48, 53, 108, **208**, 260, 261, 262, 263, 294
Save 33, 41, 203, 208, 235, 261
    executable 41
    limits 261
    literal 41
    objects 33, 41, 208
    type 235
savetype 235
scale 62, 63, 66, 75, 109, **209**
scalefont 87, 90, 111, 156, 183, **210**
Scan conversion 8
    limitations 10
Scanner 20
sccbatch 297
sccinteractive 298
Script 14, 263
search 48, 106, 116, **211**
Serial communication 278
    protocol 280
    status query mechanism 282
setcachedevice 101, 111, **212**
setcachelimit 111, **213**
setcharwidth 101, 111, **213**
setdash 70, 109, **214**, 261
setdefaulttimeouts 300
setdostartpage 298
seteescratch 301, 302
setflat 70, 109, **215**
setfont 87, 111, 156, **215**
setgray 70, 79, 82, 89, 109, **216**

sethsbcolor 70, 79, 109, **216**
setidlefonts 288, **301**
setjobtimeout 304
setlinecap 70, 109, **217**
setlinejoin 70, 109, **218**
setlinewidth 109, **219**
setmargins 285, **299**
setmatrix 83, 109, **219**
setmiterlimit 109, **220**
setpagetype 299
setpassword 295, **300**
setprintername 277, **296**
setrgbcolor 70, 79, 109, **221**
setsccbatch 279, **297**, 308
setsccinteractive 279, **298**
setscreen 76, 80, 83, 109, **221**
settransfer 76, 82, 83, 109, **222**, 310
show 45, 57, 58, 87, 89, 94, 111, **222**
showpage 57, 84, 111, **223**
Simple objects 27
sin 46, 105, **223**
Spacing 120, 122, 178, 228, 239
Spot function 81, 221
sqrt 46, 105, **224**
srand 47, 105, **224**
stack 53, 108, **224**
Stack operators
    See Operand stack
stackoverflow 42, 112, **224**
Stacks 35
    See also specified type
stackunderflow 112, **225**
Standard files
    See File
StandardEncoding 95, 111, **225**
start 49, 107, **225**
status 52, 108, **226**
statusdict 279, 282, 284, 285, 286, 288, 293, 294, 303, 310
stop 49, 53, 107, **226**, 290
stopped 49, 53, 107, **227**
store 48, 106, **227**
string 47, 106, **228**, 261
String 27, 235, 260
    conversion to 144
    executable 41
    limits 260
    objects 27, 29, 41

Colophon

The colophon of a book is traditionally an embellishment placed on the last page of a book or manuscript. There is usually some inscription of the scribe or printer listing the date, place, and details of publication.

The word colophon is from the Greek word "Kolophon" (κολοφων), meaning summit or final touch. Or perhaps, colophon is from the Greek word "Kolophos" (κολοφως), which was the name of the very last island in the Greek chain of islands; hence the last page was called the colophon.

Because of the special nature of this book, detailed production notes are given in the preface. The typefaces used in this book were digitized by Adobe Systems Incorporated. The body type is Times Roman with Italic and Bold. The titles, examples, and operator definitions are in Helvetica with Bold and Oblique.

Cover Design—Marshall Henrichs
Book Design—Bob Ishi
Illustrations—John Warnock
Scribe Wizardry—Brian K. Reid
Index—Steven Sorensen